D1620663

USSR:

KONSTANTIN M. SIMIS

TRANSLATED BY JACQUELINE EDWARDS
AND MITCHELL SCHNEIDER

The Corrupt Society

THE SECRET WORLD OF SOVIET CAPITALISM

SIMON AND SCHUSTER

NEW YORK

1 2 3 4 5 6 7 8 9 10

Library of Congress Cataloging in Publication Data

Simis, Konstantin M.
USSR—the corrupt society.

1. Corruption (in politics)—Soviet Union.
I. Title.
JN6529.C6S5513 1982   320.947   82-5809
ISBN 0-671-25003-5   AACR2

Contents

Foreword

O N TUESDAY morning, November 16, 1976, I was walking, engrossed in thought, toward the doors of the Institute of Soviet Legislation, where for eleven years I had been a senior research assistant, when someone called to me: "Konstantin Mikhailovich!" I turned to see a young, very fat man, a man completely unknown to me. Even in the split second before I had time to gather my thoughts I realized what had happened. I realized that my former life—the regular life of a man working for a prestigious research institute, a man integrated into normal society—was now over and that some new life was beginning, a life of which I had had no experience before: the life of a heterodox outcast.

No rational thought process led to this realization. It was the subconscious product of an instinct born of sixty years' experience of Soviet life. And when that fat young man flashed a cordial smile and invited me to get into a black car that had obligingly drawn up to us, the force of inertia was such that I even made a bit of a scene and demanded that he show me his identification card. He did so readily, and I saw that it belonged to Second Lieutenant Khokhlov of the Moscow Criminal Investigation Department. One remembers such trifles at critical moments in one's life.

I asked where they were planning to take me, but I repeat that I did all this out of simple inertia; it was perfectly clear to me what lay ahead.

All the time I was being driven home in total silence, squeezed in between two agents, all the time we were walking up the five flights to my apartment (the elevator being out of order by some strange coincidence) I was thinking of one thing only: that copies of the manuscript of this book, already prepared for sending to the United States, were lying on my writing table and on my wife's desk in her room.

We were expected. A crowd of seven or eight people were gathered in the hallway outside the apartment. I did not look at them—I saw only my wife. She was pale but outwardly calm and collected as she stood in the doorway preventing our uninvited visitors from entering our rooms. She had been holding them at bay for about forty minutes, refusing to let them in until I arrived. We said not a word to each other, but simply exchanged glances.

Then the search began. We sat on the divan, facing an Investigator Borovik, who was in charge of the operation, and we experienced that feeling of humiliating powerlessness familiar, I am sure, to millions of people who have been subjected to such a search.

As it happened, everything that might have been of interest to the KGB was in full view: the business cards of Western journalists whom we knew, books published by Russian-language presses in the West, and, most important of all, the three manuscript copies of my book.

No one but my wife knew that for about three years I had been writing a book on Soviet society and the Soviet system. It was destined for publication in the United States under the pseudonym V. Vostokov. About six months prior to the fatal day my American friends had smuggled the first version of my book into the United States. A number of United States journalists and scholars had read it and managed to transmit their comments and criticisms to me. I had made many additions, and now the final draft was lying on my writing table. One of the three copies was to have been given the next day to an American friend who would take it to the United States; the two remaining copies would be hidden in safe places.

Meanwhile the search was in full swing. Seven people were busily examining chests of drawers, carefully tapping the sides of my antique writing desk in an attempt to discover hiding places (some eluded them, but, alas, only the empty ones), thumbing through hundreds of books on our shelves, and rummaging in our laundry. One of the agents picked up from my desk the mosaic frame containing a picture of my wife, looked at it front and back, and replaced it. But the thin, sharp-nosed, bespectacled girl who had been appointed official witness in the search—actually just another KGB agent like the rest—scolded him, whereupon he began carefully taking the frame to pieces, trying to find a secret place.

Yet despite all the fuss they were making, my wife and I had a nagging feeling that the whole thing was a sham, that they were only going through the motions of a search. We soon understood why; we realized that they had already been to our apartment over the weekend while we were out of town at our rented dacha. They had picked our lock, entered the empty apartment, and carried out their real search, finding everything that might be of interest to them.

Before long we had evidence that this surmise was correct. Part of the manuscript they had taken from my writing desk now lay in front of Investigator Borovik. Turning to one of his people, he ordered, "Bring the rest to me."

Without hesitation the man walked straight to my wife's room (where no one in the search party had been yet that day) and fetched the last seventy pages of the manuscript, which had been there since Friday.

At about seven o'clock in the evening the search was over.

"Get dressed. We're leaving," said the investigator, turning to us. I naturally wondered, where to? Is this only a search or are we being arrested? I decided to come straight to the point and ask.

"What should I wear? Should I plan to spend the night in prison?"

Borovik shrugged his shoulders noncommittally.

My wife and I were put in separate cars and we started off. As soon as the cars turned down Kutuzovsky Prospekt it became clear that they were driving us to the dacha to conduct a search there too.

They searched in a lazy, totally uninterested fashion. There was only one moment when the sluggish, very low-voiced agent seemed to wake up. We had rented the dacha for the winter from a very nice young woman, and it was from her writing desk that the investigator extracted a scrap of paper that said in handwritten capital letters, "HIDING PLACE IN BACK YARD. POUR HOT MILK. HARES. FOXES."

Borovik read the note out loud and gave me an inquiring look. Although our situation was far from comic, I burst out laughing.

"What's the matter with you? Nervous laughter?" asked Borovik crossly. "Don't worry, we'll find your hiding place."

Poor Borovik. He never did find that hiding place; the note had been written by the owner of the dacha when she was seven years old.

It was past ten o'clock by the time we were once again placed in separate cars and taken back to Moscow. We crossed Kutuzovsky Prospekt and approached Sadovoye Ring. I anxiously wondered which way we would turn. If we made a right turn into Sadovoye Ring, then we would be going to the KGB's Lefortovo Prison. If we went straight through, I wasn't sure where they would be taking us.

The driver asked no questions but crossed Sadovoye Ring and Kalinin Prospekt and drove in the direction of the Kremlin. Another moment of anxiety: if we turned left, we were headed across Dzerzhinsky Square to KGB headquarters, but if we went straight ahead across the Bolshoi Kamenny Bridge, we were going to the Moscow Municipal Public Prosecutor's Office. Again without a question, the driver made a decisive left turn. It was now quite clear: we were on our way to the KGB. Then suddenly Borovik asked the driver, "What are you doing? Don't you know where we are going?" and was answered, "I'm sorry, Comrade Borovik, I wasn't thinking."

The car made a sharp U-turn and sped across the bridge toward the Public Prosecutor's Office.

We were taken to a small building next to the old mansion that housed the Office of the Public Prosecutor and placed in separate rooms. The interrogation began.

My wife refused to give evidence on the ground that the hour was very late (it was about 11:00 P.M.) and that she was tired at the end of the day. All this time she was paying careful attention to what was going on in the next room, where I was being questioned. After all, I was the author of the manuscript and it was I who was in danger of being arrested. I have a habit of coughing from time to time, and while I was nervously waiting to see what would happen next, my wife could hear comforting coughing noises through the thin partition. Soon the investigators went out, leaving her shut inside the room alone.

Then my coughing stopped, and she could hear the tramping of military boots and the slamming of the door that opened onto the street. She rushed to the door of her room and started banging loudly on it. It was immediately opened by a militiaman: "What are you knocking for?"

"I have to go to the toilet."

"You'll have to wait. I can't let you out now." And the door slammed shut again.

When she banged again, one of the investigators entered. He tried to calm my wife and asked her to be patient. But she refused to listen and kept repeating, "Where is my husband? Tell me at once what has happened to my husband!" Finally the investigator looked fixedly at my wife and said quietly, "Be calm, Dina Isaakovna. No one is going to separate you from Konstantin Mikhailovich."

He was just like many another investigator in the Public Prosecutor's Office. In the course of events his behavior toward us varied—sometimes he was merely impolite, sometimes downright provoking. But I never forgot his kindness then and I never shall.

It was after midnight when we returned home, dead tired and shaken by the events of the day. We fully realized that our previous life was all over. That life had been a settled and happy one.

My wife was a well known defense attorney with a thriving practice. In the 1960s and seventies she had become widely recognized for defending political cases, and her statements in the trials of Vladimir Bukovsky, Pavel Litvinov, Yuri Galanskoy, and other Soviet dissidents had won her the reputation of being a brave and principled lawyer, respected in liberal circles within the Soviet intelligentsia. Somehow we just became legal counsel to all the Moscow dissidents— those fighting for human rights in the USSR as well as those fighting for the right of Jews to emigrate. All this time I was a senior research assistant at the Institute of Soviet Legislation of the Ministry of Justice.

Our life was not only comfortable but interesting as well. We had a circle of close friends, and fate had granted us the joy of mixing with the real (as opposed to the party-designated) intellectual and artistic elite of our people.

I recently read in an article by a Soviet emigré that the main thing that a Soviet citizen gains by emigrating is the chance to be himself. I cannot speak for other people, but as far as my wife and I are concerned we always remained ourselves, both during the bad times of the 1940s and early fifties, when I was expelled from my assistant professorship at the Higher Diplomatic School and found it impossible to get even the humblest job simply because I was a Jew, and during the happier times, when we were both practicing attorneys. Throughout all this we retained our independence of thought and spirit. We refused to join the Communist party despite considerable pressure to do so after 1956; we never dissembled or lied in our defense statements; we never spoke at any political meetings. It was perhaps precisely because I remained myself in the Soviet Union that I felt the need to write a book in which I could tell the world everything I knew about Soviet society and the Soviet state, a book that would set down my whole experience—everything I had learned about the Soviet system from living in it for nearly sixty years.

However, I lacked the resolve necessary to shatter my life entirely; I did not want to be banished to the camps or expelled from the country. I therefore planned to have the book published secretly, under a pseudonym. I realized that, given the power of the KGB's investigative apparatus, my chances of being found out were quite high; I knew the risks I was running if I failed. It was patently clear that even if I was not put in prison, we would both lose our jobs and thereby our means of existence.

We could not get to sleep that night; we needed to talk, discuss what had happened, think aloud about what we should do next. But that was not possible, for we were absolutely convinced that everything that went on in our apartment was being listened to: every rustle was being taped.

So we lay there and spent a sleepless night.

The following weeks saw a strange sort of existence. Through inertia we continued in our former lives. Every weekend we went to the dacha and skied, attended concerts, entertained guests. I continued to work at the institute as if nothing had happened. The directors pretended they knew nothing, and I went on with my planning studies, gathered information for governmental bodies (at the time, work was under way on the draft constitution, which was adopted a year later), and spoke at learned conferences.

But parallel to that life, threatening it and rendering it illusory and fragile, was my second life, the one built around the case against me as the author of a slanderous, anti-Soviet book.

Our first interrogation was to take place on November 24, and we were particularly thorough in our preparations for it. To avoid being overheard we would go walking in the forest and discuss at length our line of conduct in the investigation. We made plans for my wife if I should be arrested, and for that eventuality I had drawn up a statement for the Western press and given it for safekeeping to a friend of ours who was a Western newspaper correspondent. He was to publish it if I was arrested.

As it happened, he had been planning a trip out of Moscow for the day of the interrogation; after protracted efforts he had finally been granted permission for this by the Press Department of the Soviet Ministry of Foreign Affairs. But my friend refused to leave and remained in Moscow to be with us on that day.

November 24 arrived. My wife was to appear at 10 A.M., and I at one in the afternoon. I accompanied her to the Public Prosecutor's Office—the same building we had been taken to on the evening of November 16—and, as we had arranged, I went off to wait for her at a nearby Metro station. She rejoined me after about an hour and a half. By that time one of our friends had arrived; he was to stay and wait with my wife to see whether or not I would come back from my interrogation. All three of us thought it likely that I would not be returning. But after three hours I did return.

After that, months went by; my wife continued with her

law practice and I with my work at the institute. But three or four times a month the telephone would ring and a polite, rather characterless voice would speak: "Hello, Konstantin Mikhailovich, Chief Investigator Pantiukhin here. I must have a chat with you; could you call round at such and such a time?"

And if the date did not suit me for whatever reason, the polite voice readily agreed to a mutually convenient time. Then the day of the interrogation would arrive and I would dress as experienced people do in the Soviet Union when they know they might end up in prison. I would put into my pocket a cake of soap, a toothbrush (toothpaste is not allowed in prison), and a spare pair of socks and set off either to the Municipal Public Prosecutor's Office or to Lefortovo Prison, the home of the KGB's Investigation Department. One of our friends would come over to our apartment and share the painful hours of suspense with my wife, waiting with her to see whether I would telephone after three or four hours to say that I was coming home or whether there would be no telephone call, which meant I would be away for the night.

This went on until Tuesday, May 19, 1977. On that particular day I was not expected at the institute. But early in the morning my section chief rang and asked me to be sure to come in as an urgent report had to be drawn up for the Central Committee of the CPSU (Communist Party of the Soviet Union). He said that the director of the institute expected us at 1:00 P.M. to discuss questions relating to further work on the draft constitution.

When I entered the director's office I found, apart from the director himself, the Vice-Minister of Justice and two imposing men who looked as if they were either Central Committee officials or colonels in the KGB. Over the past ten to fifteen years both types have merged to such an extent that even to the experienced eye they are difficult to distinguish.

Coldly but politely the director greeted me, and informed me that back in March he and the secretary of the party office (who was also my section chief) had been called to the Public Prosecutor's Office, where they had been given the manuscript of my book to read as well as the records of my interrogations.

"And now an extraordinary meeting of the Academic Council will be held to examine the question of whether or not you can remain at the institute. You needn't attend if you do not want to."

There was a great temptation to leave and have no part in this farce whose outcome was predetermined. But, then, that meeting too was a part of Soviet life, and I had to witness it.

The meeting began with the director's report on what had happened, including a detailed account of the contents of my book. His statement was thorough and objective. He even quoted the manuscript's most pointed—and incriminating— passages, and for the first time in the institute's fifty years of existence, words were uttered in the room of the Academic Council itself about the totalitarian power of the party apparat, its universal venality, its total lack of ideals.

The director's behavior was correct. "Have I given an accurate account of the contents of your book, Konstantin Mikhailovich?" he asked me upon concluding his report. I confirmed that he had, whereupon he added for the information of those present, "Konstantin Mikhailovich stated during the investigation that he has no regrets and repents of nothing. We have not gathered here to judge him or to determine what his book represents under criminal law. The only thing we have to decide is whether someone who holds such anti-Marxist views can be a member of our institute, whose work is guided by Marxist-Leninist principles. Can he retain the academic degree and title awarded to him in 1944? The directors consider that, because of his ideological convictions, Konstantin Mikhailovich does not satisfy the requirements set for those who work in this country's learned institutions, and that he should be dismissed from the institute and stripped of his academic degree and title. Does anyone wish to speak?''

There was no shortage of people wishing to brand me as anti-Soviet and to demand my expulsion from the institute. The events of that meeting were more like the public castigation of Chinese dissidents during the Cultural Revolution.

Those who spoke can be divided into three groups. The first were representatives of the old Stalinist party guard. According to their lights I was a real enemy, and their hatred was sincere and not faked. They were absolutely convinced that they were right in calling for arraignment before a court of law, and imprisonment. The most striking of these was Mikhail Kirichenko, a long-standing party member who had formerly held a responsible position within the apparat of the Supreme Soviet of the USSR and was then made chief of the institute's constitutional law section. He spoke with a strong Ukrainian accent and with a verve that in this case was completely sincere.

He objected to the fact that the director of the institute, who had called the meeting, had not touched on the criminal side of my behavior. ''We are all lawyers here,'' said Kirichenko in an impassioned voice. ''On behalf of the Academic Council we can and should request that the Public Prosecutor's Office bring Simis [he did not use the usual ''comrade'' or even ''citizen'' before my name] to trial and mete out severe punishment. There used to be a custom in China that when a criminal was apprehended he was tied to a post in the main square and all who passed would spit in his face. I spit in Simis' face!''

I think perhaps Kirichenko expressed most accurately the fundamentally Oriental nature of that court scene. I was truly bound hand and foot, and anyone who wanted to could spit in my face. My fate had been decided in advance; I was merely a witness to the events.

The second category of speakers were those who had been compelled to take the floor on orders from the party bureau. These included many who sympathized with and respected me. But precisely because they were afraid of being suspected of this they did not dare to speak out (although I know that one section chief—a party member—absolutely refused to comply with the party bureau's proposal despite fairly clear hints that because of his behavior he would hardly be able to retain his position at the institute). I was sad to hear them but not surprised. I knew full well how easy it is in our country to break even decent people, how easy it is to force them to behave dishonorably if their jobs are jeopardized or their chance to travel abroad threatened. But I was particularly struck by Isidor Gringolts' statement.

The lot of the career-oriented Jew in the Soviet Union is not an easy one. In order to overcome the secret party and state prohibitions on the promotion of Jews up the official ladder, in order to have a successful career, a Jew must do the same things as a Russian but with even greater zeal. The beginning of any successful career in the Soviet Union is party membership. After that, two paths can lead the Jewish academic up the ladder of a university or administrative career.

The first path is political demagogy, ideological and professional servility, toadying to the authorities. The second path is to attain a particularly high degree of perfection in one's chosen field. A Jew has to become what they call in our country an "irreplaceable specialist." He has to work two or three times as hard as his Russian colleagues, and the main point is that he has to place everything—talent, knowledge, and diligence—at the service of the administration.

Isidor Gringolts chose to take this second path. A talented and scholarly jurist, he really became the country's greatest specialist on the legal side of the CMEA (Council for Mutual Economic Assistance). He worked so hard that he managed to become a section chief in the institute, writing some very serious research papers and doing an enormous amount of completely unpaid work for the directors of the CMEA secretariat.

Gringolts' position was complicated. I had come to the institute in 1966 after a sixteen-year break in my teaching and research work. (I had been dismissed from my academic position in 1950 during the period when Jews were being persecuted.) At that time Gringolts had given me invaluable assistance. He spared neither time nor effort to go through all my research papers, and his comments were of great help to me. Everyone at the institute knew about this. They also knew that he was sympathetic toward me, that he thought highly of my work, and that he was a man with a liberal mind.

As he went up to the rostrum he looked pitiful and embarrassed. He was all hunched over and spoke in a very indistinct and hardly audible voice, muttering unconnected phrases that sometimes made no sense at all. He said that he used to respect me a great deal and how surprised he was that I, who was so well acquainted with constitutional and administrative law in the capitalist countries, could be an opponent of Soviet democracy. He told about the time that he had been present at a Bundestag meeting in West Germany and had seen for himself that Western democracy was a fiction. Gringolts ended his statement, as they all did, by demanding that I be expelled from the institute and stripped of my academic degree.

He was so humiliated that I felt sincerely sorry for him then. But a few days later he was rewarded for this humiliation: Gringolts was appointed personal legal adviser to Katushev, the Deputy Chairman of the Council of Ministers of the USSR.

Last, there was the category of speakers who regarded the whole proceedings with indifference. They took the floor on orders from the party bureau, and, while not sympathetic, they showed no hatred for me.

A secret vote was taken after the discussion. Despite the atmosphere of hysteria and ideological terror that pervaded the meeting, three out of sixteen council members voted against the motion that declared me unfit for the post of senior research assistant, dismissed me from the institute and stripped me of my academic degree and title. And I should add that I am absolutely certain that two council members who were not present at the meeting would also have voted against my expulsion.

I visited the institute three or four times after this to put my affairs in order. The majority of my former colleagues tried not to notice me and turned their backs to avoid greeting me. Despite this I could detect around me an atmosphere of sympathy and respect that showed itself in various ways. Most often it was manifested by a respectful greeting or a particularly firm handshake (albeit given when nobody else could see it). There were both comical and touching incidents.

Some of the speakers in the Academic Council had called me a double-dealer and had accused me of writing one thing for the *Proceedings* of the Institute and quite another in the book that had been confiscated during the search. This was the only accusation I considered it necessary to answer. I said at the time that my published articles did not deal with the same ideas as those developed in the book, and further, that they contained nothing that would be inconsistent with those ideas. Then, when my case was under discussion at a party meeting, the Secretary of the institute's party bureau said in his report—with naïve astonishment and unintentional respect—"But, you know, Simis really isn't a double-dealer. I've just been rereading all his articles, and I can't understand how the editorial board let them through."

But my female colleagues were the most touching of all. They turned out to be much braver than their male counterparts. Whenever I met them at the institute they did not hesitate to come up to me and express their sympathy in

loud voices, embracing me in front of everyone. This glad-
dened me, and I still remember it with emotion.

In any event my life in the official Soviet Establishment
had come to an end.

A little more than a month after my expulsion from the
institute my wife was dismissed from the bar association.
Neither of us now had work or any chance whatsoever of
finding any. Our sole source of income was my wife's pension—120 rubles a month.

Meanwhile interrogations were becoming more frequent
and the investigators' threats ever more serious. Our situation was growing more critical, and we saw no way out. It
was the KGB that pointed out the solution.

In late summer or early autumn the Chairman of the Presidium of the Moscow Bar Association, a fellow student of
mine from university days, made a point of meeting my wife
and telling her outright that the Deputy Public Prosecutor of
Moscow, who was supervising my case, had asked him to
inform us that if we applied for permission to emigrate to
Israel to be reunited with our relatives (who he knew did not
exist), we would be able to leave very soon. On the other
hand, if we were obstinate and refused to emigrate, I would
be put on trial for the book and sent to the camps.

On November 6, 1977, we left our native land forever. The
meticulous customs inspection of our luggage was behind us,
as were the farewell embraces and the tears. It seemed as if
all our scores with the Soviet motherland had been settled
and that all that remained was to climb aboard the plane to
Vienna. But just then a customs official tapped me gently on
the elbow and asked us to go with him. He politely led us to
a small room.

A man of about fifty, with a sallow, unhealthy-looking
face, introduced himself as KGB Colonel Vladimir Ivanovich. He addressed us by our first names and patronymics,
as if we were good friends, and very politely explained to us
that, although we were leaving the Soviet Union, this did not

mean that the KGB was no longer interested in our fate. He said bluntly that the KGB had the means to apply certain repressive measures against us and our relatives who remained behind if during our life abroad we did not behave ourselves "properly." He was extremely insistent in recommending that I refrain from publishing this book and that my wife refrain from public statements defending the political prisoners Aleksandr Ginzburg and Anatoly Shcharansky, whom she had agreed to represent shortly before she was disbarred.

Three hours later we stood stunned and deafened in Vienna airport. In those three hours we had been transformed from people with no rights, defenseless against KGB persecution—people like our 260 million fellow citizens—into people who were free but stripped of citizenship and social status, stripped of a lifetime's experience. We would have to start learning everything all over again, from how to use a public telephone to how to travel by bus.

It is now the spring of 1982. I am sitting at my writing desk by the window, and before me lies a hilly and tree-lined Arlington street. The whole street is in bloom. The white, pink, and purple blossoms are a delight to my eyes, used to the subdued colors of Central Russia. Exotic—to me—birds are flying about in the garden beneath my window. I already know that the bright red ones are called cardinals, but I do not know what the sky-blue ones are.

It is all so beautiful and so foreign to me.

And in front of me on my desk is the manuscript of this book.

ARLINGTON, VIRGINIA, 1978–82

Chapter I

IN PLACE OF AN INTRODUCTION

F OR THE reader to understand the place occupied by corruption in the Soviet state and Soviet society, and the way in which the machinery of that corruption functions, he must have at least a general idea about the laws that govern that state and that society and under which its people live. For people born and raised in Western countries that knowledge is not easy to acquire, even for the few who know Russian, read Soviet newspapers, and have an acquaintance with Soviet law. Even they, not having had the experience of living in the Soviet Union as ordinary citizens (perhaps only as diplomats or journalists), find it hard to understand that the newspapers constantly and deliberately paint a distorted picture of events in the country. That is because all the newspapers are in the hands of the single party—the Communist Party of the Soviet Union—which exercises monopoly rule over the country; they are carrying out the propagandistic tasks assigned them by that party.

But for the person who has grown up in a democratic country the most difficult thing to grasp is the fact that ways and means of governing the huge superpower, and the rights and duties of its citizens, are defined not by a constitution or any other written laws but by a whole body of unwritten laws, which, although not published anywhere, are perfectly well known to all Soviet citizens and are obeyed by them.

The present Soviet constitution states that the power belongs to the people, who exercise it through elected soviets —councils—and the government of the country is carried out by the Council of Ministers and other administrative bodies. The fact is, however, that true power in the Soviet Union belongs to the apparat of the Communist party, and it is the members of that apparat who are the true leaders of the country.

The constitution states that the Supreme Soviet of the USSR is to exercise supreme power in the country: it issues laws and forms and dissolves the government—that is, the Council of Ministers, which is responsible to it. But in real life the Supreme Soviet of the USSR merely rubber-stamps the decisions of the top Communist party organs. The purely decorative Supreme Soviet is necessary to give to the Soviet state a semblance of democracy.

Everything attests to the decorative, propagandistic functions of the Supreme Soviet: it is in session for a mere six days a year, and in the course of its forty-three years of existence there has *never once* been so much as a single vote against a motion submitted by the government, or even an abstention, either in the Supreme Soviet of the USSR or in the supreme soviets of any of the fifteen Union republics that make up the federation that is the USSR. The fictitious nature of the power of the supreme soviets is further borne out by the fact that never in any of these Soviet "parliaments" has any question been raised relating to lack of confidence in the government; no member of the government has even been questioned on any subject.

That government, in the form of the Council of Ministers, consisting of sixty-two ministers and fourteen chairmen of various committees, unlike the Supreme Soviet, is no decorative body: it plays an important role in the day-to-day administration of the country. But that role, as played by dozens of ministries and government committees, boils down -mainly to carrying out the decisions made by party organs, which always have the final word. This applies in equal measure to the Council of Ministers, charged with the government of the entire USSR, and to the many district executive committees, which are responsible for government on the district level. Everyone in the Soviet Union knows that any district-level decision of any importance is made in the party Raikom—the District Committee—and that the Raiispolkom—the government District Executive Committee—merely formalizes that decision (or, as Soviet bureaucratic jargon has it, translates it into the language of the soviet).

The Soviet population is much less well informed about the ''balance of power'' at the highest levels, but in those lofty reaches too the party apparat's domination of the state apparat is just as fully and openly manifest.

For a minister, even if he is a member of the Communist Party Central Committee, the head of the corresponding department of the Central Committee apparat, even if he is *not* a member of the Central Committee, is the boss. Without his sanction the minister can make no decision of the least importance.

The state's subordination to the party is clearly evident in the rules of bureaucratic protocol: where a meeting is in order, it is the department head from the Central Committee apparat who summons the minister to his office, not the other way around. True, such summonses—though they are in fact orders—are couched in the words of a request (''Nikolai Ivanovich, could you possibly come by and see me at such and such a time?''), but a minister would never make such a ''request'' of a Central Committee department head.

Here is an example from real life of the subordination of the state to the party apparat, a subordination that now raises no eyebrows. A minister (now retired) who headed one of the industrial ministries for about twenty years told me a story that put it all in a nutshell, both the position in the ruling hierarchy of each of its participants and the subordination of the state apparat to the party apparat.

My informant had arranged with another minister to transfer to him control of several enterprises. They drafted a proposed Council of Ministers resolution about the transfer and took it for approval, not to the Council of Ministers itself but rather to the department of the party Central Committee apparat that was in charge of their ministries. The department head did not endorse the proposal, and the ministers—one of whom was a member of the Central Committee, unlike the party official—did not even try to dispute his decision or appeal to the Council of Ministers. It is of course possible that they might have succeeded in such an effort with the help of the Chairman of the Council of Ministers, who was a member of the Politburo, but relations with the head of the Central Committee department, on whom they depended, would then have been ruined forever.

Thus the real power in the Soviet Union is in the hands of the country's only legal political party, whose apparat is not even mentioned in the constitution or the other laws of the land, and whose functionaries are not elected, but appointed by higher party organs. That power encompasses all spheres of public and private life; it is just as absolute on the national level as it is within each district, each region, and each Union Republic.

The party apparat's power is the more nearly complete since it extends beyond administrative matters to the entire economy of the country. All the country's resources—land, water, factories, banks, transport systems, trade and services; educational and scientific establishments; even entertainment—belong to the state, which is to say that they are under the control of the party apparat. That strengthens the party's control over society as a whole and over each citizen individually, since it turns the party into a monopoly employer, able to prevent the employment in any job of anyone who fails to observe the unwritten rules on which the party's power is based.

Not only does the party apparat wield supreme power in the country but it also governs the daily life of the country, from the activities of the Council of Ministers to those of a small factory or collective farm. Each of the nation's districts is administered by the apparat of the District Committee (Raikom) of the Communist party; each region by the apparat of the Regional Committee (Obkom); and each Union Republic by the apparat of the Republic Central Committee. The entire state, finally, is ruled by the apparat of the Central Committee of the Communist Party of the Soviet Union.

That structure is completely parallel to that of the government; every government department, dealing with every sphere of life—economic, administrative, ideological—has its own corresponding department in the apparat of the party Central Committee. Each of these departments—which in 1977 numbered seventeen, not counting the Administrative Department, and which control the broad sectors of industry, agriculture, the army, the courts, the media, and so forth —is divided into sections, and the problems of each section are divided up among various supervisors.

The Central Committee's apparat is managed by Central Committee secretaries (formally elected at the Central Committee plenum, delegates to which are chosen at the party congress), but the organ with genuine supreme power is the Politburo of the Central Committee, which consists of thirteen to fifteen members elected and dismissed by the Central Committee plenum. In each of the links of the chain of the party apparat—Raikom, Obkom, Republic Central Committee and Central Committee of the CPSU—power is personified in the First Secretary of the committee (known nowadays in the CPSU Central Committee as General Secretary). Within his link the First Secretary's power is limited by no principles of legality or public opinion or a free press (nonexistent in the Soviet Union), but only by the next-highest party organ, to which he is completely subordinate. It is those organs that appoint and depose officials of both the party and state apparats.

Formally these secretaryships are elective offices. In reality, however, the delegates to district, regional, and Central Committee plenums, whose right it is to elect them, always vote unanimously in favor of the election of a candidate proposed by the higher party body, whose name they hear for the first time on their arrival at the meeting; they vote unanimously in favor of the dismissal of a secretary with whom they may have worked for many years and whom they respect. (There are *never* any exceptions to this unanimity.)

The power of the First Secretary, on whatever stratum, as demonstrated throughout the sixty-three years of the existence of the Soviet state, is absolute and is not subject to the restraints of the law or of public scrutiny. It is this that forms the fertile ground on which corruption in the Soviet Union has flourished so luxuriantly.

Yet—apart from the stillborn constitution—there are a multitude of laws and codes that really do operate in the Soviet Union. It is on the basis of these that the courts decide on disputes between citizens, try crimes, resolve labor disputes, and so forth. Nevertheless, the principle of legality does not operate in the Soviet Union. Since the regime does not consider itself to be bound by the law, any organ within the system, from a district council to the Supreme Soviet, and any court, from a people's court to the USSR Supreme Court can—indeed, must—violate the law on orders from its opposite number in the party apparat.

A perfect illustration of regard for the law shown by the supreme state power is found in the story of how the big-time speculators on the black market in foreign currency were executed in the early 1960s. The late 1950s and early 1960s saw a flourishing black market in foreign currency. Hundreds of big- and small-time speculators in hard currency, as well as gemstones, made successful deals reckoned in the hundreds of thousands of dollars, knowing that they were risking years in prison, but not their lives. Criminal law at that time did not provide for the death sentence for such crimes.

In the 1960s the authorities mounted an offensive against the black market. Using a network of undercover agents and *agents provocateurs,* they began to pull in the speculators and hand them over to the courts, which sentenced them to varying—usually quite long—terms of imprisonment, in accordance with the penal code. But then this routine course of events was tampered with by someone over whom the party apparat had no power—the son-in-law of the all-powerful First Secretary of the Central Committee and Chairman of the Council of Ministers, Nikita Khrushchev.

His name was Alexei Adzhubei, and at the time he was the editor in chief of the "second" (according to official nomenclature) newspaper of the country, *Izvestiya.* He was a lively man and a talented journalist, and he attempted, not without success, to transform his paper from a cheerless organ read by no one into an interesting newspaper put together on Western models. In its quest for entertaining, sensational material *Izvestiya* began publishing stories about the millions that were made by the big-time foreign-currency speculators, and about the heaps of gemstones and packets of dollar bills found in their possession when they were searched. It told of the group orgies that went on in their homes and in the homes of women of their acquaintance.

During the trials of the speculators and their accomplices, *Izvestiya*'s readers, incensed by what they read, showered the paper's offices with thousands of letters demanding that they be put to death. This the courts could not do, as such a penalty was not within the terms of the law for the crime of foreign-currency speculation. When the prison sentences were reported in the paper, the flow of letters increased, and the cry of "Execute them!" became even louder and more insistent.

Adzhubei informed his omnipotent father-in-law of this, whereupon the infuriated Khrushchev (who was, in any event, easily roused to fury) summoned the Public Prosecutor General of the Soviet Union, Roman Rudenko. Rudenko related the following outcome of this encounter at several meetings of his own department. The outraged Khrushchev, with the coarseness and lack of restraint typical of him in moments of irritation, let loose a storm of vilification at Rudenko. His main question was, Why hadn't the speculators been executed? The Public Prosecutor General gingerly tried to explain to the head of the party and the government that the law did not permit the courts to do this. Khrushchev then spoke the wonderful sentence that sums up the attitude of Soviet power to legality: "Who's the boss: we or the law? We are masters over the law, not the law over us—so we have to change the law; we have to see to it that it *is* possible to execute these speculators!"

Rudenko says that he was not afraid to explain to Khrushchev that even if such a law were to be put on the books now, it would still be impossible to try the speculators under it, since no one can be tried under a law issued after the commission of a crime. But Khrushchev interrupted these arguments and told Rudenko that while such things might be impossible in bourgeois countries, they *were* possible in the Soviet Union.

On July 1, 1961, a decree of the Presidium of the Supreme Soviet of the USSR was issued. It introduced the death penalty for the crime of speculating in large sums of foreign currency. Leonid Brezhnev, Chairman of the Presidium, signed many resolutions stating that the new punishment was to be applicable to the whole group of big-time speculators. They were all tried (some for a second time) and sentenced to death.

Even Soviet judges, accustomed to their subordinate position with relation to the party apparat, had a hard time with such an evident assault on the law. The case of one of the biggest of the speculators, Rokotov, was heard in the Supreme Court of the Russian Republic and was presided over by the head of that court. Everyone present at that trial remembers the old judge coming into court to pronounce sentence: he was pale, with tears running down his cheeks. It seemed as if he was going to fall unconscious before he could read the sentence. But he read it right through, and in a shaking, scarcely audible voice he pronounced the final words, ". . . the maximum penalty: execution."

For him the President of the Supreme Court of the Russian Republic, the orders of the First Secretary of the Central Committee, Khrushchev, were more powerful than the law.

Such are the possibilities open to the First Secretary of the Central Committee of the ruling party, such is his ability to bend legality; and the First Secretary of any party committee has no fewer possibilities within the confines of his district. All institutions, courts, enterprises, all information media, are subordinate not to the law or to the government but to the will of the party First Secretary.

In a small provincial town, to which I had been blown by the wind of my legal practice, I had occasion to learn of a story that reflects the relationship between the powers that be and legality. In that little town the daughter of the First Secretary of the Raikom attended the same school as the son of a humble post office functionary. Their romance began in that school, and when they graduated they decided to marry. But the First Secretary and, in particular, his wife categorically opposed such a *mésalliance*. The girl, however, had a strong character; she refused to submit to her parents' will, whereupon her father took overt action in accordance with his notions of legality. He summoned the head of the district office of ZAGS, the Soviet registry office that is the only body authorized to register marriages, and forbade the registration of the marriage of his daughter to the son of the post office manager.

What could the young couple do? Go outside the district and register their marriage elsewhere? That was impossible; in the Soviet Union at least one of the parties must be a resident of the district in which the marriage is to be registered. Lodge a complaint about this flagrant violation of their legal rights? They did lodge complaints with the regional authorities, but all their complaints about the illegal activities of the ZAGS official were, in accordance with the unwritten laws obtaining in the Soviet Union, transmitted to the party Raikom—that is, to the father of the would-be bride.

Thus, unable to register their marriage, the couple decided to live together and moved in with the young man's mother. But they were pursued by the power of the First Secretary. The boy's mother was fired from her job (again, a violation of all the norms of labor law) and evicted from her small two-room apartment in the post office building, on the grounds of its being intended for the use of the post office manager.

The young couple was in an impossible situation. They had nowhere to live in their own town. Nor could they move outside the district in which the girl's father wielded power since they had neither money nor professions that might have enabled them to settle down in another town. So the still-unmarried couple capitulated. The girl moved back with her parents, and the boy's mother was transferred to another job, which took her—and her son—out of town.

Of course I am not claiming that "never was a story of more woe than this of [our district] Juliet and her Romeo." Provincial court records throughout the Soviet Union are full of really tragic tales concerning the tyranny and lawlessness of the local party authorities. But that small story suffices to give the reader an idea of the absolute power of the First Secretary of the party Raikom within the confines of his fiefdom and how he can disregard the country's laws whenever he deems it necessary.

The functionaries in the intermeshed party and state apparats are arranged in a huge hierarchical pyramid. At its base there are the thousands of Raikom secretaries and the chairmen of the district executive committees (the executives of local government), the heads of district offices of the KGB, the police, and certain other institutions. All have the opportunity to take bribes and receive illegal gifts.

Above them stand the secretaries of the regional committees (obkoms) of the Communist party, the chairmen of the regional executive committees and higher officials in the apparats of the regional party committees, and certain regional state organs. Together they make up the middle level of the ruling party-state apparat.

Finally, at the summit of the pyramid (apart from Politburo members and secretaries of the Central Committee of the CPSU) are the top functionaries in the apparat of the Central Committee, the chairmen of the Council of Ministers and the Presidium of the Supreme Soviet of the USSR (who are nearly always Politburo members), their deputies, members of the government of the USSR, secretaries of the central committees, and chairmen of the councils of ministers and presidiums of the supreme soviets of the fifteen Union republics.

There are very significant differences among these three levels in terms of the limits of their power and official position. What is particularly important for our topic is the even greater gap to be seen in their life-styles. That is important, because it is precisely those differences that determine the features of the corruption inherent in each of the three layers of the ruling party-state apparat.

Despite the differences, however, the corruption of the Central Committee secretary, living in his government house and provided free of charge from special government stores with all the food he needs to keep his family, and the corruption of the secretary of a remote provincial Raikom, who has none of those legalized perquisites, have a common foundation. That common foundation is power, a power unbridled by the principle of subordination to the law or by a free press or by the voice of public opinion. It is the power of the party apparat that has turned the Soviet Union, in the sixty-three years of its existence, into a country eaten away to the very core by corruption.

Chapter II

THE RULING ELITE: CORRUPTION, LEGALIZED AND ILLEGAL

"Now, why did you go and do that? You really shouldn't have bothered! We don't eat that 'town stuff' you know."

Those were the words spoken by the lady of the house my wife and I had come to visit when I handed her the cake we had brought. I knew perfectly well that in that household they did not eat "town stuff," the expression used by members of the ruling elite, among whom our hosts counted themselves, to describe any food that can be purchased in stores open to the general public. In such households, as I was aware, they eat only "Kremlin stuff"—food bought in the private stores kept exclusively for the top ruling people, food that is produced especially for those stores. But I was unable to flout the Russian tradition of never paying a visit empty-handed, and I had bought a cake at a restaurant that was famous for its cakes and pastries.

Our hostess was not a poorly educated woman, and she certainly had no intention of insulting us; we were received cordially and hospitably. But she had spent about forty years

35

of her life as a member of the ruling caste, and all those years she had lived in a world isolated from that inhabited by the bulk of the people: a closed world which that caste has created for itself.

To reach the house to which we had been invited, my wife and I first had to go through Arkhangelsky Park, the site of the celebrated Palace that had belonged to Prince Yusupov before the Revolution. On the other side of the park we found ourselves faced with a high wall topped with barbed wire and forming a horseshoe girdling a huge plot of land on the bank of Moscow River. At the checkpoint a member of our host's family pointed us out to the guard (who carried a pistol at his side) and said, "Those are ours." And then we were on the other side of the wall, on the territory of State Dacha Number One, an out-of-town residence for members of the government.

The picturesque high bank of the Moscow River was dotted with two-story cottages (not isolated by their own fences); only one house, which stood out from the rest because of its large size, was enclosed within a special—yet another—wall and protected by its own guard. That was the house known officially as Dacha Number One, which belonged to the number-two man in the regime, the late Politburo member and Chairman of the Council of Ministers, Aleksei Kosygin.

The people who had invited us, and their grown-up children—who were actually the ones we were friendly with—greeted us affably. With pride they showed us the house and its surrounding garden. The garden was truly beautiful, and we could see that it was tended by a professional even before the owners told us how satisfied they were with their gardener, as they were with their maid and their cook, all of whom attended to their home and family. They did not mention that it was not they who paid for this staff, but the state: that went without saying.

There was expensive furniture in the house, paintings on

the walls, and crystal in the cabinets, but the decor struck us as completely characterless and without a trace of the personalities and tastes of the owners. This anonymity was soon explained. In the course of the meal I accidentally broke a large crystal wineglass. When I made embarrassed apologies, our hosts' son-in-law hastened to calm me: "There is nothing of ours in the house; from the teaspoons to the grand piano, everything comes from the warehouses of the administrative section of the Council of Ministers. So go ahead! Break all the wineglasses you like—in fact, smash all the china! It will all be immediately replaced." He made no attempt to hide his sarcasm.

The head of the household was one of the most senior ministers in the government, but it was in fact his wife who was the real head of the family and the household. This made itself felt immediately and in every aspect of life. By and large it was she who led the conversation. Her judgments about people, politics, and art were expressed categorically, leaving no room for doubt. Timid attempts by her husband or her children to object or express any disagreement were cut short peremptorily. My wife and I chose to hold our tongues, having landed in this alien and, in any event, inaccessible, world of the ruling elite; we preferred to listen and observe. Our hostess was an intelligent woman and could see that we, her guests, did not share her nostalgia about Stalin's era. So she considered it necessary to tell us a story as proof that she did not look favorably on Stalin's regime. She told us that in Stalin's time the then Minister of Culture had a private movie theater in his dacha (which was right there in that very dacha settlement), to which only he, his family, and his guests had access. The other dacha owners were not allowed in. "But now everything is very democratic," she said with pride. "Now the theater is open to everyone—anyone can go and see the films."

"What about your servants—the maids, the chauffeurs?" I asked. "Do they go to the movies there too?"

"No, of course not! They have their own club. It is only the residents who are allowed in," was the answer to my provocative question.

As we walked past the Yusupov Palace and its theater, into which the servants were admitted only as ushers and stagehands, we could not help thinking of those who, in the name of the people, had taken the palaces and the privileges away from the Yusupovs, who call themselves the servants of the people and live, not in palaces but in tastelessly decorated cottages, cut off from that people by high walls, by barbed wire, by armed guards, and by pride of caste.

LEGALIZED CORRUPTION

The life of the caste that rules the Soviet Union is a closed one and not readily accessible for study. This difficulty of access exists not simply because their life is passed in special private homes or suburban communities, isolated from the rest of the country and guarded by armed sentries. (Brezhnev himself, for example, lives in a huge apartment building on Kutuzovsky Prospekt, in which he occupies a whole floor and to which he has his own private entrance that is closely guarded by KGB agents.) Equally—even more, perhaps—it is true because of the exclusiveness of the milieu, to which outsiders are hardly ever admitted.

It is only the actual members of the ruling elite, their families, and their servants who are familiar with the details of the life-style and the privileges that this elite has provided for itself. The mass media are absolutely forbidden to make available to the public any information about those privileges, but since thousands of people—chauffeurs, maids, cooks, staff of the special closed shops and hospitals that serve the ruling elite—are involved in the lives of these people, there is a constant trickle of information.

To understand the scope of the privileges and benefits that

the Soviet ruling elite has secured for itself, one must have at least a general idea of the standard of living of ordinary people in the Soviet Union. The average monthly wage for manual and office workers, according to official data in 1979, is 164 rubles, before taxes. According to my own calculations, however, the minimum required for a family of three to live modestly is 250 rubles (about $330). (I use my own figures here because the official statistics are secret and have never been published.) At the same time the salary of the Minister of Defense or the President of the Academy of Science is 2000 rubles a month, almost thirty times the legal minimum wage of 70 rubles a month. And this does not take into consideration all the legalized perquisites given to a minister or an academy president. If these are included, a minister's monthly income—without exaggeration—will run to as much as 4000 rubles, and is thus at least fifty-five to sixty times the minimum wage paid to a manual or office worker.

To put these figures into United States terms, this could be likened to the gap separating an American earning $12,000 a year from a fellow countryman whose yearly income is $700,000.

These two factors—thorough infection of the ruling apparat by corruption and material inequality—have created conditions and an atmosphere in which corruption has spread everywhere—even to people who never either give or take bribes themselves. The main privilege of the ruling elite is not really the high salaries paid to its members (which, by the way, amount to four to ten times those of ordinary white- and blue-collar workers); it is the existence of a whole network of special stores, hospitals, sanitoriums and service establishments that provide them—and no one else—with goods and services. None of these benefits or privileges are paid for by the members of the ruling caste out of their own pockets; it is the state budget or the party treasury that pays for it all.

Among the privileges that come with membership in the

highest levels of the ruling caste, the most important of all is a secure private supply of food, clothing, and other items needed for daily life. Since the forced collectivization of the peasants in the late 1920s and early 1930s, the entire country has constantly suffered from a shortage of food. The ruling elite, however—which is concentrated mainly in Moscow—gets its food supplies through the *Kremlyovskaya stolovaya* (the "Kremlin canteen"), which can be used only by people with special passes—the members of the elite, their families, and their servants.

I do not know the official name of that institution, but everyone who uses it—or has even heard of it—calls it the *Kremlyovka*.

The *Kremlyovka* system includes the dining room, a few food stores, and snack bars scattered through the buildings of the Central Committee of the CPSU, the Council of Ministers, and the Supreme Soviet of the USSR. All these facilities sell foods of particularly high quality, the like of which is never seen in ordinary stores: sausages, fish delicacies, cheeses, bread, vodka, cakes and pastries (baked to specifications in special bakeries); and dairy products, fruits and vegetables produced and grown on state farms that supply the *Kremlyovka* system exclusively. In addition, the Kremlin stores and snack bars sell imported goods that cannot be bought in normal stores: American cigarettes, Scotch whisky, and English gin.

Our hostess, the minister's wife, was right when she said that they ate no "town stuff" from the ordinary shops. The main reason for this is that anything they might get from the "town" is of immeasurably lower quality than what they find in the *Kremlyovka*. Besides, not only is the "town stuff" worse but it is also much more expensive.

Although prices in the Kremlin stores are nominally the same as prices outside, they are actually much cheaper for their high-ranking customers. The reason is a simple one: the customers in those stores pay not with money but with vouchers. Depending on an official's position in the hierarchy and on the size of his or her family, each high-level functionary receives vouchers to a certain amount, for which he or she pays approximately one-third of face value.

People with access to the *Kremlyovka* are divided into two categories: those in the first are given monthly vouchers in the amount of 80 rubles, and those in the second in the amount of 140 rubles. The vouchers can be used in two ways. One way is to pay for meals in the Kremlin dining room, at which the diner is also given a package of food— "for breakfast and lunch," as it is officially known. The meals in the *Kremlyovka* are marvelous: they are prepared from the best ingredients by first-class chefs—and under nutritional supervision, as the Kremlin Polyclinic is housed in the same building as the dining room. But few recipients of dining room vouchers use them like that—it doesn't pay. With the 80 rubles' worth of vouchers that would buy daily meals for one in the Kremlin dining room (granted, with food packages thrown in) an official can buy enough food in the Kremlin stores to provide a family of four with complete first-rate meals for a month (including caviar and other expensive delicacies such as brandy, wine, and high-grade vodka).

I was personally acquainted with three families who lived on these Kremlin rations and was able to collect information about their daily life and eating habits. I can safely say that such privileged families ate incomparably better on 80 rubles a month than an ordinary rank-and-file family of four could eat on 250 rubles, for whom even meat, chicken, and sausages are hard to come by in sufficient quantities, and expensive delicacies and fruits are out of the question.

That is why the overwhelming majority of those with access to the *Kremlyovka* prefer to spend their vouchers in the shops. Among the few who spend their vouchers in the dining rooms, there is a preponderance of people who, owing to their lofty positions, get such quantities of vouchers that they can pay for both meals in the dining rooms and sufficient food from the stores to provide for their families. Apart from them—and the unmarried people—another well represented group in the dining rooms are the neophytes, those who have recently entered the elite circles. For them the dining room plays the role of a club, where they have the opportunity to mix with high officials on a regular basis and thus cultivate connections that may be of use in their careers.

In addition to the stores and the dining rooms, there are also the Kremlin snack bars, located in the buildings of the Central Committee of the CPSU, the Council of Ministers, and the Presidium of the Supreme Soviet. In these snack bars customers pay cash, but prices are much lower than they would be outside. Even in the snack bars there is a hierarchy: different floors in each building have different types of snack bars. The snack bars on the lower floors are for low-ranking officials and their guests; the third floor serves high-ranking functionaries; and somewhere on the very highest floors is the snack bar for the elite itself.

I had occasion to eat breakfast in the second-floor snack bar in the Presidium building when, as a research assistant in the Institute of Soviet Legislation, I was involved in work on the drafting of various laws. For 80 to 90 kopecks I could get a breakfast that was better than any I might find in a good restaurant for 4 or 5 rubles. But on the second floor we could get neither American cigarettes nor Scotch: these were available only on the higher floors.

The higher the floor, the lower the prices and the wider and more luxurious the range of available merchandise.

The privileged customers of the Kremlin stores dealing in clothing and other consumer goods have access to items that either do not appear in normal stores or that take weeks to find—or that are available only under the counter by paying a bribe to the salesclerk. On the whole, it is clothing imported from the West that is most highly prized by Soviet consumers. The prices at which items are sold in the Kremlin stores are arrived at in the following way: The wholesale price paid to the Western firm is converted to rubles at the official rate ($1 = 66 kopecks). Because of this the wife of a minister or of a high Central Committee official pays about 35 to 40 rubles for a pair of imported boots that an ordinary customer would be happy to get for 120 to 140 rubles, since Western goods are rarely found in outside shops at reasonable prices.

Not only does the ruling elite have its own stores, it has its own theater-ticket agency, its own bookstore, in which its members can buy scarce volumes, and its own pharmacy, which sells imported drugs unobtainable in ordinary drugstores.

All this makes it possible for the ruling elite to enjoy material advantages that are inaccessible to ordinary citizens. In fact, everything to do with the country's rulers is exclusive and separate. They are serviced by a special network of medical establishments, including sanatoriums, clinics, and hospitals in and around Moscow, as well as many sanatoriums throughout the country, all of them responsible to the Fourth Department of the Ministry of Health.

I have had occasion to visit some friends in the main hospital of the Kremlin system, the Kuntsevo Hospital. If I were to compare what I saw there with what I can see in a good American hospital, I think that the comparison would be in favor of the latter. While in the Kuntsevo Hospital, as in American hospitals, most patients are put in semiprivate rooms, there are telephones and television sets in only some of them—those destined for the highest-ranking patients. (Once when I visited a friend who was a patient in Kuntsevo Hospital, the late Aleksei Kosygin was also a patient there. My friend told me, in a manner indicating that it was particularly noteworthy, that in the room occupied by the head of the country's government there were a telephone and a television set.) And as far as I can judge, the drugs and equipment at the disposal of an American hospital are more sophisticated and modern than they were at Kuntsevo.

At any rate, hospital conditions for Kremlin patients must be compared not with conditions in American hospitals but with those prevailing in the hospitals that care for ordinary Soviet citizens.

In one of Moscow's best hospitals, the Botkin Hospital, I have myself observed that eight to ten people per ward is the norm; in addition, however, there are always patients in beds in the hospital corridors. The food in Botkin Hospital is so bad that anyone who has the slightest opportunity to do so receives regular packages from the outside. Even the most common drugs are in constant short supply, not to mention imported preparations.

Housing for the ruling elite is also special and unlike that for ordinary people. Buildings for the privileged are built to special designs and are finished with particular luxury. The families of the ruling elite get—free of charge of course— apartments that are enormous by Soviet standards—four to five times the size of any apartment obtainable by even the most fortunate of ordinary mortals.

The ruling elite even has its own special cemeteries: the Kremlin Wall on Red Square for the most important members, and a cemetery on the grounds of what was once the Devichy Monastery for those of somewhat lower rank. And provision has also been made for a possible nuclear war: there is a special shelter designed to house the key members of the elite for months.

I once defended in court a number of specialist builders who were involved in the construction of that government shelter, located in Moscow, near the Rossiya Hotel. I learned from my clients that there is an entire town under the Moscow streets, with its own transport system consisting of electric trolleys, a self-contained, independent ventilation and electricity-supply system, a year's supply of food —even its own cinema. One of my informants told me that a tunnel several kilometers long stretches from this shelter out into the heart of the country, with its exit somewhere in the Vladimirskaya region.

All these benefits enjoyed by the ruling elite are doled out in strict accordance with rank within the ruling class. While the range of benefits is very great, the nuances of the way in which they are rationed are very delicate. For about eleven years I followed the career of a Central Committee official of my acquaintance, and I was able to observe how, as he moved up the official ladder, the spectrum of privileges he received subtly and gradually changed. When he arrived in the apparat of the Central Committee as a lowly *instruktor,* or agent, he was given 80 rubles' worth of Kremlin vouchers per month, and had the use of a Central Committee car only for himself personally when on official business. He was given the use of a state dacha outside Moscow, but only for the summer, and with no maid service. When he and his wife visited the government sanatorium (a resort with medical facilities), they had only one room and took their meals in the communal dining room; liquor was free only in strictly limited quantities.

But the years went by, and my acquaintance rose to the lofty rank of deputy head of one of the most important and prestigious departments within the Central Committee. When he reached that rung on the ladder he could buy food in the *Kremlyovka* without any limits, and in even more privileged and tightly closed shops in the system. He could order cars from the Central Committee garage at any time of the day or night and in any number—and for any reason, including that of sending his friends home after an evening of boozing at his dacha, thirty kilometers from Moscow. And that dacha, which now was his all year round, was serviced by a maid and a cook. Now when he visited a government sanatorium he was given a suite of rooms, where, if he preferred, he could also take his meals. There were no limits to the liquor he was permitted—and, again, it was free of charge.

Yet, even having won all the perquisites I have mentioned,

my acquaintance spoke to me with thinly disguised envy of the benefits accruing to those even higher up on the official ladder. These people had not only maids and cooks in their dachas but gardeners as well. They arrived at the sanatoriums with their own personal cooks; special paths on the sanatorium grounds were set aside for their walks, from which other members of the vacationing elite were excluded.

There is also an elite in the Soviet Union that stands beyond all these categories: the members of the Politburo, those thirteen to fifteen people who make up the highest body in the party apparat, the body that in reality governs the state. Without restrictions, and completely free of charge, they get anything they want in any quantity. A special office exists in the Kremlin for the purpose of providing this sector of the elite with their benefits; that office has limitless possibilities and resources.

Each Politburo member has his own personal palaces on the Black Sea in the Crimea or in the Caucasus and in the neighborhood of Moscow, although these are obviously not the private property of the official. These palaces stand in huge parks and are serviced by complete staffs of cooks, chauffeurs, gardeners, hairdressers, doctors, gamekeepers, and so on. They are screened off by high walls surmounted with barbed wire, by high-tension wires, and by a photoelectric surveillance system. Armed agents, in the command of the Special Section of the KGB Central Office, keep guard round the clock in and around the palaces and their grounds. (I learned all this from someone who for many years had been the personal barber to one of the members of the Politburo and Secretary of the Central Committee.)

The current rulers, not satisfied with the palaces of their predecessors, build themselves new ones. In the early 1970s a large building was erected in the Barvikha region near Moscow (which as early as the 1920s had already become a private vacation spot for Soviet leaders and leaders of the Communist parties of the world). This building has three floors, and each one was set aside for one of the top three dignitaries of the country—the General Secretary of the Central Committee, the Chairman of the Council of Ministers, and the Chairman of the Presidium of the Supreme Soviet (respectively, Brezhnev, Kosygin, and Podgorny). I was informed by some Moscow museum staff members that, on orders from the Ministry of Culture, about thirty pictures by famous Russian and Western artists were sent from the reserve collections of the Tretyakovskaya Gallery and the Pushkin Museum of Fine Arts to adorn the walls of that house.

Since Politburo members enjoy all these material benefits without limit or cost, their salaries can be lower than those of top-ranking ministers. Thus the 1500-ruble monthly salary of the Minister for Foreign Affairs Andrei Gromyko was reduced to 800 rubles a month on his appointment to the Politburo.

ILLEGAL CORRUPTION IN THE CENTRAL GOVERNMENT

Even though the members of the ruling elite have arrogated to themselves all those perquisites and privileges, they have not failed to take part in the universal corruption that reigns in the Soviet Union. It is difficult to imagine and even more difficult to understand their psychology. Consider, for example, an official in one of the highest posts in the party or state apparat. He is invested with enormous power; he is provided with all the good things of life (indeed, to excess), but still he contemplates committing crimes for the sake of money. However hard it may be to imagine, corruption, even in the highest stratum of the Soviet ruling elite, has become a fact, and not even a rare fact.

How can we understand what went on in the mind of Frol Kozlov? Whenever one opened a newspaper or turned on a television set in the late 1950s and early 1960s, one caught a glimpse of a man of about fifty with his hair in a tight permanent wave, and a face that positively exuded smugness. That face belonged to Frol Kozlov, the Secretary of the Central Committee of the CPSU, a member of the Politburo and the right hand of the all-powerful dictator Nikita Khrushchev—in short, the number-two man in the Soviet ruling elite. (However, as a remarkable Russian poet observed accurately, there are no "second men" in Russia: there is the first man, then all the rest are last. Let us just say that Kozlov was first among all the last men and occupied a highly privileged position from which he wielded great power.) Then all of a sudden, and completely unexpectedly, it was discovered that he was a big bribe taker. This was a chance discovery and had nothing to do with any initiative by the authorities.

Nikolay Smirnov, Chairman of the Leningrad Municipal Executive Committee, was a close friend of Kozlov's. One day Smirnov suddenly died in his car on the way to his office. It was necessary for some reason to open his office safe, and in it were found packages of precious stones and huge bundles of money. These were all clearly labeled: some belonged to Smirnov and others were the property of Kozlov.

The safe had been opened in the presence of a number of witnesses, and it was impossible to squelch the scandal. After a cursory investigation the KGB Central Office was easily able to establish that the second man in the regime, through the Chairman of the Leningrad Municipal Executive Committee, had been accepting large bribes in exchange for performing various services. He had been paid off for appointing people to responsible and prestigious posts, for general protection, for promoting people up the bureaucratic ladder of the ruling apparat, and for using his influence to halt criminal proceedings against underground businessmen wealthy enough to buy such influence with bribes amounting to hundreds of thousands of rubles. (When a Soviet public prosecutor or judge receives a telephone call from the office of the Central Committee Secretary and member of the Politburo asking him to "look into the matter carefully," he knows that such a request, in *apparachik* jargon, amounts to an order to find in favor of the defendant.)

Frol Kozlov did not lose his membership in the Politburo; he retained all his posts and privileges and, under the pretext of illness, was merely removed from active service. When Kozlov died he was buried with full state honors in the Kremlin Wall on Red Square.

Another instance of corruption at the very apex of the pyramid of power concerns the late Ekaterina Furtseva. The dizzying career of that very beautiful woman arouses as much puzzlement as astonishment. She began as a humble laboratory assistant at the Moscow Medical Institute, and her first small step upward was her election to the secretaryship of the institute's party bureau. From there her career experienced a swift and mysterious takeoff: she became First Secretary of one of the district committees of Moscow (in itself an entrée to the higher reaches of the ruling apparat). Then there was another sharp jolt upward, and Furtseva became First Secretary of the Moscow Committee of the party—one of the most prominent and prestigious posts in the ruling party apparat.

In 1957 a group of veterans of the Stalinist regime, headed by Molotov and Kaganovich, attempted to overthrow Khrushchev. Furtseva played a decisive role in organizing the counterattack. On very short notice she managed to assemble in Moscow the members of the Central Committee plenum and do what had to be done to persuade them to go along with her views. The opposition was routed, Khrushchev held onto power, and Furtseva became Minister of Culture and the first (and, thus far, the only) woman member of the Politburo.

Furtseva's career is full of such sudden rises, which are difficult to explain without accepting the version in circulation in Moscow concerning the romantic foundations of that career, a version that, among others, mentions the name of Nikita Khrushchev himself.

What prompted her to decide to build a dacha for her daughter? She built it in 1972–73, near Moscow, with state materials and state labor, paying for neither, at a cost to the state of 100,000 to 120,000 rubles.

It is highly likely that her experience of officialdom led her to build that dacha at state expense with the intention of registering it as private property in the name of her daughter.

But when her abuses were exposed, Ekaterina Furtseva retained her posts in the Central Committee of the CPSU and in the government. The ruling elite lives in complete isolation from the rest of the country, and in an atmosphere of secrecy. In the very rare instances of one of its members being found guilty of corruption, the regime does all in its considerable power to hide the fact from the people.

As difficult as it is to comprehend the psychology of high-ranking criminals and the motives that impel them to crime, it is possible to point to several factors that have combined to determine the psychological predisposition to corruption of members of the very top echelon of the class that rules the country.

The first, and probably the most important, of these causes is the fact that none of the material benefits showered on a member of the ruling elite actually belongs to him: he owns nothing. The dacha, the chauffeur-driven car—they belong to the state, and he enjoys them, along with access to the *Kremlyovka,* only while he occupies his official post. If he loses his position in the ruling apparat, he automatically —literally on the next day—loses everything that was his.

The psychological shock of such a downfall cannot fail to be traumatic. Many years after Ekaterina Furtseva was un-expectedly (to her) removed from the Politburo she related what she had had to endure to a close friend, one of the country's most famous dramatic actresses and a People's

Artist of the USSR (from whom I acquired this information). The morning after she was removed from the Politburo, Furtseva's huge black limousine, equipped with a telephone and flanked by two other limousines carrying armed guards (provided for all Politburo members), did not arrive at the entrance to her house. Instead there was a humble Volga, which conveyed her through the streets of Moscow to the Ministry of Culture without any guard. She arrived not at the special entrance to the ministry (which had been reserved only for her and her guard), but at the public entrance. On the same fateful day she received a call from the administrative section of the Council of Ministers asking her to vacate her palace outside Moscow—within a week—and to move to a far more modest dacha located in quite a different neighborhood. At the same time she was informed that she had been deprived of access to the Politburo food store and that a pass and vouchers for the Kremlin dining room would be sent to her at the ministry.

Furtseva retained her post as minister, and all this did not represent total ruin, but the result of the humiliation she had suffered was protracted psychological depression combined with an inclination to alcohol, which remained with her to the end of her life.

It is not only the precariousness of any official position (and thus of the perquisites that go with it) that acts as catalyst for corruption in the highest reaches of the ruling elite. Even high officials are mortal, and neither a job nor its benefits can be inherited. So there is a natural temptation to ensure not only one's own well-being (in case of loss of one's elite status) but also the future of the family in case of death.

Of course we cannot discount normal human greed either, the blind, often irrational greed that has been, is, and ever shall be found in all strata of society, in all epochs, and under all political systems, totalitarian and democratic alike.

Then there is another, purely psychological, factor; after years of working on the lower levels of the party-state apparat and clambering up the official ladder, the future ruler of the country psychologically adapts to a situation in which bribes and gifts are a daily routine for himself and his colleagues, who in no way consider themselves to be criminals. Then, having reached the summits of power, the official retains the same psychological model of his relationship to corruption, which is now ingrained in his attitude.

To the four factors I have enumerated I must add one more: the lack of fear of punishment and a feeling of impunity. High-ranking bribe takers are very infrequently exposed in the Soviet Union, and it may be said that cases of their being truly punished are extremely rare. The reason for this is certainly not that high-level corruption is such a dark secret; on the contrary, the members of the Soviet ruling elite live under a bell jar. Every step they (and their families) take is known by the KGB officers who are responsible for guarding them; they are accompanied everywhere—to the theater, on visits, and at home. These agents are not responsible only for guarding the members of the ruling elite; they are also engaged in secret surveillance of them.

Servants too are called on to spy on their masters. Maids, cooks, and chauffeurs are all selected by the administrative departments of the Central Committee or the Council of Ministers (the departments in charge of the everyday lives of the elite). But before a servant is engaged he is screened by the KGB, and will be hired only if he undertakes to carry out secret surveillance of his future employer. (This information came from a relative of mine who worked in the KGB Central Office from 1926 to 1972.)

Furthermore, the apartments and dachas in which the country's rulers live are filled with bugging and recording devices: every word uttered is heard by the KGB. A close friend of mine once telephoned a Vice-Minister for Foreign Affairs. After she had dialed she heard no ringing, only a soft click. Then she was able to hear everything that went on in his large apartment: water flowing from the faucet in the kitchen (where there wasn't even a telephone) and the minister's wife scolding her young son for having come home with bad grades from school.

But even though the KGB has full knowledge of the fact that the ruling elite is infected with corruption, the members of that elite remain inviolate. The fact is that, since its inception, the Soviet regime has been tolerant of the ruling elite's improbity.

The exposure of the ruling clique of Georgia is a case in point. The dubious dealings of the Georgian elite (headed by one Vasili Mzhavanadze, First Secretary of the republic's Central Committee and a Candidate Member of the Politburo) were exposed as a result of the efforts of its Minister for Internal Affairs, Edward Shevarnadze. He was at least in part motivated by ambition, but he apparently did feel genuine hatred for corruption and was truly pained by the decadence he witnessed. "Once, the Georgians were known throughout the world as a nation of warriors and poets; now they are known as swindlers," he commented bitterly at a closed meeting. (This information comes from notes taken by one of the participants in that meeting.)

For several years agents of Shevarnadze's Ministry for Internal Affairs shadowed all the leading functionaries in the party and state apparats of Georgia, as well as their families, gathering much compromising evidence. This was not a particularly difficult task, since a reckless orgy of corruption was raging almost openly in Georgia.

There was a trade in the highest posts in the party and state apparats, which had become so blatant that the underground millionaire Babunashvili was able to order for himself the post of Minister of Light Industry. Babunashvili headed a highly ramified illegal company that produced and marketed fabrics, but his ambition was not satisfied either by his multimillion-ruble income or by his business activities, and he decided that he wanted to cap his career by combining in a single person (himself) both sides of Soviet organized crime: the corrupter (underground business) and the corrupted (government).

The newspaper *The Dawn of the East* reported on February 28, 1973, that the plenum of the Communist Party of Georgia had remarked on this state of affairs. The article noted that "the not-unknown schemer Babunashvili was able to 'order' a ministerial chair," and it went on to say that this was not an isolated incident. But the newspaper made no mention whatsoever of who received the bribes resulting in ministerial appointments. These bribes went to the person with a determining voice in deciding on ministerial appointments, the First Secretary of the Communist Party Central Committee and Candidate Member of the Politburo, and to the one with whom those decisions had to be cleared, the Chairman of the Council of Ministers.

At that time I knew a number of young people in Tbilisi who did not occupy very lofty posts—they were junior officers in the Council of Ministers and in the Presidium of the Supreme Soviet—but whose jobs allowed them access to top secret information about the behind-the-scenes life of the ruling apparat. It was they who told me of the trade in ministerial and deputy ministerial posts in Georgia, and assured me that the situation was just the same in Azerbaidzhan.

At the time there were more people ready and able to pay several hundred thousand rubles for a ministerial post than there were vacancies, so when a post did open up, a competition was begun. The first move was nomination by an official sufficiently high up to be entitled to make such a nomination, such as a Secretary in the republic's party Central Committee, personnel chief to the Central Committee or the Chairman of the Council of Ministers or one of his deputies. A decisive factor in these nominations was often a clan linkage between the candidate and his proposer; in Central Asian and Transcaucasian republics, family ties are one of the most important factors determining the composition of the ruling apparat.

Even at this early stage the size of the bribe to be paid for the nomination would have been discussed, but the real battle began only when it became clear just who the possible candidates were. Then, as my informants told me, amused, something very like an auction would sometimes take place behind the scenes, although the victor was not always the highest bidder. That is because the competition was not merely among the aspirants for the vacant post; it was also a competition among the recipients of their bribes, so the most influential patron had the best chance of winning.

All my information points to a going rate in those years for ministerial posts ranging from 100,000 rubles for the not very prestigious (or lucrative) post of Minister for Social Security up to 250,000 to 300,000 rubles for such bottomless feeding troughs as the Ministry of Trade or the Ministry of Light Industry. Not cheap, of course, but once installed in his post, the minister would be able to derive considerable income from it by peddling, in his turn, jobs as sector and territory chiefs (which, in a ministry like that of Light Industry, could fetch 100,000 to 125,000 rubles).

The top functionaries in the apparats of the party Central Committee and the Council of Ministers divided the republic up into zones of influence. This division would more often than not be on the basis of tribal origin, for even today the old tribal fragmentation of Georgia plays an important role in influencing the life of the republic. A Mingrelian, an Imeretian, a Svanetian, or an Adzhar considers himself a Mingrelian, an Imeretian, a Svanetian, or an Adzhar first and a Georgian second; when he enters the ruling elite, he naturally becomes the protector of his fellow tribesmen and his region—which becomes his fiefdom. He places his relatives and devoted friends in key positions, and, of course, receives regular tribute payments through his protégés.

Following the purge of the ruling apparat, this phenomenon was shamefacedly mentioned at a plenum of the Georgian Central Committee: "Several leading officials divide the republic into spheres of influence; they take under their patronage individual districts, towns and Party organizations; each has his own 'favorites' " (*Dawn of the East,* February 28, 1973).

A special mark was left on corruption among the Georgian elite by the wives of the first and second secretaries of the party Central Committee, Mzhavanadze and Vasili Churkin. They were both named Tamara and were known in Georgia as "the Tsarinas Tamara." (A Tsarina Tamara ruled Georgia in the twelfth century, and her memory has survived in popular folklore.)

The two Tamaras played a tangible role in the administration of the republic—and of course in the corruption too. It was well known that with their assistance one could be nominated to a lucrative or prestigious post. It was equally well known that the influential ladies were loath to accept Soviet rubles in payment for their services; they preferred either foreign hard currency or merchandise such as precious stones (but only very large ones), paintings by important artists, or antiques.

Underground businessmen enjoyed the particular good graces of the two Central Committee wives; it was through these millionaires that the Tamaras' collections of precious stones and works of art grew. Each Tamara had her own clients, among whom was to be the underground multimillionaire N. A. Laziashvili, a client of Tamara Mzhavanadze.

After the exposures and the purge Laziashvili was put on trial, and his case was written up in the republic and even the national press. They wrote about the scale of his criminal activities and about the millions he had made from them; they did not write about his having been a welcome visitor at the home of the First Secretary of the Central Committee of the republic's Communist party or about his having maintained ongoing business connections with the Secretary's wife.

The two Tamaras were the talk of the whole republic, yet

when Mzhavanadze and his clique were exposed, the plenum of the party Central Committee mentioned them only in the following delicate way: "Family members began to act as surrogates for their high-ranking husbands, and problems of state came to be resolved within a narrow circle of family members and friends" (*Dawn of the East*, February 28, 1973).

Shevarnadze made careful and unhurried preparations for his exposure of the corrupt ruling elite. An official from the Ministry of Internal Affairs who was a participant in the operation told me that even within the ministry apparat no one was informed about the minister's intentions. Shevarnadze had to conceal those intentions from everyone, but especially from the republic's KGB, which was led by a general who was utterly loyal to Mzhavanadze. When Shevarnadze issued instructions that surveillance was to include members of the ruling elite, he explained this as necessary in order to expose criminals who had wormed their way into the trust of honest Communists in responsible positions.

Finally Shevarnadze considered that the time was ripe. He had received intelligence reports from Moscow stating the flight number, date, and arrival time in Tbilisi of a big-time speculator on the Moscow black market in foreign currency, who, he had also been informed, usually carried precious stones for Tamara Mzhavanadze. Shevarnadze asked his colleagues in the Moscow Ministry for Internal Affairs to let the speculator board the plane in Moscow without touching her, and promised them that she would be taken when she disembarked in Tbilisi airport. My informant from the Georgian ministry who had participated in this affair told me that the operation had been carefully worked out in every detail: the speculator was to be stopped as she descended the stairs from the airplane in Tbilisi by a special group of agents responsible directly to the minister and taken for searching and questioning to the ministry. When the precious stones were discovered she would be given the chance of providing detailed information about whom the stones were destined for in exchange for the promise of a light sentence at her trial. (Trade in precious stones is a very serious crime, punishable by long prison terms or even by death.)

But that plan was never carried out. When the plane had landed and taxied to a halt near the terminal building a group of men in civilian clothes were waiting, all looking very much alike (as plainclothes policemen do the world over). They had identified the woman from photographs and were about to act when a huge black limousine drove up to the foot of the stairs, a limousine well known to every operative agent in Tbilisi. Tamara Mzhavanadze stepped out of it, embraced her Moscow guest as she came down the stairs, and ushered her into the car.

All the agents could do was to stare at the departing limousine of the First Secretary of the Central Committee of the Communist Party of Georgia. There was no sense in following it to learn the Moscow speculator's destination; it was clear enough that she was being driven directly to the private residence of the First Secretary, which the operatives—or anyone else for that matter—could not enter uninvited.

It was then decided that the gem dealer would be arrested after her departure from the Secretary's house, even though she would no longer have the compromising merchandise in her possession. There was a hope that she might be intimidated into providing the needed evidence. Even this plan failed. The guest was driven by Tamara Mzhavanadze right back to the staircase leading to the Moscow flight and was seen off with another warm embrace. Tamara stood on the tarmac until the airplane had taxied to the runway and taken off, all the while casting contemptuous glances at the group of agents.

The fact that Tamara Mzhavanadze went to the airport herself to meet the speculator with her precious stones (a thing she had never done before) proved that there had been a leak close to Shevarnadze and that the Mzhavanadze family had already been informed of the action being planned against it. Delays were dangerous, so Shevarnadze decided to go to Moscow immediately and submit his dossier of compromising evidence to Brezhnev.

It was toward the end of the summer of 1972. The First Secretary of the Central Committee of the Communist Party of Georgia was, as was his wont, passing the summer in his country residences—in the mountains on Lake Ritsa and in Gagra on the Black Sea coast.

On August 10, the republic's newspaper reported that the First Secretary had received the Secretary of the Central Committee of the Israeli Communist Party and his wife, who were vacationing in Georgia and whom he "warmly and fraternally welcomed." After he had fraternally welcomed the Israeli party Secretary and his wife, Mzhavanadze, according to a newspaper report of September 20, received a delegation from the German Democratic Republic. On the thirtieth a sudden extraordinary plenary session of the Georgian Central Committee was convened, which "complied with Mzhavanadze's request that he be permitted to retire on pension, for reasons of age" and elected Shevarnadze as First Secretary of the Central Committee on instructions from Moscow.

Virtually the entire ruling apparat of Georgia (both party and state) was removed for reasons of health, pensioned off, or, indeed, dismissed without any reason being given. Thirteen members of the government of the republic were removed; the Chairman of the Council of Ministers, the Chairman of the Presidium of the Supreme Soviet, all the top people in the apparat of the party Central Committee, the President of the Supreme Court and the Public Prosecutor of Georgia. The decrees removing all these officials from their posts were published in the republic's Russian-language newspaper, *Dawn of the East,* during 1972 and 1973.

But that was the limit of the purge. Not a single one of the ousted bribe takers faced a trial, and nearly all of them retained their party membership and, consequently, the possibility of again occupying leading posts in industry or in the ruling apparat. Mzhavanadze himself lost his candidate membership of the Politburo (on December 1972 at a plenum of the Central Committee of the CPSU), although he remained a member of the Communist party, and was granted a special pension of the kind usually provided for members and candidate members of the Politburo who have fallen out of favor, a pension amounting to about five times the maximum pension available to ordinary citizens.

Only Churkin, the Second Secretary of the Georgian Party Central Committee, was expelled from the party. Despite that he was given a post of the *nomenklatura,* the schedule of positions that can be held only by party members, subject to ratification by the party Obkom or the Central Committee. He was named to the post of Deputy Chairman of the Consumers' Union of the Kalininskaya region in the Russian Soviet Federal Socialist Republic (RSFSR).

The principal intermediaries in the transfer of the bribes, the two Tamaras, were also let off scot-free. The ones who landed up in court were the givers of the bribes, those who had purchased posts and academic credentials. Similar trials were held in Georgia between 1974 and 1977.

In the 1970s a bitter struggle developed between two clans within the ruling elite of Uzbekistan. On one side was the clan of one Sharaf Rashidov, the First Secretary of the Central Committee of the republic's Communist party and a Candidate Member of the Politburo. Opposing it was the clan within which Mankul Kurbanov and Yaggar Nasreddinova (respectively Chairman of the Council of Ministers of Uzbekistan and Chairwoman of the Presidium of the Supreme Soviet) had joined forces.

The main tactic employed by both sides in this struggle was sending revelatory denunciations to Moscow. Each clan had its own protectors (who acted by no means selflessly) within the apparat of the Moscow Central Committee, through whom it tried to compromise its opponents in the eyes of Brezhnev and other secretaries of the Central Committee of the CPSU. Denunciations fell fast and furious, each clan accusing the other of bribery, disruption of work, and falsifying triumphant reports about the fulfillment of the plans for the cotton harvest. (Cotton is Uzbekistan's principal crop and is of national importance). It must be said that these denunciations were quite true: there was wholesale corruption in the ruling circles of the republic.

From court cases later heard in Tashkent at local assizes of the USSR Supreme Court (in which Moscow defense attorneys participated) and from informants privy to information about the party and state rulers of Uzbekistan, I know that the leaders of that republic were paid regular tribute by chairmen of collective farms and managers of state farms, tribute in cash and in sheep, whole herds of which would be driven for them from mountain pastures into the capital. The owners of underground private enterprises made monthly protection payments in the form of money, gemstones, and, very often, in accordance with Asian tastes and traditions, valuable handmade rugs.

Each major official had his own sphere of influence and his own clientele by whom he was paid regular tribute in return for protection. For example, all the little shops and stalls in the Alai bazaar in the old part of Tashkent paid their tribute to Kurbanov, Chairman of the Council of Ministers.

But there was one underground business sector that made its payments to everyone: to the secretaries of the republic Central Committee, to the government leaders, to the Minister for Internal Affairs, to the head of the DCMSP (Department to Combat the Misappropriation of Socialist Property), and to many others besides. That sector was concerned with the cultivation and preparation of illegal drugs, the most dangerous—and the most profitable—business of all.

Apart from regular payments for protection and for connivance at illegal activities, bribes were also paid for the provision of specific services: appointments to lucrative and prestigious jobs, not-guilty verdicts in trials, and academic degrees. Chairwoman of the Presidium of the Supreme Soviet of Uzbekistan Nasreddinova, for example, traded in pardons, and her rates were well known: for the Presidium of the Supreme Soviet to issue an official pardon after someone had been convicted of a serious felony the cost would be 100,000 rubles. Pulat Khodzhaev, President of the Supreme Court, charged from 25,000 to 100,000 rubles for a verdict of not guilty.

The war between the rival clans in the ruling apparat of the republic continued, with each side scoring its share of successes, but the Moscow Central Committee tried its best to avoid an open, scandalous wholesale exposure of the ruling elite of Uzbekistan. They tried to defuse the situation by removing Nasreddinova (who had been exceedingly active in the intrigues in Uzbekistan). This they did by promoting her: she was "elected" (that is, appointed by the Central Committee of the CPSU) Chairwoman of the Council of Nationalities of the Supreme Soviet, one of the two houses of the Soviet parliament.

But in 1975 there came a turning point in the clan warfare. Taking advantage of the party apparat's dominance over the state apparat, Rashidov (First Secretary of the Central Committee of the Communist Party), with the assistance of the republic's KGB (formally subordinate to the Council of Ministers), collected a body of evidence of the corruption of his opponents. He took this evidence to Moscow and managed to get permission to conduct a purge. It is the view of my Uzbekistan informants that it was because of his insistence that it was decided to hold several open trials of members of the ruling elite of the republic.

To avoid scandalously compromising the regime, it was decided not to institute proceedings against Nasreddinova in her new and highly prestigious Council of Nationalities post.

She remained a member of the Communist party but was quietly transferred to one of the many deputy ministerial posts in the USSR ministries of the textile industry.

The first to stand trial was the President of the Supreme Court, Pulat Khodzhaev, and the next was the Chairman of the republic's Council of Ministers, Kurbanov.

The complete picture of corruption among the Uzbek ruling elite was not drawn during the trials, which took place between 1976 and 1977. The investigators on the case put a stop to any attempts by witnesses or defendants to extend the range of instances being examined and, consequently, the range of possible defendants. Kurbanov was particularly difficult to control in this respect. During the investigation and the trial, which took place in the presence of the public (a carefully selected public: only people with special passes were permitted to witness the trial), the investigators and the presiding member of the USSR Supreme Court all confined themselves to an examination of certain specific charges of individual instances of bribery on the part of the defendants, the President of the Supreme Court and the Chairman of the Council of Ministers.

Both of them pleaded not guilty, and since the bribes in question had not been received directly by the defendants, but had rather been passed on through middlemen (or whole chains of middlemen), their lawyers argued that the evidence of their guilt was far from incontrovertible. Indeed, the USSR Supreme Court rejected some of the charges as unproven. But both were found guilty, although a leniency unusual in Soviet justice was displayed toward them. To put this leniency in proper perspective I shall cite the case of the head of a driving school in Moscow's Baumansky district, who was sentenced to seven years in prison for having accepted 25- or 30-ruble bribes from pupils for whom he secured drivers' licenses; he was charged with having received altogether 1050 rubles in bribes. This is in great contrast to the two officials, who occupied very high positions in the ruling apparat of Uzbekistan and were found guilty of having taken hundreds of thousands of rubles in bribes; they were condemned to eight years (for the President of the Supreme Court) and ten years (for the Chairman of the Council of Ministers).

This atypical leniency was not the result of an arbitrary decision by the judges; the sentences were worked out beforehand at a very high level within the apparat of the Central Committee of the CPSU. Those sentences once more attest to the central authorities' tolerant attitude toward corruption in the top strata of the ruling party and state apparats.

Why are the authorities so tolerant of a corruption that has penetrated their own ranks? This tolerance—in a regime that is so forthright and ruthless in punishing all other crimes—is due first and foremost to the fact that too high a proportion of the members of the ruling elite is itself involved in the corruption. The proportion is so great that not even the all-powerful Politburo wants to risk a general purge of the ruling elite or the open confrontation with this elite that would result.

Another reason is the regime's fear of destroying a legend that has been built up over sixty years by the propaganda machinery of the Soviet Union and the foreign Communist parties—the legend of the infallibility of the Communist Party of the Soviet Union and its leadership, made up of chastely honest "servants of the people" whose personal needs are few and modest.

CHAPTER III

THE DISTRICT MAFIA

I WAS once on a train journey to the town of Salekhard in the center of the Yamal-Nenetsky National Okrug* near the Arctic Circle. I passed through concentration-camp country, and through the window I saw the names of stations flash by, names that brought back memories of the worst islands in the Gulag Archipelago: Inta, Pechora . . .

I was on my way to defend a man by the name of Berlin (his real name). The little I knew of his case left me completely bewildered. Berlin was a prominent figure in Salekhard, the director of the transcontinental telegraph communications department, responsible directly to the Ministry of Communications and not to the local authorities. He was a member of the Okrug Council of Deputies and by law was entitled to immunity from prosecution. However, he had been charged by the local public prosecutor's office with misuse of office and had even been arrested and im-

---

* An Okrug is a subdivision of the *krai*, or territory, based on the nationality of its inhabitants. (Trans. note)

prisoned. The whole thing was entirely counter to Soviet provincial ways.

While I was sitting in the office of the deputy public prosecutor of the okrug (who, contrary to generally accepted practice, was personally investigating the case) I took a look at the documents in the case, compiled during the investigation, and as I read, my perplexity, far from being allayed, grew ever greater. All the charges against Berlin consisted of mere trifles, routine matters in the life of any Soviet economic executive. He was charged with actions that are unavoidable for the manager of any Soviet enterprise, bereft, as he is, of independence and the right to manage the resources of the enterprise entrusted to him.

Those responsible for the investigation had not even charged Berlin with committing these misdemeanors for mercenary motives, a fact that, legally speaking, made the prosecution's position totally invalid. According to Article 170 of the Criminal Code, under which Berlin had been charged, only actions that are both inconsistent with the interests of the service and committed for mercenary motives or for personal gain are deemed criminal. When I pointed this out to the public prosecutor and tried to get to the bottom of the whole thing, he was evasive. Finally, however, he hinted that his office had nothing to do with the case and that he was only carrying out orders from the party bosses.

I went to see my client in the prison, a solid building made of stout pine beams. A tall, corpulent man met me, his hair, according to prison regulations, cropped close to the scalp but still clearly showing the gray. His manner was that of someone used to giving orders, authoritative and confident in his right to power. The mystery of why he had been charged and arrested was explained very simply. Since he was answerable directly to Moscow, Berlin felt independent of the local authorities. So when the First Secretary of the Okruzhkom (Okrug Committee) of the Communist Party imperiously demanded (demanded, not requested) that Berlin should give him materials and workmen to build a private house with all modern conveniences (in Salekhard at that time only Berlin and his deputies had homes like that), and further, that he should provide firewood for Okruzhkom staff members, Berlin refused, and did not greatly concern himself with couching his refusal in diplomatic terms.

The Secretary did not have the power to fire Berlin, but he saw to it that the okrug inspectorate sent their officers to Berlin's establishment. The result was a report enumerating all Berlin's violations, and this report formed the basis for an indictment. On the personal orders of the First Secretary, the Okrug Council of Deputies stripped Berlin of his immunity, and the prosecutor instituted criminal proceedings against him and issued a warrant for his arrest.

Since it would be impossible to get a fair verdict at the okrug court—it was obvious that the judge, prosecutor, and even the accounting experts would do what the First Secretary of the Okrug Committee of the Communist Party wanted—my task was to use the trial to prepare the case for the hearing at the Supreme Court.

The okrug court sentenced Berlin to a year's imprisonment and directed him to pay for the damages "caused by his actions against the state" (in reality there was no damage and nothing to pay). It was the Supreme Court of the RSFSR itself that revoked the sentence and completely acquitted Berlin. However, the happy ending was not quite so happy, for when he was released from prison Berlin felt it necessary to resign from his job and leave the Yamal-Nenetsky Okrug where he had lived and worked for almost twenty years. He had chosen not to abide by the rules, not to become a tributary of the okrug mafia, but in doing so he had learned a harsh lesson: that no one could flout the rules laid down by the local elite.

That is how the district elite deals with those who do not

pay their dues. But what are these "dues" and what role do they play in the life of the Soviet provinces?

Because of the limitations on the state budget and party funds, the ruling elite of the country is incapable of providing the lower levels of the gigantic ruling apparat with the same privileges they have secured for themselves. All the secretaries of district committees, chairmen of district executive committees, directors of district offices, and other such officials have to look after their own interests by themselves. Their official salaries are not large (for example, a district committee secretary might earn 250 rubles a month), but on the other hand they wield great power in the life of their districts, and they can make up for what they do not get from the state and party by using this power to extort payments in goods and services from people who are dependent on them. This lower stratum comprises tens of thousands of party and state functionaries who represent power in the provinces and who are the backbone of the ruling class. They are the main buttress of central power, of which they are the representatives. Consequently the supreme authorities have to accept the fact that the local authorities compensate for their lack of official perquisites by accepting payments in money and in kind.

Once I had to stay in a small district center of the Arkhangelsk region, on the shores of the White Sea. I had to remain for about five weeks to take part in a trial, and since the only hotel in town was terrible, I preferred to rent a room in a private house.

The landlord of this house worked as a foreman in a butter plant and his wife was a bookkeeper in the district consumer's union. Her brother—a former legal adviser to a Moscow factory—was staying with them. He was the man who helped me learn much about the life of this district center.

As he was retired, the former jurist was able to observe life in this small town. Every morning he would walk to the post office to buy two-day-old Moscow newspapers. The post office was located on the same square as the various state and party institutions. As he sat alongside the other pensioners on a bench in the square and read the papers he used to notice trucks loaded with cabbages, whole carcasses of meat, dry-cured or fresh fish, or enormous forty-liter milk cans regularly driving up to these offices. Once even a truckload of hay rolled up to the district police department building. Whenever a truck drove up to the entrance of an office building, the employees would leap out and lend a hand in taking the produce inside or to the spacious backyard.

The visitor from Moscow struck up acquaintances with a few of the retired local people who always gathered in the public garden to read the Moscow newspapers and have a leisurely chat about the vicissitudes of the international situation. Among them were former civil servants, book-keepers, and salesclerks. They were able to give exhaustive answers to all his questions, and he soon learned from them that the trucks were delivering state farm and collective farm produce to the employees of the district institutions, produce that they needed to feed themselves as well as for winter fodder for their livestock.

The townspeople explained to him, with a thorough knowledge of the subject, that the First Secretary of the District Committee, "Himself," was a fair, unpretentious (that is, democratic and not arrogant) boss and that he held the law in respect. Accordingly, everything that was delivered was divided equally among the employees, irrespective of their positions. They paid for all the meat, fish, and honey they took—not as much as they would pay in the shops, of course, but at the same prices that the heads of the state and collective farms charge when they sometimes allow a small amount of produce to be made available from their warehouses and sold to the workers at prices one-fifth to one-tenth those charged in the stores. As for the rest—the hay and the vegetables—the employees in some offices paid the same low prices, and in others they paid nothing at all.

The former legal adviser attempted to explain to his local acquaintances that all this was illegal and that the state and collective farm managers were misappropriating socialist property and that the directors of the district institutions, including the District Committee Secretary, were accessories to the crime and even inciters to crime. No one he spoke to shared his indignation. Everyone regarded all this as perfectly normal, day-to-day routine that did not deserve any particular attention. Not only did the locals not condemn the system of merchandise payoffs, they fully approved of it, considering it unavoidable, since without it, as they explained to the visitor, a rank-and-file office worker would find it impossible to live.

The locals he talked to also held the same view about the gifts received by the bosses. They were unanimous in their approval of the First Secretary because he was a modest man, taking only what he needed and nothing more and not allowing his wife to take more than she needed. With one voice too they deplored the behavior of the Chairman of the District Executive Committee and related that he had taken over for his own dwelling a large building that had been intended for a kindergarten (he gave his old house—a much smaller one—to the kindergarten), which the district building office had, completely free of charge, fitted out with a luxury hitherto unknown in the town. In disapproving tones they stated that the car belonging to the district motor transport bureau was permanently—and, naturally, free of charge —at the disposal of the Chairman's wife, and they said much else besides.

And soon the jurist was able to observe with his own eyes the workings of the gift system. The whole town was alive with rumors about the forthcoming marriage of the son of the Chairman of the District Executive Committee. Everyone knew that the wedding would be celebrated on a grand scale in the town's only restaurant and that there would be more than a hundred guests present. Officialdom was agog, and everyone was anxious to be invited. Whether or not one had received an invitation became a matter of prestige, an indicator of one's position in the hierarchy of the local elite.

The restaurant was closed to the public for a whole week. Carcasses of calves and suckling pigs, smoked and fresh fish, and much else besides were brought in from all corners of the district. On the day of the wedding a crowd gathered in front of the restaurant to have a look at the festivities (my informant was among them), and everyone saw a bus drive up to the restaurant and discharge two dozen old women all dressed in embroidered antique country costumes. It was a celebrated folk choir that specialized in ancient North Russian songs. Through the open windows the crowd could hear the old women charm the local elite with their ceremonial wedding songs.

My landlady, as bookkeeper of the consumer's union, to which the restaurant belonged, learned what the Chairman of the Executive Committee had paid for the reception: eighty-five kopecks a head. She could only hazard a guess at how much the wedding—including the dozens of bottles of vodka, wine, and champagne—had actually cost the restaurant. But the visitor's indignation at all this was not understood by his relatives, who, while they did not receive any gifts themselves, did not condemn people who did; they were simply somewhat envious of them, just as anyone would be of someone who was better off than himself.

My landlady and her husband told me many interesting things, disregarding the fact that they were divulging local secrets. The landlady told us that each month all the local cooperative shops delivered packets of money to the chairman of the consumer's union, part of which he took himself and part of which he passed on to someone in the District

Committee (she did not know to whom exactly). He also sent part to the regional consumer's union in the main town of the region. Her husband related that his dairy regularly delivered butter and sour cream to the houses of the most important bosses of the district.

It was then that the legal consultant from Moscow decided to expose what he called "these plunderers who had ensconced themselves in the leadership of the district and who were a disgrace to the Soviet regime and the Communist party."

I advised him to complain directly to Moscow. But as a jurist he was accustomed to observing the rules of hierarchy, so he first wrote to the regional bodies—the Communist party committee and the public prosecutor's office. He received no answers, but his faith in justice and legality were not shaken. So he wrote to Moscow, to the Central Committee of the Communist Party of the Soviet Union and the USSR Public Prosecutor's Office, which notified him that his complaints had been forwarded to be examined by the competent regional organizations and that he would be informed of their findings.

He did not have to wait long for a reply. Soon his hospitable relative was summoned to the District Committee (he was a party member), where the Second Secretary told him that unless his relative returned immediately to Moscow and stopped writing denunciations he would be fired and life would be made impossible for him and his wife. There was nothing to be done; my informant could not destroy the life of his relatives, so he capitulated, accepted the committee's ultimatum, and returned home to Moscow.

The picture painted above is a typical one. In remote parts of the country the system of tribute has become a characteristic and generally accepted form of corruption on the lower rungs of the ladder of the ruling class. Its salient feature is that, besides accepting bribes for performing some definite action, the members of the district elite receive gifts in kind and in the form of services from everyone dependent on them. And since all institutions and enterprises in the district are in such a position of dependence, the range of goods and services that might be offered is limited only by the possibilities of the district itself. A fairly coherent and nearly complete picture of the way the system of tributes operates in remote areas can be formed on the basis of court case documents, articles in the Soviet press, eyewitness accounts, and my own observations.

In small provincial towns there are no "Kremlin 'Care packages' " like the ones to which the ruling elite in Moscow have access, nor are there any of the restricted stores where the governing classes can buy food. In fact, people in the small far-off towns, especially in Russia itself, cannot get hold of the necessary staple foods, in the normal way, even for money and at the regular state prices. The ordinary people in these towns still live, as they did in the past, mainly by subsistence farming. They cultivate their own garden plots and, if at all possible, keep a goat or a cow; in addition, they buy things in the marketplace. Members of the local ruling elite, on the other hand, live mainly on tribute. And, depending on the season and local climatic conditions, there is an abundant and constant flow from the state and collective farms to the pantries and kitchens of the top district employees: tons of fruit and vegetables, meat and fish, jars of honey, basketfuls of eggs, thousands of liters of homemade country wines, and sundry other victuals.

The best (usually the only) restaurant in every town has a small room whose key is held by the manager. This room is opened only for select persons—those belonging to the local elite and their guests. They are not served the same food as the simple folk in the public dining room; they are given dishes that are specially prepared from a separate food supply. More often than not they eat and—it goes without saying—drink in such a place absolutely free of charge.

These provincial towns have nothing like the garages belonging to the Central Committee and the Council of Ministers, from which anyone in the higher levels of the apparat may order any number of cars at any time of day or night. The District Committee and the District Executive Committee may have one or two cars, and these are all that the ruling elite has at its disposal. However, they do have access to any vehicles, whether passenger cars or trucks, that belong to the district motor transport establishment or indeed to any local department.

On orders from the District Committee Secretary, state vehicles, completely free of charge, will take the Secretary, his family, and his friends hunting, fishing, or out for a picnic. Or they will transport furniture or building materials from the main town of the region or even from Moscow if needed to repair the Secretary's private house.

There are no government houses in these provincial towns, as there are in Moscow, on Granovsky Street or Serafimovich Street, nor are there any special apartment buildings like those erected for government officials in the larger regional centers. On the other hand, the remote areas do have chairmen of collective farms and directors of state farms who, at the bidding of the District Committee, use farm funds to foot the bills for the construction of private residences for the local ruling elite, to the tune of tens of thousands of rubles. They also have construction organizations with managers who are prepared to allocate state building materials for these private ventures, materials that might have been intended for kindergarten or hospital projects. Finally, there are village and district soviets that will violate the law and issue orders to designate tracts of land for these private residences.

A list of tributes in the form of services could be continued *ad infinitum:* free automobile repairs in the garages of state enterprises; household repairs at no cost made by the district construction offices; workers from local state enterprises sent during working hours to tend gardens of the officials, and so on.

The circle of people who belong to the elite of a district and who enjoy the fruits of the tribute system cannot of course be precisely delineated. But each member of this circle receives personal tributes in accordance with his position in the district hierarchy and with how much power he wields and the areas over which it extends. Accordingly, a First Secretary of a District Committee of the Communist Party is at the apex of this hierarchy, followed by a Chairman of the District Executive Committee, for their power is universal and extends to everything in the district. Therefore each is able to make use of the services of any institution or enterprise in the district and to receive gifts from all the state and collective farms. These officials accept all this not in return for any specific service but just for a generally favorable attitude and for their patronage. They are given tributes simply because power over the whole district is concentrated in their hands; they are offered services to make sure that they do not use their power against the giver, to forestall any possible trouble, and to ensure that if one of their tributaries was threatened by prosecution they would exercise their authority to defend him or her.

This type of relationship between district rulers and the managers of enterprises and institutions who are subordinate to them is based on the total power of the party-state apparat and the fact that it is not subject to the law or checked by public opinion and the press. Another major factor is that in the Soviet Union there exists not one single manager—even the most unshakably, incorruptibly honest of them—who is capable of running his enterprise or institution effectively without breaking the law. Because of that a manager's happiness and peace of mind hinge on the people who wield the power in the district, on whether or not they will look favorably on his exaggerated reports on fulfillment of planned targets and on his breaches of the law and of their own instructions on financial and material expenditures.

But few managers exploit their official positions merely in order to get things done in their respective institutions or enterprises. There are a number of other reasons as well—not the least of which is the need to find the money to pay for all the tributes they have to distribute!—that impel them to misconduct in their own mercenary interests. It is in this way that opportunities for payoffs are opened up to district public prosecutors and police chiefs.

Neither prosecutors nor police chiefs occupy very exalted positions in the district hierarchy; often they are not even members of the bureau of the District Committee (one of the sure signs of membership in the district elite). But they do have a certain amount of say in whether or not criminal proceedings are to be instituted against a store or restaurant manager or the head of a state or collective farm, and, accordingly, these people have become the obedient tributaries of the police and public prosecutors' offices.

The district financial, sanitation, veterinary, and fire inspectors do not have much power at all, although each of them in his own sphere can make a certain amount of trouble for the director of an institution or enterprise. The financial inspector can audit the books, expose criminal manipulations and falsifications, and draw up a report that leaves no choice but to request the public prosecutor to institute criminal proceedings.

Sanitary and fire inspectors are authorized to make reports about violations of health or fire laws and temporarily close down a store or restaurant or impose a fine on its manager.

In large cities too, such as regional centers, capitals of republics, and Moscow itself, the local ruling elite takes advantage of its position to obtain tributes. In these places, however, the tribute system takes on a somewhat different form and operates much less blatantly than its rural counterpart. But despite the fact that the regional or central administration may be in close proximity, the system is still unchanging and ubiquitous in large cities.

Information about this urban version of the tribute system never leaks out into the Soviet press, and I know of no case of a top employee of the party-state apparat being prosecuted for having taken advantage of it. Nevertheless I was able to collect information about tribute accepted by the district elite in the large cities from my own experience as a lawyer, as well as from court files and by questioning members of the elite and food-store employees.

In cases of this kind it is only the employees of shops, restaurants, and cafés who are ever indicted; their privileged clients never appear in court, even as witnesses. Managers of stores and restaurants, salesclerks, and refreshment-bar waiters are most often accused of pilfering or of cheating customers.

As in the provinces, the district elite in the large cities have free use of automobiles belonging to the various district institutions and enterprises, and of garage services to repair their own cars. Lacking in the large cities are the collective and state farms to provide the elite with produce, but this function is performed by the state stores and restaurants.

In each district of a major city there are two or three food shops especially set aside for the local elite. Neither their outward aspect, the range of goods on the shelves, nor the mass of customers crowded into them distinguishes them from dozens of other shops. However, behind the scenes—in the managers' offices and in the stockrooms—everything is different: the privileged social status of the customers, the assortment of goods, and even the prices.

An example of a typical Moscow arrangement was revealed in its every detail during the trial of seventeen employees of Food Shop Number Five, situated not far from Luzhniki Stadium (which was the center for the 1980 Olympic Games). Nearly all the store's employees were charged —from the sixteen-year-old trainee salesclerk to the hoary old manager, retired Air Force Lieutenant Colonel Boris

Adamov. (I am giving his real name 'since he died in the camps while serving out his sentence.)

Food Shop Number Five had been designated to serve the ruling elite of one of the Moscow districts. The shop had a list of the district's state and party staff members who were to be afforded privileges. In cases when someone had to be added to or removed from the list the Raikom inspector charged with the supervision of trade would telephone the manager. (The inspector himself also took advantage of the store's facilities, of course.) People who had been ejected from the elite generally understood the inevitable consequences and never visited the store again. Those who tried to exercise their privileges, having lost the right to them, were not openly barred from the store, but various transparent pretexts were used to keep the goods out of their hands, such as the claim of a lack of supplies or the manager's having no time to serve them.

The tribute routine went something like this: Once or twice a week the wives of the top Raikom and Raiispolkom staff members would visit the store. They would inquire about what was available and would hand over a list of what they required. While the order was being filled they would wait in the manager's office, to which the wrapped packages would be brought. The manager would then tell the customer the amount of her bill. For delicacies, wine, vodka, and cognac, either the full price would be charged or no charge would be made at all (the latter mostly on the eve of an important state holiday, when the Raikom would give instructions to prepare holiday gift packages for executive employees). The other goods would go for one-third to one-half the list price.

Apart from the top staffs of the Raikom and Raiispolkom, there were other members of the elite who were not on the list at Food Shop Number Five but who still enjoyed preferential service. For example, the District Chief of Police and the chief of the Department to Combat Misappropriation of

Socialist Property (DCMS) were regular customers. But they would come and select what they wanted in person, not through their wives, the subtlety in procedure indicating that their status as privileged clients was not as official as that of the employees of the party and state organs. On the other hand, nothing they procured from the store—food or liquor—ever cost them a kopeck, and this was indicative of the fact that the store was more directly dependent upon the police than on the district leadership in general.

There were others as well, not leading officials at all, who also had to be given free merchandise on a regular basis: the sanitation inspector (fortunately she was a woman who did not very often demand such expensive drinks as fine cognac and vodka), the fire inspector (who, on the other hand, was mainly interested in such strong liquors), a police precinct representative, as well as some completely unexpected characters, such as the technician from the local telephone station.

The number of people given favors by Food Shop Number Five was established in court—about forty in all. Since the store's assistant manager (who was also on trial) kept a "black" ledger in which she had entered all the illegal receipts and expenditures, it was possible to ascertain approximately how much the favors had cost the store: they attained the very impressive sum of about 90,000 rubles a year.

The case of the employees of Food Shop Number Five was by no means unique. There were several similar cases in Moscow and Leningrad, and the picture of the tribute system as shown in the documents of these cases differs only in minor details from what went on in Food Shop Number Five.

In the various districts of a regional town, on the other hand, the mechanics are somewhat different. In recent years food supplies to the Russian provinces have become ever poorer. In the overwhelming majority of regional centers (not to mention the smaller district centers) even the most essential staples such as meat, fish, poultry, sausages, dairy products, and vegetables cannot be bought in stores open to the general public. This situation can be partly overcome by purchasing some things in the market at prices that through 1978 were running three to three and a half times shop prices. (According to information that has reached me from the Soviet Union, they were five to six times the prices charged in stores as of August 1979.)

Given this supply situation, it is obvious that the few insignificant morsels that do reach the stores in regional centers do not get as far as the ordinary shopper but find their way either onto the black market or into the hands of all those on whom the peace of mind and happiness of the store manager depend—members of the local elite, the police, the public prosecutor's office, and the various inspectors. And as a rule even these privileged clients (apart from the police) pay full-scale prices.

Despite this system of tributes and favors, food-store managers do not tolerate actual losses; the only loss they can take is the one they describe as "lost profit"—the difference between the state price of an item and the price it would bring on the black market.

Where did the manager of Food Shop Number Five get hold of the ninety thousand rubles he needed to cover the cost of tributes and favors? How can collective and state farms manage to deliver truckloads of provisions to the local elite free of charge?

To anyone acquainted with this aspect of Soviet life the answer to all these questions is perfectly obvious: illegally. Only by committing theft, by cheating the government and their customers, and by falsifying the accounts are officials and managers of state farms, collective farms, food stores and restaurants able to bear the burden of the tribute system. And so the permanent corruption of the ruling elite at the district level has given birth to a system of true organized crime. In essence, this is the story of the Soviet district mafia. A reader unfamiliar with the Soviet system of government would be quite justified in asking, "Why don't these people just refuse to pay the price? What could happen in a modern state to someone who will not take on the obligations of making such payoffs?" The story about the prosecution of my defendant Berlin, with which I began this chapter, offers the answer.

It is interesting now to note how the district mafia guarantees the impunity of those who do pay tributes, even when they have committed real crimes. In the Soviet Union there are two big holidays at the beginning of May: the International Day of Workers' Solidarity on the first, and Victory Day on the ninth. On those days, as on other Soviet and church holidays, a binge of hard drinking lasting several days traditionally takes place in the Russian villages. At the beginning of May 1978 the entire male population of the "Bolshevik" State Farm in Kolchugino in the Vladimir region was dead drunk and incapable of any work. The bosses had left for another village "to have a good time" (to get drunk themselves). The herdsmen and the drivers were also having a good time. Meanwhile the supplies of fodder had run out at the farm, and as there was no one to go and fetch more, the cows were not fed for more than a week. In addition, a long period of rain set in, and the roads to the farm became impassable for vehicles and even for pedestrians.

On May 11, when all those hearties finally managed to fight their way through to the farm, they found 16 cows already dead of starvation and the remaining 200-odd lying in a weakened state before their gnawed-down wooden troughs. But there was nothing for them to eat, since the workers had not yet recovered from their ten-day binge, and no one was fit to fetch the fodder even if the tractors had been able to make it through the mud. The cattle had to be fed with rotten straw that had been lying in the fields under the snow all winter. The next day the poisoned cattle were struck with murrain, and 219 died.

The damages caused by the murrain amounted to 40,000

rubles, and the scandal was so huge that the manager of the state farm and the others directly implicated had to be brought to trial. (As I see it, this was done only under pressure from regional authorities.) And even so, the culprits got off virtually scot-free. The Raikom expelled no one from the party; no one lost his job; and the District People's Court gave them all suspended sentences (which had been previously arranged with the Raikom). Instead of the culprits having to repay the 40,000 rubles lost by the farm as a result of their drunken negligence, they had to pay back only 10 percent of it, and even then they were allowed to pay it out over seven years.

This story about how the Raikom protects its tributaries was related in *The Literary Gazette* (No. 5, 1979) and is typical not only for Russia but for any of the Union republics.

What strikes one mostly in this example, as in others, is the utterly blatant and fearless way in which the district elite acts, covering up criminals who are harmful to the very state to whose ruling class that elite itself belongs. Their complete indifference to the interests of that state is striking.

The fight against organized crime has always presented major difficulties for any state in whatever political system. In a democratic country such as the United States the difficulties stem from a respect for legality and the basic principles of justice. The police know the heads of the Mafia families and their whereabouts, but they do not have sufficient evidence to submit to a court of law in order that criminal proceedings might be instituted.

In a totalitarian state like the Soviet Union, on the other hand, the fight against organized crime encounters quite different obstacles, obstacles that stem from the fact that crime has practically enveloped the whole country and the entire lower levels of the party-state apparat.

The district mafia in the Soviet Union is invulnerable to attack from within the district itself. Its power could be destroyed only by the higher apparat of the Obkom on the regional level of the party if the Obkom were to replace the district leaders and fire or transfer the major figures of the district's criminal world. But in the Soviet Union that is a rare and extraordinary occurrence, and, considering the way in which the Soviet organized-crime system normally operates, the likelihood of its happening is extremely slight and may on the whole be discounted. For in normal circumstances the upper levels in the ruling apparat are perfectly well informed about what is going on in the districts but prefer to accept it.

It is quite easy to find evidence of this fact in articles that have appeared in the Soviet press. In columns entitled "Following Our Action" or "After Criticism" which appear in all the central papers published in Moscow (e.g., Pravda, Izvestia, Literaturnaia Gazeta) hundreds of articles are published each year informing us that the bureau of a certain Obkom or Raikom has disciplined a district official or the manager of an institution or enterprise for actions that are in fact violations of the criminal code, such as misuse of office for mercenary purposes, overstating the amount of work actually done in order to obtain illegal bonuses (tantamount to embezzlement of state funds), falsification of accounts, and so forth. These articles almost never say that the offenders have been indicted and tried in courts of law.

A feature article in *Pravda* (the official organ of the Central Committee of the Communist Party of the Soviet Union) that publicly exposes the criminal deeds of managers of district institutions and enterprises who belong to the district mafia is as effective and incontrovertible as a court sentence would be. But even that sort of article is very seldom as punitive as it sets out to be, and more often than not the Raikom or Obkom will cushion its impact by reporting to the newspaper and the Central Committee that the culprits have been apprehended, removed from their respective posts, and disciplined by the party. But this party discipline does practically no damage to the interests of the offenders. After they are removed from one post they immediately—or after a short interim—are given another, no less prestigious and lucrative, in the same region, or even manage to be promoted.

Strange as it may seem, the typical way in which the district and regional levels of the party-state apparat sabotage the central government's attempts to combat the district mafia has been described in the pages of *Pravda*. One of the numerous articles devoted to that subject appeared on September 2, 1979.

The action takes place in the Saratov region, Ivanteevo district: "Certain leading officials in the district, to put it mildly, did not always observe the norms of party ethics or at times even of our legislation. However, the bureau of the Raikom and its First Secretary N. Misiura shut their eyes to this and even connived at the offenses." An interpretation of the jargon traditionally used by the Soviet press when writing about the misdeeds of government officials reveals that the district elite, headed by the First Secretary of the Raikom, took lavish and unabashed advantage of the tribute system.

According to a letter from the Chairman of the District Party Control Committee, several Obkom inspectors had visited the district and had stated that "the acts described in the letter were indeed committed." The *Pravda* article continues: "The matter was taken up by the Obkom bureau. However, the participants in the Ivanteevo saga got off with scolding reprimands and mild words about 'looking out' and 'paying attention.' "

Following this inaction by the Obkom a devastating feature article was published in *Pravda*. A whole year passed after the article appeared. And at the end of that year, what steps were taken by the Saratov Obkom after the all-powerful Central Committee of the Communist Party of the Soviet Union had demanded that the Ivanteevo story be given a "principled, party-minded evaluation"? Some members of the district mafia, including First Secretary Misiura, were transferred to high posts in the regional center, while the chairman of the Raiispolkom continued to occupy his post. But the Chairman of the Control Committee, who had been so bold as to expose the affair, was dropped from the district elite; he was not reelected to his post in the bureau of the Raikom.

Regarding the regional party-state apparat's protection of the district mafia, I must agree with the words of the author of the *Pravda* article, "Unfortunately, these examples are not isolated ones."

Thus the regional apparat does nothing to combat corruption at the district level, and the central authorities can achieve success in this struggle only with great difficulty, by sabotaging the regional party organs. But even the central authorities do not devote much attention to fighting district corruption, and make only extremely rare use of their unlimited law-enforcement powers to deal with the district mafias.

What are the reasons for this tolerance? First, the district elite is linked to the ruling apparat by a chain of corruption, and a portion of the never-ending tributes and bribes flows in a constant stream from the district centers to the regional centers. But the second, and principal, reason for the district mafia's impunity is that virtually all districts of the country are afflicted with corruption, and to struggle against it effectively would require total and constant purging of the ruling apparat in all the districts of all the regions of the country. The ruling clique of the Soviet Union is not prepared to destabilize the government apparat in that way.

Even if the district mafia could be dealt some blows, albeit not fatal ones, from above, it still remains absolutely invulnerable to any attempt to combat its activities from within the district itself. Furthermore, it is always able to strike a counterblow and give short shrift to anyone who encroaches upon its power. More than once I have witnessed the mafia dealing with its enemies. The following is typical of the way they ordinarily operate. My sources of information are the documents of a criminal case, conversations with people who took part in the events, and my own personal impressions.

I once came across an unusual client in the waiting room of my legal consultation office: a man in the uniform of a police colonel. He and his wife had been awaiting my arrival. The colonel was an experienced man of the world. He was taciturn and rather gloomy about their prospects in the case on which they sought my help. His wife, however, was seething with indignation and was firmly convinced that justice would triumph and that vice would be punished. The case concerned her father somewhere in the depths of the Arkhangelsk region who had been arrested and accused of slandering leading district officials.

The investigation was over and the case had been passed to the court, so the colonel could not help his father-in-law by using his official influence. What he could do was to engage a lawyer from Moscow who—unlike a local lawyer—would not be afraid to enter into a fight with the local powers.

In the USSR, members of the bar are allowed to plead before any court in the country. An agreement is reached with the client, who pays for all traveling expenses and accommodations. During the years of my law practice I made many business trips throughout the country, sometimes to the most Godforsaken places. I enjoyed these trips, first, because I had a chance to observe the life of the Soviet province, and second, because arguing before provincial courts involved sharp and even dangerous fighting against the local mafia on behalf of men and women who were being unfairly prosecuted.

So a week later I set off for the village of Ustye, buried

deep in the forests of the Arkhangelsk region. I arrived there by train and by hitching rides on trucks; the last ten miles I covered on foot. I studied my client's case and listened to what he, his sons, and his friends had to say. Gradually the life of the district began to unfold for me.

Agriculture played a secondary role in the economy of the Ustye district. The bedrock of life, the main resource of the district, was timber. Timber stations, which fell trees and carry out the rough processing of the logs, are scattered throughout the territory, a territory that is equal in area to half of Belgium. These stations are vital to the economy of the district. The Obkom bosses evaluate the work of the district managers on the basis of how successfully they have fulfilled the timber plans. A no less important feature of the life of Ustye, however, is that the timber stations are the chief contributors to the district elite.

The Soviet Union is one of the most heavily wooded countries in the world, and yet timber in the form of logs and planks is one of the most sought-after and scarce materials for any enterprise or collective farm. For how can anything be built without timber? But the Soviet state sees timber as a prime export and the source of badly needed dollars. For that reason timber products are strictly controlled, and the timber stations are allowed to ship them only with special documents issued by the appropriate government organs. People who require timber and have not been issued the necessary documents have only one recourse: to send their agents directly to the timber stations and procure the much-needed planks and logs by bribery.

Such is the abundant and inexhaustible source of the money the directors use for gifts that go straight into the pockets of the district elite (and naturally for their own enrichment as well).

In the Arkhangelsk region every timber station is an island lost in a sea of forests, isolated from the whole world and even from the district center because of impassable roads. A timber station is a settlement consisting of nothing more than the office building, a club, a canteen, and a store. The people live either in their own small houses, which resemble peasant *izbas,* or else in barracks-style hostels—long, one-story buildings consisting of several dozen smallish rooms. Each family occupies one room—even if there are four or six people in the family—and uses one of the two large kitchens. There are no toilets, baths, or even running water in these barracks.

An outpost like this is ruled—and ruled like a dictatorship —by the director of the timber station. It is he who decides who shall be given work at the station (and there is nowhere else to work), and whether the work is to be easy and lucrative or hard and badly paid.

My client, a man called Popov (all the names in this story are real), lived in one of these communities and worked as a tractor driver. A certain Romanov was the director of the station, and his wife was in charge of the store and the canteen, which provided monopoly services to the settlement. The Romanovs ruled the timber station and the entire community like despots. The husband was thin and small of stature and looked comical next to his tall wife with her enormous girth, yet everyone—including Madame Romanova herself—quaked in his presence. He was a spiteful and vindictive man and did not brook the slightest display of discontent. As in any kingdom, the Romanov pair were assisted in ruling their domains by courtiers who constituted the elite of the community: the Secretary of the party bureau, the Chairman of the local trade union committee, and the foremen and section managers. In addition, there was naturally a network of secret informers that had been organized by the director himself.

The retinue of courtiers kept an eye on the inhabitants of the community, and twice a month—on paydays—they skimmed off part of the workers' wages and gave the money they collected to the director. To make sure that they were not keeping back any money for themselves, they in turn were watched by the director's spies—even more closely than the ordinary workers were, in fact. The director distributed the loot himself; he gave his assistants their rather meager share and kept the bulk for himself. This sum was used to pay regular tribute to those district bosses Romanov felt it important to cultivate. In particular, regular payments were made to the Raikom secretaries and the chairmen of the Raiispolkom, while smaller and more sporadically paid sums went to the District Chief of Police and to the public prosecutor of the district.

The store and canteen were Mrs. Romanova's domain, and here it was she who had unlimited power. She fixed prices for everything that was in demand, taking no notice of the official state prices that she was—theoretically— obliged to charge. She also drew up the list of people who were to receive particularly scarce items. The food in the canteen was so miserable that even the undemanding loggers who spent weeks on end in the forest and were accustomed to bad food sometimes could not contain themselves and would raise hell with the cook and the waitresses. (The men were afraid of Mrs. Romanova herself and behaved meekly when she was around.) Added to that, the canteen's customers were mercilessly cheated: they usually got a little more than three-quarters of the amount they had paid for.

However, the exploitation of the inhabitants of the settlement did not end here, for they were under another obligation, that of doing unpaid work for the Romanov family. The Romanovs owned a house with a large garden, and at the merest hint by "the missus," as Romanov called his wife to her face and behind her back, anyone in the settlement was obliged to work in the garden, make repairs to the house, or attend to the Romanov family's needs, all for nothing.

The Romanovs had ruled over the timber station and the community in this way for many years. In all this time no one had attempted to throw off their yoke. Everyone knew that sending a complaint about them "to the district" was useless; they were all aware that the Romanovs duly shared their booty with all the right people, starting with the First Secretary of the Raikom.

In 1972, however, someone did appear who was not afraid to do battle with the almighty rulers of the timber station. Popov was the best tractor driver on the station, and in a community that was almost universally addicted to hard drinking he was particularly remarkable for the fact that he and his sons were teetotalers. It was while serving at the front during the war that Sergeant Popov had joined the Communist party. And he was still one of those Communists, a rare breed in the Soviet Union nowadays, who religiously believe everything printed in the Soviet newspapers about the justice and democratic nature of the Soviet system, that the workers are in control of the country, and other such pronouncements. Popov explained the situation in Ustye to himself and others by saying that there just happened to be dishonest people among those in charge. He was piously convinced that it was enough to inform the higher levels of the party about the disgraceful things that were going on to have all the criminals expelled from the party and severely punished.

And so Popov set about exposing them. He wrote detailed letters to the party Obkom and to the regional newspaper. Soon he was asked to go to Ustye where the representative of the Raikom sat with him and tried to talk him out of writing complaints. He employed demagogery as well as appeals to his sense of duty to the Party and his conscientiousness as a Communist, who should not undermine the authority of the Party leadership—and, of course, he employed threats. But Popov wrote further, even more detailed letters to the Central Committee of the Communist Party of the Soviet Union and to *Pravda*. The officials at the Central Committee and at *Pravda* informed him that his letters had been transmitted to the Obkom of the party for examination.

This time Popov was spoken to by the First Secretary of the Raikom himself, and now without demagogery or cajolery. He was simply presented with an ultimatum: "Unless you stop writing denunciations I'll fire you and expel you from the party."

After this meeting Popov sent off a new batch of complaints to Moscow, again to the Central Committee and *Pravda,* but this time he added a new address to his distribution list: the Public Prosecutor General of the USSR. (I am able to trace this because these complaints, as well as the previous ones, had all been neatly filed by the investigator in the dossier I was reading.) Popov was not summoned again to the Raikom, but at the timber station's Party bureau meeting, the personal case of Communist Party of the Soviet Union member Popov was examined, and party member Popov was accused of slandering the party leaders of the district and the director of the timber station. The Secretary of the bureau, one of Romanov's closest accomplices, easily got a decision passed to expel Popov from the party "for slandering and discrediting the party leadership." Orders soon followed from the station's director: Popov was dismissed from his job.

Once more Popov sent off a heap of complaints to Moscow and at the same time filed suit with the district people's court to be reinstated in his job. Although there could be no question that his suit was justified, the court rejected it, while Moscow continued to inform him that his complaints were being examined by the appropriate regional organs. Despite everything, Popov still believed in the ultimate triumph of justice and kept sending more and more complaints to Moscow.

Matters then came to a head. One morning a local police officer handed Popov a summons to the district public prosecutor's office to meet with an investigator. Popov did not return home from Ustye. In the public prosecutor's office he was shown a decision to prosecute him under Article 130 of the criminal code of the Russian Soviet Federal Socialist Republic "for spreading slanders known to be false discrediting the Citizens Romanov." He was then shown a warrant for his arrest signed by the district prosecutor and was escorted to a detention cell.

The people's court heard the case against Popov in the community club. The district prosecutor was there in person to support the state's charge (a very rare occurrence for district public prosecutors' offices). The Romanovs appeared in court as the aggrieved parties.

There was an atmosphere of tense expectation in the room, which was packed with people from the community. At first everything went as the prosecutor and judge had planned. The timber station workers, when summoned as witnesses for the prosecution, testified without exception that they had never given anyone a single kopeck of money out of their wages, that the store and the canteen could not be better run, and that if they ever had to work in the director's garden or make repairs to his house, they were always given extra remuneration for that work.

All my attempts to elicit truthful testimony from them during my cross-examinations were unsuccessful. Then a woman, not old but very emaciated, took the witness stand. I knew that she had been left a widow with two small children after her husband had fallen while drunk onto the blade of a circular saw in the sawmill, that she could not work at the factory as she had no one to leave her children with, and that she could scarcely make ends meet on the tiny widow's pension she received. I also knew that her position was virtually that of an ever-faithful servant to the Romanov family.

At first she behaved like the other witnesses and testified that "the missus" paid her for all her work and regularly gave her money, food, and old clothes. But one had the distinct feeling that she was extremely tense and was having a hard time forcing herself to speak. Knowing the situation, I asked her whether she took the children with her when she was working at the Romanovs' or whether she left them at home.

"I left them at home. They're very small: one girl is three, the other is five."

"Who minded them for you? Who fed them?"

"No one. Sometimes the old woman next door would look in and feed them."

"Why didn't you take the children with you to the Romanovs'?"

Silence.

I repeated my question. She shrugged her shoulders and answered reluctantly, "The missus didn't allow it."

"Did you ever ask her permission?"

A long silence. . . . then an explosion! This was no longer courtroom testimony but incoherent, hysterical shouting about how that "Romanov cow" wouldn't let her bring the children with her because she was afraid she would have to feed them; that for a day's really hard physical labor the missus would give her a few lumps of sugar "for the children"; that after long and humiliating begging she would be given one ruble; and that she would be torn to pieces for the slightest blunder, for a single broken plate.

Hysteria is infectious in a crowd, and this crowd was tense to begin with. What happened in that courtroom cannot be imagined. Witnesses who had already been questioned jumped up and demanded that the judge allow them to take the stand again. Even people who were there merely as spectators started shouting; in reality, each of them was a witness and could testify to what had happened in the timber station and the community.

After the judge and prosecutor managed to calm everybody down, the cross-examination took a totally different course: the dam had burst. One after another they took the stand—new witnesses and those who had already testified but who were recalled at my insistence. They told the court about what really went on at the station. Nothing could hold back the stream of disclosures, neither the shouts of the public prosecutor nor the opposition of the judge, who threatened the witnesses with prosecution for perjury, as they had made totally different statements during the preliminary examination.

None of this had the slightest influence on the outcome of the case. Popov was sentenced to two years' imprisonment in an "ordinary regime" labor camp. I appealed the verdict, but after considering my complaint the regional court did not alter the sentence. And even though the Supreme Court of the RSFSR revoked the sentence and dropped the case, Popov had already spent about six months in prison and in the camps. He returned ready to continue his fight for truth, but his sons, and especially their wives, could not endure more threats and the renewed pressure. The Popovs were forced to sell their house and leave the Ustye district.

Massive and ubiquitous corruption at the district level of the party-state apparat has forged such close ties between it and the criminal world that there is every justification for saying that a system of organized crime has come into existence in the Soviet Union, a system that has permeated the political power centers of the districts as well as the administrative apparat, the legal system, and key economic positions. Although not conceived as such by its creators, this Soviet variety of organized crime naturally is derived from and has become an organic part of the dictatorship of the apparat of the only political party in the country, the Communist Party of the Soviet Union. Organized crime in the Soviet Union bears the stamp of the Soviet political system, the Soviet economy, and, in general, everything that may be lumped together as the Soviet regime. Its paradoxical nature is shown by precisely those factors.

The paradox lies first of all in the fact that the district underworld is not made up of gangsters, drug peddlers, or white slavers. The criminal world of the districts includes store and restaurant managers and directors of state enterprises, institutions, and collective and state farms. They are all members of this ruling monopoly—the Communist party —and their principal professional activities are absolutely legal and aboveboard. But there is another, secondary—and inevitable—side to their activities, which, although inseparable from the operation of their institutions or enterprises, is nevertheless criminal. Therefore all these upstanding Communists who regularly pay their party membership dues, these members of the raikoms and raiispolkoms, these pillars of the regime, still make up one of the two components of the system of organized crime that pervades the districts of the nation.

The second component in this system is also made up not of gangsters or mafia families but of members of the lowest ranks of the ruling party-state apparat, and this is also highly typical of the system of organized crime in the Soviet Union.

The final characteristic of the system is that the ruling district elite acts in the name of the party as racketeers and extortionists of tribute, and that it is the criminal world *per se* who must pay through the nose to the district apparat.

Thus it happens that the system of organized regional crime combines with the political regime and the economic system of the country and becomes an inseparable component of them.

CHAPTER IV

JUSTICE FOR SALE

I === I

I N THE courtroom of the Moscow Municipal Law Courts
everyone was standing: the judge, the two People's Assessors, the twenty-seven defendants, the public and we, the
lawyers. We were all listening to the sentence in a case concerning an underground business, in which a group of sharp
dealers had used a number of state knitted-goods factories
to set up a regular—and illegal—private company. The company had been organized and directed by one of the many
members of a well-known Moscow circle of underground
multimillionaires.

"In the name of the Russian Soviet Federal Socialist Republic . . ." The President of the court began to read out the
sentence. It was a lengthy reading and took more than two
hours. The sentence gave all the details of the production
and sale of the goods, the evidence against each of the defendants, and, of course, their terms of imprisonment. Various
figures flashed by: seven, eight, and ten years' hard labor for
the salesclerks working in state stores who had illegally sold
the company's products and twelve-, thirteen-, and fifteen-

year terms for those who had organized and managed the production side. Some had pleaded guilty and some not guilty; some were young and some were old; but they were all condemned to substantial terms in the labor camps.

The sobs and muffled shouts of the wives and mothers of the accused could be heard in the courtroom. Suddenly everyone fell silent and there was a hush in the room: "The guilt of Isaak Solomonovich Koifman [the name is changed] in this case has not been established. . . . Isaak Solomonovich Koifman is acquitted owing to lack of evidence. He is to be released from the custody of this court."

When this decision was read out I was standing next to Koifman's lawyer, one of Moscow's best defense attorneys and an old friend from university days. He turned to me and said in a serious and somewhat sad voice, "Honestly, this has nothing to do with me." And I believed him. I knew that Koifman had not been acquitted because of a brilliant defense. I even knew that the bribe had been actually given by another lawyer involved in the case, and that he had handed it to the judge, a member of the Moscow Municipal Law Courts. All this was no secret to us lawyers, who regularly worked on important cases of this kind; we knew very well which judges were on the take and through what channels to reach them.

The scene is Moscow, capital of the Soviet Union; the time is the 1940s and 1950s, years of rampant corruption in Moscow's courts and public prosecutors' offices. Even during the period I am describing, no judge often went so far as flatly to acquit the big wheels of underground business, the leading figures in the big trials. The reasons for such an acquittal would have been too obvious and the risk for the judge would have been too great.

In this case the resulting scandal was so great that the Public Prosecutor of the Russian Soviet Federal Socialist Republic appealed the verdict to the Supreme Court of the Republic, demanding that it be annulled and that the case be retried. This appeal was granted, and the case was returned to the Moscow Municipal Court, but this time Koifman was tried by a different judge. He was acquitted again. The prosecutor protested the verdict a second time, and the Supreme Court yet again revoked the not-guilty verdict. A third member of the Moscow court tried the case, but the outcome was the same: not guilty.

This time the public prosecutor's office acknowledged its impotence and capitulated. The verdict was unshakable.

The public prosecutor's office and the court system were established in the Soviet Union in the 1920s, and they survive to this day without any radical changes. Investigators from the public prosecutor's office and the police carry out inquiries in all criminal cases except for political cases and those involving foreigners, which are handled by the KGB. The investigative apparat is subordinate not to the courts but to the public prosecutor's office, which is responsible for the legality of an inquiry.

Formally, the public prosecutor's office is responsible to no one, and its apparat is built on the hierarchical pyramid principle. At the top is the Public Prosecutor General of the USSR, who is appointed by the Supreme Soviet of the USSR. He appoints public prosecutors for the Union republics, which in turn appoint regional public prosecutors. These latter appoint the district public prosecutors.

Justice in the Soviet Union is administered by a system of courts culminating in the Supreme Court of the USSR, whose members are nominated by the Supreme Soviet. Each Union Republic has its own Supreme Court, elected by the Supreme Soviet of the Republic. Each region has a regional court, elected by its Council of Deputies, and each district has a people's court, elected directly by the people of the region.

All criminal and civil cases are initially examined by a judge and two assessors; appeals cases are heard by three members of the court without assessors. Although by law the people's assessors have the same rights as judges, in practice their role is reduced to nothing. While they are present with the judge in the deliberation room where criminal sentences and civil judgments are formulated, they are totally suppressed by the authority of the representative of state power and by his professional knowledge of the law. In my seventeen years of practice I only twice came across situations in which the assessors attempted to challenge a verdict that they considered unjust.

That is a brief and very general picture of the Soviet judicial system. Now, in the 1980s, this very system has been ravaged by two parallel scourges: dependence on party and state authorities, and corruption.

Conditions were extremely propitious in the country for the spread of an epidemic of corruption. At the beginning, during, and just after the war, everyone who worked in the legal system was doomed to eke out a half-starved existence, along with the entire underprivileged population of the country. The food they were able to get with their ration cards merely prevented them from dying of hunger.

But at the same time everything was easily obtainable on the black market—bread, milk, meat, vodka . . . In Moscow a people's judge earned 110 to 120 rubles a month and a public prosecutor 140 to 150 rubles, while, at black market prices, a kilogram of wheat bread cost 12 rubles and a half-liter bottle of vodka cost 70 to 80 rubles. Toward the end of the war the state set up its own black market, and state commercial shops appeared, in which no ration card was needed to buy any quantity of marvelous food; commercial restaurants opened where one could spend an evening eating a sumptuous meal and listening to jazz. But the monthly salary of a people's judge would just about cover the cost of dinner in a commercial restaurant.

Life became somewhat easier during the 1950s for civil

servants and people on fixed incomes. Contrary to the logic of socioeconomic theory, however, judicial corruption became, if anything, even more widespread and brazen during those years.

The 1940s and 1950s saw an extraordinary growth of the world of illegal businesses. Since that world was illegal, it was easy prey for the police, the prosecutors' offices, and the judges, who were all trading in justice because it was impossible for them to live a decent life on their salaries from the state—and who, or what, could stop them? A belief in the sanctity of the law? Respect for their own positions in the state system? Self-respect bred of their sense of independence within that system? Awareness of the importance of their functions for society?

But where could all these ideas and feelings come from in a country whose system of justice had from the very outset been in the service of the party-state apparat—had, indeed, been subordinate to it?

According to the Soviet constitution—in the law on the judicial system and the provision on the Public Prosecutor's Office of the USSR—the courts are independent and subordinate only to the law. In actual fact, however, each court and each organ of the public prosecutor's office is subject to its respective contact point with the party apparat.

The Communist party is able to interfere with the courts and prosecutors not only because all judges and employees of the public prosecutor's office are members of the party (or of its affiliated youth organization, the Komsomol), and are therefore bound by party rules to abide by the instructions of party organs as a matter of party discipline—which doubtless plays an important role—but primarily because of the over-all subordination of all organs of state power and government, without exception (including the courts and public prosecutors' offices), to the party apparat.

This subservience of the courts and public prosecutors' offices is shown not only in the fact that they are obliged to abide by the party's general policies; it is also made manifest in the treatment of specific cases, both civil and criminal. There is an unwritten but universally followed law in the Soviet Union: that judges, prosecutors, and investigators, whether party members or not, must carry out the party's instructions even in individual cases.

This does not mean, of course, that *all* cases that are investigated by public prosecutors or tried in the courts are *always* decided according to instructions from the party. The overwhelming majority of cases are decided by investigators, prosecutors, and judges without any instructions from any quarter. However, whenever the party apparat has an interest in the outcome of a case, it can impose whatever decision suits it.

Of course, according to the strict letter of the law, either the prosecutor or the judge could refuse to carry out the party's instructions and could make his own decision in the case, but any prosecutor or judge is very well aware of the consequences of such a refusal to comply: either immediate or imminent dismissal. It is a simple matter of the appropriate party organ issuing an instruction to the recalcitrant public prosecutor's office official. The procedure for dismissing such an official is the same as it would be in any government department.

To get rid of a judge, who is elected to a five-year term in the Soviet Union, is somewhat more complicated but still quite possible. The party body has only to wait patiently until the judge is up for reelection, and then it has the last word. The lists of candidates to be placed on the ballot (which in the Soviet Union is tantamount to being elected, as only one candidate is put forward for each vacancy) must be approved by the party, and any judge whose name has been struck off by any of the party committees stands no chance of reelection.

The dependence of the courts and prosecutors' offices on the party apparat is completely institutionalized. This phenomenon allows the party apparat bosses to use their influence without fear of being exposed or punished. I am familiar with only one exception to this rule, but it is precisely the exception that proves the rule.

In the 1950s and early 1960s a man called Galushko (his real name) was First Secretary of the Raikom of the Kuibyshevsky district of Moscow and a member of the bureau of the Municipal Committee—that is to say, he was someone with a fairly elevated position in the hierarchy of the ruling apparat.

An engineer by training, Galushko had made a brilliant career and was approaching further promotion: in the leading cadres section of the Central Committee his candidacy had already been confirmed for the post of Deputy Minister for Foreign Trade. But apart from his life as a successful party functionary, Galushko had a second life, that of an enterprising bribe taker. Over a period of several years he had taken bribes from relatives and partners of those who operated underground businesses and who were on trial or under investigation.

The go-between and supplier of clients was the Chairman of the District Executive Committee, an old friend who owed his job to Galushko. After a bribe had been handed over (its size fluctuating between 25,000 and 100,000 rubles), Galushko summoned to his office the official from the district public prosecutor's office or the district DCSMP who was leading the investigation or the people's judge who would be trying the case.

If he was facing a people's judge, Galushko would demand a verdict ensuring the defendant's release. If he was dealing with an official from the public prosecutor's office or the DCSMP, he would give orders that the investigation should be dropped and the prisoner released. Without asking any questions about the substance of the charges or about the conclusiveness of the evidence, Galushko would quite categorically demand that his instructions be obeyed.

He acted quite openly, as though he were speaking in the name of the District Committee. Sometimes his interlocutor tried to voice some objections, pointing out the heinousness of the crime or that, on the basis of all the evidence, the defendants were unquestionably guilty. On such occasions Galushko would become rude and aggressive.

All these judges, prosecutors, and DCMSP officials to whom Galushko gave orders were questioned in court at his trial. They all said that any attempt—not to argue; one doesn't argue with the First Secretary of the District Committee—merely to explain the situation provoked the same threatening questions: "What's up with you? Sick of being a people's judge?" or "What's the matter? Doesn't your party card make you feel ashamed of yourself? Where did you find it? On a garbage dump?"

Nevertheless in the end Galushko was appearing in court at his own trial, but only because the machinery of power had operated in violation of the rules. This violation became possible because of the involvement of two characters who committed acts that were atypical of Soviet officials and not provided for in the unwritten rules on the functioning of the machinery of power. The first transgressor of these rules was a really young man, a trainee investigator in the district division of the DCMSP, fresh from the university.

He was still full of youthful illusions and naïvely believed everything his professors had told him about "the sanctity of socialist legality" and "the independence of the judiciary as guaranteed by the constitution of the socialist state, which is the most democratic state in the world." When the young man's boss—the head of the district division—ordered him to prepare a decision dropping a criminal case against a group of underground businessmen which he had been investigating, the young investigator refused to do it. The information that they were orders from the First Secretary of the District Committee did not help.

"You cannot have reported the case to him correctly.

I'll go and see him and explain that there must be some misunderstanding, because all the defendants have already pleaded guilty and have testified to their crimes in full detail,'' he told his boss.

The young investigator managed to get in to see Galushko, but did not succeed in explaining the case to him. Galushko rudely interrupted his very first words and bawled at him, promising to take away his party card.

After Galushko had booted him out of his office the young investigator demonstrated extraordinary persistence for a Soviet official and got an interview with General Grishin (his real name), the head of the Moscow DCMSP. And here we meet the second character in the tale of Galushko's downfall who made up his mind to break the system's unwritten rules.

Grishin was a young opportunistic careerist who had just received his general's epaulets. Unlike the investigator who had come to see him, he was not naïve but was fully conversant with all the rules by which the power system operated. But temperamentally he was a reckless gambler and a lover of adventure (qualities that are almost unheard of in the Soviet bureaucracy).

Grishin believed the young investigator's story, realized what was behind Galushko's demands, and decided to take the risky step of exposing Galushko, hoping to make a lightning-fast leap upward in his career into the bargain. And here he committed a violation—unprecedented in its audacity—of all the rules, written and unwritten. Without permission from the First Secretary of the Moscow Communist Party Committee, and without the sanction of the public prosecutor (he did not even bother to seek their authorization since he knew full well that he would be given nothing but a categorical refusal), Grishin took the law into his own hands and conducted a search of the office of this First Secretary of the District Committee and member of the bureau of the Moscow Committee.

During the search 70,000 rubles were found in the safe.

Galushko, scared out of his wits and bewildered, was taken to the Moscow division of the DCMSP, and there in Grishin's office he confessed everything and in his own hand wrote out a statement relating all his crimes and naming all his accomplices.

Grishin took Galushko's handwritten testimony and visited the First Secretary of the Moscow Committee of the party, who found himself in the hopeless situation of being compelled to authorize Galushko's arrest and trial.

Galushko was tried in the Moscow Municipal Court in closed sessions, at which I was present. Hearing a case of this kind in closed session was a blatant violation of the law, since legally there was nothing to justify such proceedings. However, there were things that the party apparat did not want to become general knowledge, such as the unlimited power of high-ranking party officials and the presence of corruption among them. And so, on orders from the Moscow Committee, the doors in Galushko's trial were shut tight.

Galushko was sentenced to eight years' imprisonment. But General Grishin had miscalculated; he did not forge a brilliant career on the basis of his exposure of Galushko. His actions were not viewed with rapture either by the Moscow Committee, which was compromised by the whole affair, or by the Central Committee. At the orders of the Moscow Committee, the KGB began a concentrated operation against him. He was put under surveillance, undercover KGB agents infiltrated his staff, and his telephone was tapped twenty-four hours a day. About a year later Grishin was arrested and convicted of misuse of office.

In Galushko's story, only the fact that a high-ranking party functionary was exposed and tried is unique and extraordinary; in no other aspect is the story anything but typical.

Thus the dependence of the legal system on the party apparat has played a fatal role in the history of Soviet justice: it has acted as a catalyst for corruption.

Needless to say, any honest person in any society, whether democratic or totalitarian, cannot help feeling indignant about corruption. Trading in justice is particularly abhorrent to any lawyer, and the things that I have described as having happened during those years gave me a constant feeling of profound disgust.

I and other lawyers who were not involved in corruption still had to defend cases in which bribes had been given. We were called upon because a qualified defense is needed even if bribery has occurred. In doing this work not only did I categorically refuse to give my clients any advice that had anything even remotely to do with corruption, however indirectly, but I even requested them not to inform me about that side of the matter.

If, contrary to my wishes, I was told all the details, it was not simply because my clients trusted me and were not afraid that I might inform on them. No. When they told me of all the upheavals in their dealings with the middlemen who handed over the bribes or with the judges who promised a successful outcome in return for a bribe, they may have realized they were talking about indictable offenses, but they did not perceive their conduct as being in any way immoral.

And when the middle-aged wife of a client named the impressive cost of the verdict that had saved her old husband from twelve years' imprisonment in a hard-labor camp, could I really find it in me to morally condemn her? Could I put my hand piously on my heart and try to convince her not to resort to bribery, and tell her that if her husband was not guilty, then sooner or later we would see that justice was done through legal means? Of course not. I knew the Soviet legal system, including what goes on behind the scenes, and I had no right to promise anything of the sort.

I knew that I was not dealing with murderers, thieves, or rapists. I knew that the people on trial were merely accused of being engaged in private enterprise or trade—that is to say, of activities which in any democratic country are considered normal and lawful but which in the Soviet Union are punished by long years of imprisonment or even by execution. And I was aware that in most cases the bribes were given to obtain verdicts that were correct and in keeping with law.

In the series of corruption trials held at the beginning of the 1960s, in which more than two hundred investigators, public prosecutors, and judges were convicted, a special legal study was undertaken for each trial. Highly qualified jurists studied each case in which the accused had accepted bribes. They had to determine whether the decision made by the investigator or prosecutor or the verdict passed by the judge in return for the bribe was in fact correct and in keeping with the law.

As it turned out, the figures for all trials were extremely consistent: in 65 to 70 percent of cases, decisions and verdicts handed down in consideration of bribes were fully correct and in keeping with the law. In other words, legal verdicts and decisions were being brought—those that should have been handed down in the first place, without the need for bribes.

The question naturally arises: Is there any need to give bribes to achieve legal results? In the Soviet Union that need does exist, for in the Soviet judicial system one can never be certain of achieving legal results by legal means alone. Indeed, there is a very high probability that for various reasons having nothing to do with the law an investigator's decision or a judge's verdict will not be a lawful one. At the same time there is only a very slight chance of obtaining a review of an illegal decision by legal means. This was shown very convincingly in a case decision described below.

There were eighteen watchmakers in the dock of the Moscow Municipal Court charged with buying and reselling gold and imported watches. The entire accusation was based on the evidence of a secret informant from the Moscow Criminal Investigation Department. The informant was clearly an *agent provocateur* and had himself organized and taken part in the criminal operations. But the prosecuting authorities decided not to call him as a witness. Despite the vehement objections of the defense, which demanded that the informant be examined, the court went along with the prosecutor and handed down a verdict on the sole basis of the written testimony given by the informant during the preliminary investigation—which is categorically prohibited by law. On the basis of his evidence, seventeen of the accused were found guilty, both those who had pleaded guilty and those who had pleaded not guilty. As for the eighteenth, the same evidence was deemed insufficient and he was acquitted. This man's lawyer and the judge had previously worked together as people's judges in one of the Moscow districts.

Seventeen appeals were sent to the Supreme Court of the Russian Soviet Federal Socialist Republic and they were all turned down. All subsequent attempts to have the verdict reviewed by the inspectorate proved futile, even though the defense took the case to the highest levels—the Prosecutor General of the USSR and the Supreme Court of the USSR.

Out of eighteen defendants only one was given a fair trial, and that one fair trial had been bought.

This provides the context for understanding my attitude toward some of my clients who had bribed judges or investigators in an attempt to mitigate the plight of their relatives. All the same, whenever I was aware that I was defending a case in which bribes had been given, agonizing doubts entered my mind. Should I deny such people my services? But the Soviet law does not give attorneys such a right. Should I pass the information on to the authority? I didn't consider that as a possibility. Nothing was left but to ignore the *fait accompli* and try to perform my professional duty.

I am not sure that this way is perfect, but I could not find a better one.

In nine out of the fifteen Union republics that make up the Soviet Union (that is, in three Transcaucasian republics—Georgia, Azerbaidzhan and Armenia—five Central Asian republics—Uzbekistan, Turkmenistan, Tadzhikistan, Kirgizia, and Kazakhstan—and the Union Republic of Moldavia) and also in districts far away from the capital cities and main centers of the remaining six republics, corruption in the investigative and public prosecutor systems and among the judges, whatever form it may take, is the rule rather than the exception. My information for this statement is based on court case materials, my own observations made during seventeen years of travel throughout the country as a practicing defense attorney, the tales told me by my Moscow and provincial colleagues, and the information given by clients who had dealt with other Moscow lawyers.

Imagine a small town hundreds of kilometers away from the main town of the district or cut off from it because of the lack of road or rail connections. Throughout my years of legal practice I had occasion to stay in many such desolate spots. And everywhere I went, a picture emerged on the basis of my own observations or because of what the local people or my colleagues there told me—a picture of total corruption of the police, the investigative organs, and the people's courts. But it was a type of corruption that was somehow surprisingly patriarchal and drably provincial. The simple customs and relationships were such that, used to the formality and alienation of the Moscow courts and public prosecutors' offices, I sometimes began to imagine that a time machine had transported me back to the first half of the nineteenth century, to the provincial Russia of Gogol.

Once my law practice brought me to a remote town in the Arkhangelsk region. While working on the case I was able to observe the local judge receiving callers. Early one summer morning I was sitting in the courtroom, where about twenty petitioners had gathered, patiently waiting to see the judge. Finally the door of the judge's chambers opened and a middle-aged man appeared, with an unshaven face, wearing his jacket right over his undershirt and with felt boots on his feet although it was a hot day. He invited the first one on line to step inside. The petitioners went in one by one. Almost everyone who entered the room carried either a package wrapped in a white scarf or a clay jug or a pot. They all left the room empty-handed.

It is usual in such out-of-the-way areas for the several investigators, two or three judges, and the one or at most two lawyers who work with them on a daily basis to establish a business relationship. In professional life there exists an official barrier that should separate lawyers from the administrators of the law. But with the familiar relations inevitably established in these circumstances, the feeling of such a barrier is lost. And as a sense of the importance and sanctity of the law is absent on both sides, familiarity in personal relations is easily carried over into an excessively familiar attitude toward justice.

The concept of a bribe being a criminal act is lost even to the participants. The lawyer simply has a preliminary conference with the investigator or judge about the prospects of the case, the amount of money that the lawyer will receive from his client if the outcome is successful, and how that money is to be divided.

Or there is the other type of corruption, typical in the provincial town, where all members of the party and bureaucratic elite know one another, where everyone meets every day at work and at the district and regional conferences, and where everyone fishes or hunts or plays cards together. In these circumstances anyone who needs to can always find someone he knows among this elite and ask the official to put in a word for the relative who has already been taken into custody.

Let us say the chief of the agriculture department of the District Executive Committee happens to be in the council corridor and meets the people's judge, who is there on business. The head of the agriculture department takes the judge aside and says to him quite informally, "Listen, Ivan Semyonovich, you're on the such-and-such case. I know the man well; he's a good fellow. Well . . . it was a holiday and he had a drop too much to drink and made a bit of a scene. Give him a hand, will you? He won't remain in your debt for long, I give you my word."

So Ivan Semyonovich "gives him a hand," and whereas, according to Article 206, Part 2, of the Criminal Code, the man should be given a minimum term of one year in the camps, he is sentenced to a year of corrective labor at his normal place of work and a 20 percent cut in pay. And the man brings the judge something from his personal garden plot, either a few sacks of potatoes—which in autumn in the Russian provinces people lay in for the whole winter—or else half of the pig traditionally slaughtered on Christmas eve. Or he simply gives him a hundred or a couple of hundred rubles. There is no prearranged formal agreement for all this; it is just a gift of gratitude to someone who helped out during a difficult time. The judge does not consider himself corrupt at all, nor does the accused think that he has done anything wrong.

If you were to ask him, he would answer with amazement, "What do you mean, a bribe? We didn't arrange anything beforehand, like 'If you give me the verdict, I'll give you two hundred rubles'! It's just gratitude for a good turn."

The centuries-old Eastern tradition of baksheesh and the party apparat's management of the Soviet system that I discussed in Chapter One have combined to form an organized system of corruption in the Transcaucasian and Central Asian republics which has become truly universal in those parts. The judicial organs in those republics have been affected as well.

I knew a good deal about this long before I had any personal contact with it. I knew that the price for being "elected" to the post of people's judge, district prosecutor, or investigator (all of whom earned a mere 150 to 180 rubles a month) was 30,000 to 40,000 rubles. I knew from my Georgian, Armenian, and Azerbaidzhani fellow students who went back to their homes to practice law about investigators in the Department to Combat the Misappropriation of State Property and the public prosecutors who had built magnificent town and country houses (the cost of a house being equivalent to fifty years' salary) and about much else besides.

But still when I first came into direct contact with the Georgian legal system I was absolutely stunned. A prominent underground businessman from Tbilisi called Dandashvili (the name is changed), whose son had been sentenced to death by the Supreme Court of Georgia, had asked me to appeal the sentence to the Supreme Court of the USSR.

My client had been accused of killing someone in a drunken brawl. When he was arrested, his father bribed someone to have him sent to the prison hospital, and again bribed someone to organize his escape. For a year "the boy"—as the father called his twenty-five-year-old son—lived under a false name (on a passport bought from the Tbilisi police) in a town in the Urals, and every month received a sizable sum from his father. He would have gone on living there as long as he had to if he had not been arrested, under his false name, on a charge of gang rape. His real name was soon established and he was extradited to Tbilisi. He was tried for both crimes simultaneously and was sentenced to death. He pleaded not guilty on both counts of murder and rape, alleging that the victim of her own accord had had sexual intercourse with him and his friend.

The miracles started as soon as I set foot in the vaulted edifice of the Tbilisi Palace of Justice, an old ramshackle place that housed both the Supreme Court and the Public Prosecutor's Office of the Republic of Georgia. I had flown into Tbilisi in the morning, had immediately got hold of an interpreter, and set off to the court to begin examining the case. It was a Friday, and I complained to my Georgian friend and colleague that I would lose two days, Saturday and Sunday, during which I would not be able to read up on the case.

"What do you mean? We'll arrange it all for you now." After a brief exchange with my client's father he set off for the chief clerk's office. He returned five minutes later and informed me that everything was in order and that I could take the file with me to the hotel and keep it for Saturday and Sunday. (I later discovered that this had cost only fifty rubles.) But the main shock came in the evening of the same day when the father mentioned quite casually, "Let's go over to the prison now; you can have a talk with the boy."

Meetings with those sentenced to death are as a rule prohibited in the Soviet Union. Even the defense attorney needs special permission for an interview, and that is by no means always given. But the relatives of someone condemned to death are never allowed to see him at all. Nevertheless, although we had no permission, we arrived at the prison and went straight to the warden's office. And so I spent about an hour alone with Dandashvili junior in the office of the warden of the prison. I gave him some chocolate, which is categorically prohibited even for ordinary criminals, let alone for those sentenced to death. I felt I should try to calm him and cheer him up, but he seemed not to need that very much. He was firmly convinced that his father would, as he said, "buy him off."

The Supreme Court of the USSR revoked the sentence and the case was ordered to be retried in the Supreme Court of Georgia.

Soon the father came to Moscow, not so much to come to an understanding with me as to buy a very expensive set of Yugoslav furniture. "The public prosecutor was very keen to have it," he explained. When I asked which public prosecutor, he answered, obviously amazed at my being so slow on the uptake, "What do you mean, which public prosecutor? Naturally, the furniture is for the person who's going to prosecute, my boy! He's bought a house for a hundred thousand, a Volga [car] for twenty-five thousand, and now he badly needs some furniture."

I was amazed at the sheer brazenness of the public prosecutor, who, with a monthly salary of 180 rubles, not only blithely spent 125,000 on a house and car without fear of being found out but was not afraid of the gift of a roomful of furniture from the father of someone whom he would prosecute in the name of the state. If a scandal were to break, the bribe would be very easy to prove on the basis of the railway shipping receipts alone.

The case was successfully concluded. The prosecutor upheld the charge but asked the court to impose thirteen years' imprisonment instead of the possible maximum sentence. (The Yugoslav furniture was by this time in the dining room of the new house.) The prosecutor's request was practically a guarantee that the defendant's life would be spared, as it is only in extremely rare cases that Soviet courts hand down a sentence harsher than the one suggested by the prosecutor.

I subsequently visited Georgia many times and ceased to be amazed when a client said that he needed a lawyer who was considered a specialist on such-and-such a judge. I realized he was talking about a lawyer through whom the judge in question would accept a bribe without fear. I was no longer amazed at the famous and widespread Georgian hospitality shown by local judges and prosecutors to visiting lawyers from Moscow; I now knew very well where the money for all this came from.

But sometimes even the Georgians' tradition of hospitality and their enormous charm cannot mask the cynical and revolting nature of the corruption that has eroded that small nation's judicial system. A colleague from Moscow and I arrived once in Sukhumi, a health resort on the Black Sea.

We had been working in the Public Prosecutor's Office of the Abkhazian Autonomous Republic in Georgia, examining a criminal case in which more than twenty people had been indicted.

We were given a warm welcome by the investigator and our local colleagues. An invitation from the investigator himself soon followed. It was to a big party consisting of about fifteen people—judges, investigators, and lawyers—and it was held in a private room in a seaside restaurant. The manager of the restaurant was personally in charge of the waiters who served us and personally gave instructions to the chef. The dishes were expensive and exotic even by the generous standards of Georgian cuisine. We were not given the cheap local wine, but venerable cognacs—by the bottle. But when the copious meal was over, no check was produced. When I expressed surprise at this, my local colleague (who had graduated from Moscow University) explained that the restaurant manager had a special relationship with the Public Prosecutor's Office and the police.

"Don't worry about him. It's in his own interests to pay for the meal. This restaurant brings him hundreds of thousands of rubles a year, so it's to his advantage to entertain the bosses from the police and the prosecutor's office, and even to make regular payments to them. In return for that he can sleep peacefully, without fear of inspections or searches."

"But how is it that they're not afraid to flaunt their connections so openly? After all, there were fifteen of us here; someone could inform the authorities and then both the investigator and the manager would be in for it. Even if they weren't prosecuted, they'd certainly be fired from their jobs and expelled from the party."

My colleague just shrugged his shoulders. "Who would write denunciations here? And to whom? Everybody lives like that in these parts; everybody has similar connections. If someone did write a denunciation, many people would suffer. Could he write to the Regional Committee? The Central Committee of Georgia? The Public Prosecutor's Office of the Republic? The people who work there are the same as we are; they do the same sort of things, and they're not about to bite the hand that feeds them. It's our hand that feeds them, and the money goes from us in a direct line up to the very top.''

"But what if a denunciation is sent to Moscow?'' I asked.

"That's nothing to worry about either. Moscow sends back a complaint to Tbilisi for us to investigate, and everything's okay. And do you think the informer would get away with it? You know what happened to Vakhtang, don't you?''

I did know Vakhtang's story. He had been a small-time businessman in Tbilisi and an important professional middleman for passing on bribes to officials in the Georgian public prosecutor's office and the Ministry of Internal Affairs. He had apparently cheated his accomplices and had not given them their full share of an enormous bribe, so he was dropped from the game. No one would have anything to do with him. His apartment was burglarized twice. He became embittered and started sending allegations to Moscow, to the Central Committee of the Communist Party of the Soviet Union, to the Public Prosecutor General of the USSR. He exposed judges, investigators, lawyers, and even the Public Prosecutor of the Republic. He named cases, sums of money, the people who had employed him to pass on bribes and those to whom the bribes were given.

His exposé was so specific and horrendous that Moscow sent the head of the USSR Public Prosecutor's Inspectorate to look into the matter. The prosecutor started by examining the files for the cases in which Vakhtang claimed he had passed on bribes, and then asked to see Vakhtang himself. But Vakhtang didn't make it; the evening before the meeting he was crushed to death by a truck that drove up onto the sidewalk. The driver was arrested, but was soon released.

Although he had once been convicted of theft, the court psychiatrist found him deeply schizophrenic and incompetent to stand trial for running over the man.

Moscow in the 1940s, 1950s, and the beginning of the 1960s: generalized corruption affecting the city's entire legal system. "Entire" is no exaggeration: it extended from investigators in the district prosecutors' offices right up to the apparat of the Public Prosecutor's Office of the USSR; from people's judges to members of the Supreme Court of the Russian Republic. Everything was afflicted by the plague of corruption. It was truly like an epidemic. Those who were free from infection were regarded as freaks; infected people were considered the norm, and, as always happens during epidemics, they in turn infected the healthy ones. The presumption was: every functionary of the legal system is infected by corruption. There was nothing extraordinary about one employee offering a bribe to another, even though those involved might be complete strangers to each other.

In the trial of court and public prosecutor's office personnel of the Moscow region one particular episode stands out. A new investigator arrived at the public prosecutor's office of the Balashikhinski district, and he was soon entrusted with an enquiry into a case of misappropriations in the district consumers' union. The case involved the entire commercial world of the district, and a go-between presently appeared to see the assistant prosecutor, who for many years had had close contacts with that world. They discussed ways of hushing the case up, and the cost of doing so. Agreement was speedily reached. Testifying during the corruption trial, this assistant public prosecutor related with Olympian calm that he had called the new investigator into his office and had suggested that he conduct his investigation in such a way as to keep the number of defendants to a minimum and confine himself to implicating only minor characters, so that it would look like a case of petty embezzlement.

The presiding judge, who was a member of the Supreme Court of the Russian Soviet Federal Socialist Republic and whose reputation was beyond any suspicion, asked in complete amazement, "How is it that you weren't afraid to make such a suggestion to a complete stranger? What a risk you were running!"

The defendant answered in a tone of equal amazement, "What do you mean, 'risk'? I knew he was experienced on the job; he ought to have known how things were done by that time."

"But what if he refused to go along with the deal?" the judge asked.

The answer was absolutely categorical. "In that case one of the defendants' relatives would write to our office stating that the investigator had extorted a bribe from him. We would then hand the case over to one of our people, and the denunciation would be kept for safekeeping in our district public prosecutor's desk, just in case it ever crossed the new investigator's mind to report our conversation. Then he could always be threatened with the statement being sent to the public prosecutor of the region."*

As a matter of fact, none of this was ever necessary, as the new investigator proved to be "one of our people" and therefore trustworthy.

The mafia of bribe takers dominated the justice of Moscow during these years.

The head of the investigation department, O——n, was in charge of organized corruption in the Moscow regional office. He had held the job for many years and had established relations of trust with many district investigators and public prosecutors. He had also managed to select a staff of inspectors who were devoted to him personally. Within the re-

* Here, as elsewhere in the book, dialogue is quoted not from official court records but from my own notes taken down during the trials.

gional public prosecutor's office, and even in that of the Russian Republic, he commanded great authority and complete trust, and because of that all his decisions on cases under investigation by the district prosecutors were as good as final. O——n's organization had a monopoly on corruption in the investigative apparat of the Moscow region. For all that, of course, the district investigators were able to accept bribes without sharing the bounty with anyone, but only for very insignificant cases, checked by the regional inspectors. If O——n so much as suspected that the wheels had been oiled by a bribe he had not shared in, then he mercilessly reversed the investigator's decision.

According to Soviet law, any criminal verdict or civil decision handed down by people's or regional courts may be appealed either by the defense or the prosecution. The appellate court is authorized to overturn any verdict or decision or even to invalidate it and return the case for retrial by the same court, although of course with a different judge. Because of this there was always the risk that the findings handed down by a lower court in return for a bribe might subsequently be revoked, and that when the case was reexamined by the second judge the verdict or decision would be quite different. Naturally, for the first judge this would be accompanied by the unpleasant prospect of having to refund the bribe money.

In order to eliminate the risk of such a turnaround and in order to set the "corruption business" on a solid footing, judges needed to have one of two types of illegal connections; either in the appeals court charged with examining complaints against their verdicts or among their own colleagues who might have to reexamine a case after the sentence had been revoked. These connections were forged, grew strong, and gradually turned into permanent channels for the distribution of multiple bribes.

The prosecutors who actually argue the state's cases in court are not completely independent. A prosecutor arguing a case may request the court to hand down a longer or shorter term of imprisonment in accordance with the relevant article of the criminal code without submitting his request for prior approval. However, for him to request a sentence not involving imprisonment or to ask the court to dismiss the charges and advise an acquittal is only possible with permission from his superiors. Therefore the guarantee that a given sentence will result from a bribe can be offered only by building up a group on the vertical principle—that is, with the participation of officials higher up in the chain of command.

Such criminal groups were always being set up in those years, sometimes just for piloting some important case safely past the judicial reefs. From time to time the membership of these groups stabilized and they ran for years like well-oiled machines. In many instances their activities were revealed (for instance, the groups operating in the Kiev, Volgograd, Balashikhinski and Podolsk districts of the Moscow city and Moscow region) and their members were convicted. Other groups broke up of their own accord, went under cover, and ceased operations.

In the municipal and regional courts, there were organizations of judges who tried cases of economic crime. Although these associations were informal, they were stable; they pursued a single goal and worked according to a standard arrangement. Their aim was to make sure that verdicts handed down in return for bribes were not overturned. This was achieved by prior agreement that if a verdict was annulled by a higher court, then whichever member of the group was assigned to retry the case would see to it that the first sentence was repeated.

The judges in these groups were a mixed bag. Some of them lived in high style, and during the lunch break would eat in expensive restaurants. Their clothes were made by the best tailors in town, and for weekends they would fly to Sochi—a fashionable Black Sea resort—with their girlfriends of the moment, spending two or three times their monthly salary on each trip. Others went about in shabby, shapeless suits and for lunch would go down to the basement canteen of the court building, which is famous for its bad food, and eat a meal for seventy kopecks; they were saving their money. One judge in that group, a middle-aged woman with a faded complexion, who always went around in the same dress of indeterminate color and nondescript shape, once had some repair work done in her apartment while she was out of town. When the painters stripped away the wallpaper they discovered a hiding place hollowed out of the wall and stuffed with bundles of cash amounting to more than fifty years' salary for a judge.

The whole orgy of corruption climaxed in a wave of trials that swept through the Moscow legal system at the beginning of the 1960s. In the space of one and a half to two years roughly twenty trials were held in which about three hundred investigators, prosecutors, and judges were convicted of taking bribes. There was not a single public prosecutor's office or court in Moscow (apart from the Supreme Court of the USSR) that did not see some of its staff on trial. A whole new staff had to be recruited in some of Moscow's districts, for in those places not a single people's judge, investigator, or public prosecutor remained. The majority of them were indicted for bribe taking, and the rest got away with dismissal because of a lack of evidence beyond very well founded suspicions.

These arrests and dismissals affected the Moscow Public Prosecutor's Office, the Moscow Municipal Court and the Supreme Court of the Russian Soviet Federal Socialist Republic (whose chief of reception was prosecuted on a charge of having acted as middleman between the bribe givers and members of the court). The Moscow Regional Court and Regional Public Prosecutor's Office were subjected to a particularly radical purge—in fact it was there that the wave of trials really got its start.

The operation was prepared in absolute secrecy by an elite team of special investigators from the Public Prosecutor's Office of the USSR, and was assisted by the KGB, which handled all shadowing, wiretapping, infiltration, and so forth. One day, to everyone's complete amazement, Nicholas Shepilov (his real name), one of the most brilliant judges of the Moscow Regional Court, was caught red-handed in a bookstore being given a packet of money and was arrested.

He was taken, dazed and shaken, straight to the office of an investigator, who proceeded to inform the judge of certain facts gathered by the KGB, such as who was bribing him and for what, thus showing him how much the prosecutor's office knew about his crimes. Then he left Shepilov alone in the room, after suggesting that he write down everything he knew about bribes he and other judges had taken. In return for this honest show of repentance—and for the information—the investigator promised Shepilov that he would face charges only for the one incident in which he was caught red-handed, and that he would be sentenced to not more than three years' imprisonment. He sealed his promise with his "word of honor as a Communist."

So Shepilov started writing. He wrote many hours a day for several days and conscientiously tried to remember everything he knew about corruption in the Moscow Regional Court system. And what he knew was almost everything about practically all the members of the court, from the middleman who passed the bribes up to the bribe takers in the Moscow Regional Public Prosecutor's Office.

In a week the arrests began: members' of the Regional Court, clerks, staff from the regional public prosecutor's office, lawyers. As each person was arrested he was given the same offer by the investigator that Shepilov had been given: to write a confession naming more and more names in exchange for "clemency." The avalanche had started, and more and more people were finding themselves in its path and buried before they had even heard its rumblings. The number of arrests soon passed the hundred mark.

What was the reason for this fever of confessional remorse? A few sincerely wanted to cleanse themselves of the filth with which they were covered and which they had ceased to notice in the turmoil of day-to-day living. They became aware of it again when they were left alone with their consciences in the silence of solitary prison cells. But for most people the main motive was fear of unavoidable punishment and a desire to win the leniency of the investigators and judges at any cost. But they miscalculated, for they were shown no mercy. It was by no means always taken into account that the only evidence against them consisted of their own confessions. Some refused to confess and spent nine months in prison before their trials. At that time there was no death penalty for bribery, but generous terms of imprisonment—twelve, thirteen, fifteen years—were doled out.

I remember that we questioned Shepilov as a witness during one of the trials that had arisen from his "penitential" evidence. He was brought under escort from the hard-labor camp where he was serving his sentence, terribly thin, with a pale, hunger-swollen face and a shaven head. Dressed in his baggy prison uniform, he reminded me of the patients in a mental asylum. Indeed, Shepilov was on the verge of madness. The camp had exhausted him with work beyond his strength and systematic undernourishment, but what tortured him most of all was the feeling that he had so readily allowed himself to be cheated by the investigator; that he had condemned himself to many years of imprisonment.

Now, on the witness stand, he denied everything he had accused himself and others of doing. He played the fool, mimicking the judge and the prosecutor, making faces, and mocking himself. Finally he became quite hysterical and the guard took him away, wailing and writhing convulsively.

Not everyone behaved that way during the investigations and trials. Some never flinched, confessed nothing, and slandered no one. But that was not easy to do. A man called Spektor (his real name), who was assistant public prosecutor for the Moscow region, was among those who resisted all forms of pressure—blackmail, threats, promises. The slanderous testimony of witnesses and their accomplices at the pretrial confrontation fazed him not at all. He was twice "mistakenly" thrown into cells with hard-core criminals who were informed that they had a public prosecutor as a guest. (The fact that this public prosecutor was a Jew—a *Zhid*—to boot, they could tell for themselves.)

Spektor underwent terrible physical torment during those days, but still he came to court and pleaded not guilty. (To this day I do not know whether Spektor was a criminal or the victim of slander.) He defended himself competently and courageously during the trial. In his final statement he told the court about the torture he had endured during the investigation, and he spoke about the tragedy of a man who had been wrongly accused. He spoke with sincerity and passion. Suddenly he fell silent. Then he said very quietly, "I feel ill, I feel ill. I must have a rest."

"That doesn't matter. Go on with your statement," retorted the judge.

But Spektor did not continue. He suddenly staggered and collapsed at the feet of the person beside him. His wife shrieked and rushed forward, holding out a bottle of heart medicine, but the court guards forced her back. All twenty-nine defendants broke out into a collective, hysterical wail. One of them, a metal worker, hefted a heavy oak bench and uttered an incessant, frenzied cry of "Fucking bosses! Fucking bosses!" The lawyers were shouting; the public was shouting.

The judge announced a recess immediately and an ambulance was called. But it was too late, for Spektor was dead.

Thus ended the "blatant" period, but that was not the end of corruption; it was merely curtailed and became more discreet. For the most part it disappeared far into the underground. Bribes are still given and taken, but now the dealings are surrounded by a cautious atmosphere of conspiracy.

Even in the 1970s my clients told me of cases in which they had given bribes to obtain leniency for their relatives. In one such case an official of the Public Prosecutor's Office of the RSFSR was bribed to appeal a guilty verdict that had entered into force. In another case a member of the Supreme Court of the RSFSR was bribed to secure a reduced sentence when the appeals board considered a complaint. I also have other information about cases of successful and unexposed corruption in the 1970s in Moscow.

From time to time corruption scandals still do surface. As recently as the period from 1974 to 1976, people's judges of the Kievsky and Babushkinsky districts of Moscow were convicted of bribe taking along with several district investigators, and a large group of investigators from the Criminal Investigation Department of the Ministry of Internal Affairs was tried by the Supreme Court of the RSFSR on corruption charges.

Nevertheless, in recent years justice in the big cities has been faring relatively well: there is at least no mass, organized corruption.

CHAPTER V

CORRUPTION AND INDUSTRY

THE SIVERSKY facility, intended for major repairs on tractor engines, was certified by special act of the Inspection
Commission, dated December 28, 1978. (The date is not in-
cidental, the end of the year is the time when the construction industry takes stock of the fulfillment of the year's plan.
Nonfulfillment threatens the workers with loss of bonuses
and the managers with even greater troubles.) On February
16, 1979, the Minister of Agricultural Machinery issued an
order putting that plant into operation and establishing a plan
assignment for it. At the same time, the old plant, which it
replaced and which had previously handled all the repairs,
was closed. The minister's order referred to the Inspection
Commission's certificate, which stated that "the plant is
ready to commence operation and to achieve its full production capacity."

In fact, of the fifty-one facilities that were to make up the
plant, fourteen were more or less ready, while work had not
even begun on nine of them. The other twenty-eight were
described by the journalist who wrote up the scandal as fol-

lows: "Rearing up on the trash-bestrewn site were half-built boxes and smashed-up trenches piled high with broken bricks and lumps of dried cement."

How did the commission come to approve this plant as ready for operation? But the commission never *did* approve the "plant"; not only did it never see all the smashed-up trenches and half-completed workshop buildings but all the commission members never even met together. The head people in the Leningrad regional office of the Ministry for Agricultural Machinery merely collected signatures from all the members of the commission. The stubborn ones, who refused to sign the certificate, were replaced by others who were more obliging. In cases where such substitution was impossible, the signatures were simply forged.

For more than a year the plant—which in fact never existed—appeared in statistical reports, and its output, as laid down by the plan, was included in those reports as having been produced. Meanwhile the broken-down tractors stood there with no work being done on them, since the old plant had been closed and the new one existed only in the reports of the Central Statistical Office.

The lists of registered, operating factories in the Soviet Union include several that exist only on paper. Nevertheless the Gosplans (government planning department) set out production assignments for them and the Central Statistical Office includes in its reports the quantities they have "produced." In the space of a single year two national publications published articles about no less than five such phantom factories (*Pravda,* January 31, October 20, November 22, 1979, and January 30, 1980; *The Literary Gazette,* No. 23, 1979).

On the first of January 1973 several groups of high-standing functionaries in the apparat of the Central Committee of the CPSU and that committee's Committee for People's Control conducted spot checks of construction warehouses in fourteen of Moscow's largest and best known factories.

They were checking on goods that, according to factory accounts, had been manufactured by December 31, 1972, in fulfillment of the year's plan. The results were astonishing: in not one of the fourteen facilities inspected did they find that the reported goods had actually been produced in full. The officials who had conducted the raid (from one of whom I received this information) met the following day and had to acknowledge the total victory of *pripiska*.

The word *pripiska* means the inclusion of false information in the accounts of an enterprise, in which the volume of work done is exaggerated or jobs are listed as completed that have not been done at all. This definition, however, does not provide a full idea of the influence of *pripiska* on the Soviet economy and even on the lives of all Soviet citizens. It might give the reader who is unfamiliar with the ways of Soviet society the impression that *pripiska* involves merely cheating the administration or the authorities, but that impression would be wrong. In reality, the *pripiska* system is necessary and useful not only to the party doing the cheating but also to the party that is being cheated.

And what about the ministries, Gosplans? The Central Committee of the CPSU? The government? Surely *they* need to be given information reflecting the true state of the country's economy? Surely *they* are interested in honesty among those reporting to them? That is true to a certain extent, but another factor comes into play as well: each inflated figure reported by each individual enterprise climbs higher and higher through the bureaucracy until finally, after passing through the computers, it becomes part of the final report of the Central Statistical Office of the USSR (under the Council of Ministers) on the fulfillment of the plan. Once compiled, that report becomes a major instrument of Soviet propaganda.

And this system of *pripiska* exists despite a whole network of bodies across the face of the Soviet Union created to check on the accuracy of the accounts of the various enterprises and institutions throughout the country.

One would therefore think that the managers of enterprises would be unable to "cook the books" regularly for years on end without exposure or punishment. That would be the commonsense thought, but in the Soviet economy, total and permanent control gets along excellently with total and permanent falsification, common sense notwithstanding. That peaceful coexistence is made possible, again, by the eternal, the ineradicable bribe.

That corruption among the auditors has in recent decades become endemic is borne out by court cases, the Soviet press, and, finally, by the fact that figures continue to be falsified, year in and year out, in all the country's enterprises, while only a handful of these frauds are exposed.

That sensitive barometer, the law court, has proven beyond question that the practice of bribing auditors and high-ranking inspectorate personnel is extremely widespread and common. In any "economic" criminal case—that is, any case in which the manager of an enterprise is on trial for misappropriation or other abuses—the theme of the "blindness" of the auditors inevitably arises. These inspectors usually play the role of witnesses in the trials, although everyone, including the judges, understands the reasons for their "blindness" when they examined the activities of the defendants.

Sometimes the inspectors are cast in more fitting roles—those of defendants. There have been cases, albeit infrequently, in which all the seats in the dock have been occupied by inspectors (as, for example, in the case tried by the Azerbaidzhan Supreme Court in 1976 in which the entire staff of the state inspectorate of the Ministry of Trade was indicted: twenty-four inspectors and their chief).

Despite the atmosphere of corruption prevailing in relations between inspectors and the heads of enterprises, both of those groups quite often make efforts to mask the true nature of those relations. That is why bribes in the form of gifts and hospitality, as opposed to cash payments, play a not insignificant—even a dominant—role.

Bribes in kind have become especially widespread in cases where they are destined not for the ordinary state inspectors but for the more powerful officials of higher organs when they arrive to check up on the activities of the bodies for which they are responsible. Humanly speaking, this is easy to understand. A cash bribe spells things out clearly—there is no way to dissemble, either to oneself or with regard to possible consequences, and each bribe taker cannot but think about what will happen to him if he is caught and what will be his defense against charges.

But it is not the gift that has become the most widespread form of bribery in these cases: the most common of all is the hospitality bribe. This includes meals in restaurants, hunting or fishing trips, and drinking binges or sex orgies.

The psychological calculations of the heads of enterprises are very accurate here: they take account of the time-honored national traditions of hospitality (not only Russian but Caucasian and Asian as well), and the other tradition, also national, of breaking away from the control of the family to go on a spree in a distant town. A Soviet official is always psychologically prepared to go on a spree at the expense of his subordinates. This bribery must be paid for, and enterprises set up special funds (in the jargon of economic planners, "brandy funds"). Visitors' houses and hunting lodges are maintained, and female attendants, suitably attractive and obliging, are selected.

Regular and abundant information about this form of corruption is published in the Soviet press. I have picked one from among the many published stories. I chose it not only because it gives a picturesque outline of corruption but because it gives a complete idea of the real-life face of bribery by hospitality. I chose it also because the unpublished details were made known to me by utterly reliable sources.

In the Volga town of Kuibyshev a major construction organization built a small hotel with guest rooms and a sauna especially for visiting inspectors and officials. The hotel stood in a park surrounded by a tall fence topped with barbed wire, and the entrance was strictly patrolled by guards, each one rated a master in wrestling. Apart from these guards, the hotel staff included a cook and some fishermen charged with providing the freshest of fish, including the celebrated Volga sterlet. There was also a team of maids. Their duties included not only cleaning the rooms but sleeping with the guests as well. But two maids to entertain many guests were obviously inadequate, since group sex orgies would often be organized in the sauna for the delectation of the visitors and the regional Kuibyshev leaders. Hence, an additional duty fell to the wrestler-guards: that of procuring more women.

Under various pretexts, the guards would entice young women and schoolgirls to the hotel, rape them, and photograph the act. They then presented their victims with a choice: either the photographs would be sent to their parents, bosses, or teachers or the girls would come to the hotel when summoned and sleep with whomever they were told to sleep with. Most of the young women, crushed by the horror of their experience, capitulated to the threat and became staff prostitutes for the hotel, participating in the sauna orgies. There were some, however, who were not afraid to tell their parents everything and file complaints with the regional public prosecutor's office and the police. These complaints contained hard facts, dates, and names, but in response came the unvarying reply: "Upon checking your statement it has been impossible to corroborate the facts. It has not been deemed that grounds exist for the institution of criminal proceedings against X under Article 117 of the Criminal Code of the RSFSR [rape]."

So the pleasure hotel, with its sauna, continued to flourish. It is not clear from the article published in *The Literary Gazette* what the secret of this invulnerability was. The article describes in fair detail how the visiting inspectors from Moscow and other high-ranking officials amused themselves there, but for reasons that are absolutely clear the article says nothing about the fact that among the regular visitors to the little hotel on the picturesque banks of the Volga were also leading functionaries in the regional committee of the party and top police and officials from the prosecutor's office.

Even when the sordid facts of rape and orgies in the sauna with minors became widely known in Moscow, the regional leadership continued to protect the hotel's hospitable owners. But owing to interest in the case by *The Literary Gazette,* which had good ongoing relations with the administrative department of the Central Committee and with the public prosecutor's office, the authorities did not succeed in suppressing the scandal. Those managers responsible were charged with misappropriation of state property and misuse of office, and the wrestler-guards were charged with group rape. But even then the Communist party Regional Committee continued to stand up for the construction organization managers. They put pressure on the regional court that was examining the case; the guards (whom no one was protecting) were condemned, under the full severity of the law, to lengthy prison terms, but the managers went virtually scot-free: they all received suspended sentences with the exception of one of the secondary culprits who became the scapegoat. He was made a victim and was sentenced to six years in prison.

Why are all the businesses of the country forced to resort to the help of *pripiski* and other tricks? And why do the authorities have to connive with these measures? The answer can be found in the economic conditions that prevail in the Soviet System.

In 1966 a high-quality coated-paper mill run by the Kama Paper Combine manufactured ten thousand tons of low-grade paper instead of the forty thousand tons of high-grade paper called for by the requirements of its plan.

The first reason for this was that the Austrian-made machine tools sent to the mill were already obsolete at the time. Some of them had to be rejected, and the remainder could be put into service only after the employees had modernized them as best as they could. The second reason was that the shipments of kaolin—the principal material in the production of coated papers—received by the mill were of such poor quality that it was absolutely impossible to use them to make a high-quality product.

Seven years went by, and in 1973 the same machine tools —which had been considered unsuitable in 1966—were still in use, and the kaolin delivered to the mill was of the same low grade. The output had fallen from ten thousand tons to six thousand (*The Literary Gazette,* No. 35, 1973).

Anyone unfamiliar with life in the Soviet Union, whether an economist or simply a person with common sense, would naturally ask: "Why did the paper mill manager accept the unusable Austrian machine tools? Why did he suffer with them for seven years instead of replacing them with suitable equipment? Why did he accept substandard kaolin for all those years instead of switching to another supplier and getting the quality product he needed?" In short, why did the manager not act in accordance with elementary management logic in the interest of his enterprise?

For anyone familiar with the Soviet economic system, however, the answer to all these questions is self-evident: the manager acted the way he did because according to the laws of the Soviet Union he had no right to act otherwise.

In the strictly centralized Soviet economic system everything is determined by a plan drawn up by the appropriate state and party organs. All economic and commercial factors for enterprises and construction projects are planned at the same time. All these plans, for sectors by the dozen and enterprises and new buildings by the hundred thousand, establish not only what an enterprise must produce—the type and quantity of goods—not only what factory and other buildings are to be built and where but also the kind of raw materials they will be allocated, and in what quantity; what equipment they will receive from which suppliers; as well as to whom, and in what quantities, they will sell their goods. That is why enterprises and construction projects are unable to obtain materials and equipment as they see fit and on sites they deem to be the most favorable for their needs.

And so the manager of an enterprise manufacturing tens of millions of rubles' worth of goods cannot reject the machine tools that have been sent to him in accordance with the delivery plan even if he already knows that they are no good, and he has to accept materials that he knows to be unsuitable even though he is fully aware that the goods manufactured from them will be of poor quality. This is so not because he has no rights in the law but because planned deliveries result in his being able to receive nothing in return for the machinery and materials he rejects.

While the manager of a Soviet enterprise controls the millions of rubles that go to pay for the centralized planned deliveries, he still does not have the right to spend even a thousand rubles of those millions as he himself sees fit. Since the actions of all managers are strictly predetermined and they have no freedom of choice in making management decisions, there would appear to be no place for corruption in the economic system. But in fact, it is just this hypercentralized and hypercontrolled management system that has engendered such all-pervasive corruption in industry that it is fair to say that alongside the official economic system a second, unofficial economic system has arisen and is functioning. These are so closely interconnected that the first, official system is incapable of functioning without the support of the second, the unofficial system—that is, without recourse to corrupt means.

The official economic system confronts the manager of an enterprise or construction project with a tough demand: to fulfill the assigned plan on time and completely. The prosperity of white- and blue-collar workers depends on the fulfillment of the plan: if it is fulfilled they receive a bonus that augments their annual salary by about 20 to 25 percent. The career and peace of mind of the manager also depend on the fulfillment of the plan: if he "gives the plan," as they say, he will be forgiven a multitude of sins—even outright violations of the law, including the criminal code. But if he "wrecks the plan," then nothing can help him, not even the fact that it was not his fault that the plan was "wrecked," but that of the planning and supply organs, which did not deliver the required materials or equipment.

This happens so often in Soviet industry that it can be said that, as a rule, the state planning and supply organs do not provide construction projects with sufficient equipment and materials. But the duty to fulfill the plan is none the less binding on project and enterprise managers; they are faced with the need to procure, by any and all means, everything not supplied by the state, everything without which their plans cannot be fulfilled.

What means, then, do they use? There exists no legal way to procure the needed goods in the Soviet Union. But there is one way by which everything required to "give the plan" can be obtained: corruption.

With the universal skeleton key of bribery they obtain orders from the officials in charge of allocating materials and equipment; they obtain from suppliers what has already been allocated to them by state orders; they obtain the means of shipping the merchandise.

Court cases and articles in the Soviet press have shown quite definitely that plant, factory, and construction project representatives are compelled to bribe officials in the ministries, Gosplans, and committees that deal with supplies—high-, middle-, and low-level officials alike. These representatives have to bribe them not only in order to obtain additional, unplanned items, but also to make sure that the officials do their jobs conscientiously, that they make out the orders for the materials and equipment already allocated to the enterprise by higher state organs.

The bribes taken by middle-level officials in ministries and Gosplans are not large; sometimes they are amazingly paltry. Often gifts such as a meal in an expensive restaurant or a few bottles of brandy or a bottle of French perfume are considered bribe enough to get action from an official who is not too high up.

Middle-ranking officials quite often receive bribes not only in the form of gifts and meals but in the form of cash as well. But the sums involved in these bribes, judging by court records, are relatively small: these people do not turn their noses up at even 50 rubles, and in their circles 200 rubles is considered to be a large bribe.

A completely different corruption scenario is played out when the bribe takers are officials in the higher echelons of the apparat—chiefs of central offices and trusts, their deputies, and, of course, deputy ministers. Here the bribes must be reckoned in the thousands and tens of thousands of rubles. Court records show that an important Ministry of Agriculture official accepted three thousand rubles in exchange for an order for five hundred cubic meters of lumber allocated over and above the plan. In return for supplying a huge state farm in the Rostov region with equipment and spare parts, the head of the central office of the State Committee for Agricultural Machinery of the RSFSR would receive twenty-five thousand rubles a year.

Massive bribery within the apparats of the ministries that govern the Soviet economy is a factor of enormous importance having a tangible influence on the life of the entire country. It is quite easy to show, through examples taken from court cases and the Soviet press, how threads of corruption stretch from the Moscow offices of the ministries out through the whole country, and to demonstrate how those threads bind a leading ministerial official with a working man in a remote provincial town in a unified system of national corruption.

The following is an example taken from court documents. The chief of one of the central offices of the Ministry of Transport Engineering, his first deputy, and several of his closest colleagues regularly took bribes from the director of a large motor transport establishment in a town in the Stavropol district. Those bribes were to obtain orders for trucks, cars, and spare parts. The relationship was well established and stable. The ministry officials received 1500 to 2000 rubles and more for each order. Moreover, the director of the motor transport establishment rented a Moscow apartment for them all year round for the purpose of debauchery and orgies. When he visited Moscow he would procure prostitutes for them and would take them out to restaurants.

Those who paid for the *dolce vita* of those ministry officials were the drivers at the motor transport establishment in that far-off provincial town: for each spare part needed to repair their vehicles they paid their director 100 to 150 rubles, and for each new vehicle 2000 to 3000 rubles. Naturally the drivers could not afford to pay such sums out of their wages (140 to 150 rubles a month); they obtained the money by taking on "left-hand" journeys—using state vehicles fueled with state gasoline to transport private cargoes and passengers for ready cash.

And so the enterprise or construction project has obtained the order for the materials or equipment it needs. It would seem that the only thing remaining to be done would be to fill the order—to send it on to the supplier and wait for the shipment.

That is indeed what should happen, according to the relationship between enterprises as laid down in the law. But let us take an example from real life. In January 1979 a Saratov-based organization that constructed gigantic hydroelectric power stations on the Volga River had received less than a quarter of the metal specified by its plan, while another Saratov construction organization had received less than one-tenth (*The Literary Gazette,* No. 26, 1979).

In real life an enterprise, having received its authorization and needing the right goods on time and in sufficient quantity, is compelled, as a rule, to resort to corruption. Virtually the only way to fill an order is to pay a bribe either to the manager of the supplier enterprise or to the employees who are responsible for shipping the goods—or, indeed, to both.

This is one of those rare instances where I am able to back up my own evaluation based on observation and on my legal career with an authoritative general conclusion published in the pages of the official organ of the Central Committee of the Communist Party of the Soviet Union, *Pravda.* The issue dated June 28, 1976, tells the story of a sales employee of the enormous Novolipetsky Metals Combine who accepted bribes from the representatives of client enterprises in return for filling their metals orders. The bribes ranged from trifles —a bottle of champagne or a box of candy—to large items such as television sets or furniture. The main point of the article was that the employee always did accept bribes and did so quite openly—she even used to receive them in the mail. And this went on for several years.

I have related this story not because of the absolutely trivial and utterly typical situation it presents (although perhaps it is significant because of its very triviality) but because of the general conclusion drawn by the author of the article: that, when traveling on business to obtain needed goods from suppliers, all representatives of state enterprises carry with them presents to be used as bribes, which are always at the expense of their enterprises.

Is it possible to combat this kind of corruption? Is it possible to refuse to pay these bribes and to lodge a complaint with the appropriate authorities demanding that the solicitor of the bribe be prosecuted, or at least dismissed from his job?

In principle, of course, it is possible. But even Soviet publications clearly show the futility of such struggle. I cite a true, illustrative example demonstrating that in relations between state enterprises bribery is the norm and deviation from that norm brings with it appropriate punishment. (The truth of the story is absolute; it was related to me by one of the two main protagonists.)

In the town of N—— there was, and is still, an electric motor plant. The plant always met its production plans, and sometimes even exceeded them by a small margin. The secret behind the plant's prosperity was that twice a year a staff member would arrive in Moscow on a visit to the factory that supplied their ball bearings and would there hand the warehouse manager a sum equivalent to six months' salary for a painter in the motor plant, the post held by the warehouse manager.

This idyll continued for many years, but then the head of the electric motor plant came to Moscow to attend a meeting. He ran into an old friend from student days who had risen to the lofty position of deputy minister. That evening, over a friendly dinner, they reminisced about their youth, and each complained to the other about the difficulties encountered in his job. The plant manager complained about his problems with supplies, and, in passing, boasted about the way he had managed to guarantee his supply of ball bearings. The deputy minister was outraged. He chastised the plant manager and personally promised that the ball bearings would reach the town of N—— punctually on the condition that relations between the plant and the warehouse manager were severed. (The ball bearing factory came under his authority.)

The deputy minister did everything in his power to keep his promise. He summoned the manager of the ball bearing factory and asked him as a personal favor to see to it that the bearings were shipped to N—— as scheduled.

Everything was done in accordance with the rules of the official economic system; all levels of that system were involved in the process from the deputy minister to the factory warehouse manager. But the cogs of the unofficial economic system were neglected, so the official system could not work; the electric motor plant did not receive its ball bearings on time; its plan was not fulfilled; the workers did not receive their bonuses; and the manager was reprimanded by the minister.

After a while the courier from N—— once more made his trek to Moscow and delivered to the warehouse manager his salary for the previous six months—and, to everyone's satisfaction, everything went on as before.

I stated earlier in this chapter that the manager of an enterprise in the Soviet Union does not have the right to spend even a thousand rubles from its treasury, so the reader may be wondering where the money for all these bribes comes from. Surely the manager's own salary, which amounts to a few hundred rubles a month, does not provide the thousands that are regularly paid out to officials in the ministries and to his suppliers.

Of course not. The managers of enterprises and construction projects come by their bribery funds from within their own organizations; and to do this they use methods that go far beyond the bounds of legality. Based on the evidence of thousands of criminal cases and on articles in the Soviet press, I can state that there are three widespread methods by which managers of enterprises and construction projects obtain the fuel for the corruption engine: cash.

The following will be familiar to anyone who has ever closely observed a Soviet factory or a Soviet construction site. On paydays and bonus days someone stands alongside the cashier's window with a list. He listens to each name as it is announced to the cashier and checks it against his list. He finds the name, calls the employee aside, and speaks to him in a low voice. The employee then hands over some of the money he has just received. The keeper of the list standing by the cashier's window is acting on behalf of the administration; his job is to pass along to the administration the money he takes from the workers.

The following is drawn from a prosecution statement in a court case, and it sheds some light on the situation. Through workshop foremen and other authorized agents, the manager of an engineering plant systematically placed a levy on his workers of from 30 to 100 percent of their bonuses, free allowances from the trade union, rewards for efficiency proposals, and fictitious wages paid for work not done. When the plant manager was first prosecuted, the public prosecutor's office was compelled by the Raikom to drop proceedings. Despite this the case was handed up to the court on instructions from Moscow, but the Raikom put pressure on the judge to be lenient in his sentencing.

Two puzzling questions immediately come up. Why did the employees part so readily with their money? And why did the Raikom rally to the defense of the crooked plant manager? The Raikom ordered the public prosecutor's office to call a halt to the prosecution because they knew that the manager was exacting payment from his workers not for personal enrichment but for use as bribes and gifts for all the people on whom the plant's supplies of materials and equipment depended—that is, from the Raikom's point of view, in the interests of the plant.

The workers relinquished their money so willingly because, although the money is in their names on the books, in fact it is not really owed to them at all. The administration needs ready cash to ensure that the plant gets what it needs —what it cannot get through state channels—and it comes to an arrangement with its workers that money to which they are really not entitled will be paid to them so that they can kick it back to the administration.

The second method for obtaining cash is through the use of "dead souls." At the end of the twentieth century "dead souls" may in fact be either dead or alive—they may never even have existed. All three types of "dead souls" are officially taken on the staff of an enterprise or organization, while they do not in fact work there—not even the living ones. But their salaries are paid regularly, collected on their behalf by people who are unquestionably alive and real—the managers of the enterprises and institutions. It does happen, of course, that this money is appropriated for purposes of personal gain, but more often than not it goes for the payment of bribes to obtain materials, equipment, and authorization orders.

The enterprise and construction project managers pick "dead souls" everywhere. Some of them, not blessed with such powers of imagination, often make use of the telephone directory, from which they copy out the names they need. Still others simply draw their "dead souls" names from among their relatives, sometimes alive and sometimes really and truly deceased.

Perhaps the most complicated challenge faced by investigators was the case of the manager of a district repairs and building office in the ancient town of Ruza near Moscow. To ensure that his "dead souls" really were dead, he went out to the municipal cemetery and meticulously copied down the names of dead people from the gravestones and entered them on his list. These names included some people who had been buried even before Napoleon's invasion, to which Ruza fell victim in 1812.

But the principal and most widespread means of obtaining cash is to authorize salary payments to workers for work they have not done (manual workers in the Soviet Union are paid by the job), and then to repeat the now familiar procedure: money paid out by means of false payment orders is kicked back, in whole or in part, to the administration. But including on the books factory and building-site work that was never done is only the first, and least important, link in the all-embracing network of falsification and deception that has become an integral part of the Soviet economy.

CHAPTER VI

THE UNDERGROUND
BUSINESS WORLD

THE FOLLOWING is based on the documents of a case heard in 1964 in Moscow Municipal Court. The defendants were a group of underground businessmen.

A sprawling eleven-room apartment—seven families (about a score of people), a single kitchen, a single bathroom, a single toilet. The sort of place that houses ordinary, average people: workers, doctors, engineers. In the enormous kitchen stand seven tables, and there are two gas ranges on which the women take turns cooking dinners and breakfasts. Here there are no secrets; everyone knows everything there is to know about everyone else—who eats what and who buys what.

The family of the workshop foreman of a small hosiery mill in no way stands out from the other six families in the apartment. The neighbors see the wife preparing dinner and breakfast from the cheapest ingredients: curd pancakes from *tvorog*—a fresh cheese—bought for 26 kopecks a package from the dairy shop; ready-made meat patties—*kotleti*—purchased for 6 kopecks apiece; potatoes; macaroni; sometimes some soup made from a scrap of meat. But the neighbors do not see that later, when everyone else is asleep, these meals are flushed down the toilet or tossed into the garbage pail. Nor do they know that in the back room—the smaller of the two occupied by the workshop foreman and his family—another meal is being prepared on a small electric hotplate that is kept hidden under the table, draped with a long tablecloth. The second meal consists of the most expensive ingredients, the hardest to come by under Soviet conditions. The neighbors also do not know that the foreman's refrigerator—which stands not in the kitchen but right in this little room—is packed with expensive delicacies that none of them can afford. And even if the others could afford the prices, they would be unable to find the foodstuffs in the shops.

When the family of the workshop foreman dines, it does so behind closed doors. Two meals are set out on the table: the meal cooked in the kitchen, in full view of the neighbors, and the one prepared in the back room. Should any of the neighbors knock on the door during mealtime, the good meal is whisked from the table and hidden in the back room. It was not until the foreman was arrested and the neighbors were summoned by the investigators and then called upon to appear in court that they learned that the humble hosiery mill foreman, who always dressed in an old, cheap suit and often-mended shoes, was a millionaire. A real millionaire—the owner of a factory that provided him with an annual income higher than the combined wages of all the other six families in the apartment.

Everyone knows that the Soviet state is the monopoly owner of all means of production and all land, and that private enterprise is a crime in the Soviet Union. But not even all those who live there know that in the Soviet Union there are many private enterprises in operation alongside the state factories. A network of private factories is spread across the whole country; these factories manufacture goods to the value of many hundreds of millions—perhaps even billions —of rubles.

Of course private industry in the Soviet Union does not manufacture machinery or automobiles; it does, however, compete successfully with the state in the manufacture of clothing and items such as sewing notions. Its principal competitive weapon is its efficiency and flexibility in following fashions. State factories will take years to begin production of a new style of shoe or sweater: they require months to develop a new model and further months, even years, to get the prototype approved by all the state organs. Private enterprise, on the other hand, is restricted by nothing apart from its own technical capacity. The minute the owner of a private business sees a new fashionable item (usually from the West, where most Soviet fashions begin), he buys one on the black market and starts turning out copies in his own factory.

The tenacity of the entrepreneurial instinct, of private initiative, is really amazing. Neither the full nationalization of industry nor the seemingly insuperable obstacles that this places in the path of private enterprise nor the threat of harsh punishment (even capital punishment) has been able to curb the vigor of those human qualities. Underground private enterprise gets its strongest foothold in the smaller factories, either those parts of the *promkooperatsiya* (industrial cooperation) system, known officially as cooperative artels, or those attached to collective farms or state voluntary organizations, known as production workshops.

The infiltration takes place in the following way. A private enterprise will coexist, under the same name and under the same roof, with a state factory. This kind of private operation cannot exist on its own without the cover of the state facility. In this symbiotic relationship the state factory operates perfectly normally. It is run by an officially appointed manager and technical supervisor, and it manufactures goods as called for by the state plan, goods that appear on the factory's books and are distributed through commercial channels for sale. In criminal cases dealing with this sort of underground operations such goods are referred to as being "accounted for." But alongside these official goods the same factory is manufacturing goods whose existence is not reflected in any documents; they are unaccounted for, or, to use underground business jargon, "left-hand" goods.

The "left-hand" goods are produced with the same equipment, operated and supervised by the same personnel, as the official goods. But the raw materials and other supplies needed for their manufacture and the labor costs are paid for not by the official factory administration but by some private person. This person owns the goods, sells them, and profits by their sale. It would not be irregular to call such a person the owner of a private enterprise. Tens of thousands of these underground factories scattered throughout the country manufacture knitwear, shoes, sunglasses, recordings of Western popular music, handbags, and many other goods much in demand by consumers.

There are other major centers of underground entrepreneurship besides Moscow: Odessa, Riga, Tbilisi, and many others. In each of these centers there has arisen a circle of stable business and personal connections. Furthermore, there are such close links between the various centers that an underground system of private industry may be said to exist alongside the official state system.

There are companies and multimillion-ruble family clans that own dozens of factories and have access to a tentacular sales network, but there are also small-time entrepreneurs, who do not always own even a whole factory, but only a single workshop.

THE UNDERGROUND ENTREPRENEURIAL MILIEU

In the course of my seventeen years as a practicing attorney I defended in court dozens of people with connections to underground enterprise, and I unfailingly enjoyed the complete trust of my clients as well as that of their partners who had not been arrested. This gave me the opportunity to get to know their milieu well, to learn its customs and characteristics. I met all sorts of underground businessmen. There were crude, petty swindlers among them, but I also met major personalities and talented organizers, who knew how to operate on a grand scale, who were fascinated by the actual process of business, and for whom that process of *making* money—not the money itself—had become the real aim.

I recall one particular client who was conducted under escort to an office in Moscow's Butyrskaya Prison. He was about seventy years old, a massive man, and his every movement was an expression of self-assurance and self-esteem. He was not the biggest of wheels, but he still owned two factories manufacturing hosiery and underwear which brought him an annual income of several hundred thousand rubles. Over the years of his long life he had amassed capital that the investigator had estimated at about three million rubles.

As I came to know him better I began to appreciate the native wit and worldly wisdom that had allowed this scarcely literate Jew to become a millionaire and to win universal respect in the world of business. Once, when we were sitting in the office sorting through the expert accountant's labyrinthine opinion, I put the question to him, "Tell me, Abram Isaakovich, why didn't you retire ten years ago? Why did you continue to do business, to take risks? You knew very well that even if you and your children lived a hundred years you could never spend even half of what you had saved." And this man, threatened with many years in prison—perhaps with death—looked at me with surprise, and even with reproach. "Don't you understand? Do you really think I need the money? I need my life! And my life is my business." And he was only one of the many underground millionaires I met who, while knowing full well that they were risking their freedom, could not force themselves to give up their businesses and retire, calmly and fearlessly to spend the wealth earned after many years of daily risk. Some among them of course were possessed by a devil of greed, a senseless thirst for profit. Among both sorts I came across striking personalities who met tragic fates.

After the war the Silberg brothers (not their real name) were demobilized from the army and returned to Moscow. They soon realized that they could not bank on their being veterans of the front, decorated with military honors, to help them find good jobs. They were Jews, and the policy of discrimination against Jews was being pursued in the Soviet Union with particular consistency and openness after the victory over Nazi Germany. Jews were banned from all prominent posts in the party and state apparats. Jewish engineers had a hard time finding employment in industry; if they were hired, it was only for insignificant, poorly paid jobs.

The Silberg brothers were not willing to accept jobs as rank-and-file factory engineers at a hundred twenty rubles a month, but they did need to find some work; they needed to find a way to put their energies and abilities to use. So they went into underground business. On their discharge from the army they each received the large sum of money awarded to demobilized officers; besides that they earned money through the sale of war "trophies" they had brought back with them from Germany and Hungary—articles taken from shops and houses abandoned by people who were fleeing from the advancing Soviet army. With this initial capital they acquired a single workshop in a factory. It produced artificial leather shopping bags.

The brothers turned out to be talented businessmen, and in a few years they headed a company that owned at least ten factories manufacturing artificial leather, artificial-leather goods, and all sorts of synthetic-fiber products.

Given the illegality of the operation, the sales network they organized was highly ramified; through it they sold, nation-wide, millions of rubles' worth of artificial-leather bags, coats, and jackets and knitted underwear, shirts, and so forth.

Naturally, a firm operating on such a large scale could not escape the notice of the Moscow DCMSP, with its well developed network of secret informers. Subsequent events showed that they kept a special dossier on the Silberg brothers' company. This dossier did not give a full picture of all their commercial operations, but it did provide a fairly accurate outline of the general structure of the company and of the nature of its activities. (A bookkeeper in one of the company's factories turned out to be an informer.)

But the fact that the DCMSP knew what was going on had nothing to do with the fate of the Silbergs. Every month the brothers handed out between 5,000 and 10,000 rubles to the top people in the DCMSP—each one, of course, being paid according to his rank. One day, however, a rank-and-file DCMSP officer leaked the existence of the Silberg dossier to a well known journalist who covered, and still covers, crime and legal stories for *Izvestiya*. This influential journalist, who had connections in the Central Committee apparat, took an interest in this material, but the DCMSP chiefs would not show him the entire dossier, invoking the confidentiality of secret informers. They were, however, compelled to give him something, and the journalist began sifting through the material on the brothers' company. In these circumstances the DCMSP chiefs were powerless to save the Silbergs. They warned them immediately of the danger threatening them and of the impending searches so that they might have time to secrete their money and valuables.

When all this was taking place, however, one of the top chiefs of the DCMSP was on vacation at a health resort. The brothers still cherished the hope that he might be able to do something to save the day, and a special courier was dispatched to him. (None of the brothers could make the trip as they were all under round-the-clock surveillance.) The courier, officially, held the insignificant post of workshop foreman in one of the company's factories, but in fact he was among the most highly trusted deputies of the Silbergs and was virtually director-general of the whole operation. It was into his hands that the brothers entrusted the suitcase filled with half a million rubles intended for the DCMSP general.

The courier—a small, soft-spoken man—told me several years later how frightened he was carrying such a sum of cash and that he did not loosen his grip on that suitcase even when he went to the toilet. When he had found the general in the sanatorium for the government elite and had put the appropriate proposals to him, the general asked for twenty-four hours in which to fly to Moscow in order to become personally acquainted with the situation. The following day he gave his answer: the dossier would disappear from the DCMSP's files and the company would be saved from total destruction. However, the youngest brother, Solomon, would have to be sacrificed, along with a couple of factories in which he had been particularly active. Solomon was selected as the victim mainly because his playboy life-style had made him conspicuous and especially vulnerable, and he was thus a perfect choice for the protagonist of the article the journalist was writing for his paper.

Even before I began to study the case of Solomon Silberg et al (there were twenty-eight other defendants—workshop supervisors and foremen, bookkeepers, warehouse managers, and stockroom employees) I had read a long article about him in the newspaper. The journalist had described in great detail his wardrobe, including more than a hundred imported neckties and two dozen suits, the wardrobe of his wife, a ballerina in the Bolshoi Theater, as well as other details of the life of the underground millionaire.

All these details had a very definite purpose: to stir up

hatred in the breast of the ordinary newspaper reader (who as a rule has only one suit to get him through all four seasons of the year) for these Jewish swindlers who had robbed the Russian people and were wallowing in luxury. The author achieved his purpose, and on the first day of the trial the courtroom and all the corridors leading to it were packed with curious onlookers eager to get a glimpse of the millionaire Jew. What they saw was a tall man of about forty with handsome, prominent features and a mane of completely gray hair. Solomon Silberg walked, as prisoners are meant to walk, between two escorts, with his hands folded behind his back, hobbling along on the artificial leg that replaced the limb he had lost in the war.

He walked with his head held high, showing not a shadow of embarrassment, affably greeting his friends and relations in the crowd. Three months later he walked out of the courtroom just as calmly, between his two escorts, having heard his sentence: fifteen years in strict regime camps.*

It is almost impossible for a person with one leg to survive fifteen years in such a camp unless the camp authorities provide him with special protection. Solomon Silberg died in the camp seven years after his trial.

Each of the major underground enterprise centers has its own well established milieu, which encompasses everyone with any connection to private industry. It includes the pow-

* There are four kinds of camps in the Soviet Union: regular, strict, severe, and special. The harshness of punishment and degree of restriction of the rights of convicts depend on the kind of camp regime. The chief restrictions are on the right to correspond, to meet with relatives and to receive parcels of food. For example, the convict serving a sentence in a camp with a "regular" regime is allowed to mail three letters every month, to meet his relatives five times a year and, after he has served half his sentence, to receive three ten-pound parcels of food a year. The convict in a "strict" camp is allowed to mail one letter every month, to meet his relatives twice a year and, after serving half his sentence, to receive one ten-pound parcel of food a year. Prisoners live in barracks, except for those in the "special" camps, who live in jails.

erful family concerns with control of many enterprises and the independent operators, as well as the salespeople through whom all their products are sold.

For historical reasons the underground business world in the large cities of Russia, the Ukraine, and the Baltic republics has been predominantly Jewish. Under tsarist laws, Russian Jewry had been herded into the Pale of Settlement and subjected to legalized discrimination. When they were liberated by the February Revolution (not, as is usually thought, the October Revolution), the Jews eagerly threw themselves into those spheres of life that had previously been closed to them. Thousands of young men and women from the Jewish *shtetls* flocked to the capital cities and the major university towns. The most gifted and morally sensitive of them entered the professions of science, the arts, and literature; the less talented and the power-hungry joined the Communist party, the party and state apparats, the Red Army or the Cheka,* and by the 1920s Jews had a prominent place in the ruling apparat and in the arts and sciences.

But during—and especially after—the war, Stalin suddenly and quite openly adopted a policy of discrimination against the Jews. The party and state hierarchies were almost completely purged of Jews, and anti-Jewish policies in institute and university admissions and in hiring were rigorously implemented on orders from the Central Committee. The result was that large numbers of Jews, not members of the intelligentsia, and not having won academic or professional standing, found that they were forced into underground businesses. This process was particularly blatant immediately after the end of the war.

In the early 1960s I defended a Jew by the strange name of Glukhoi ("deaf"—not his real name). Before the war Glukhoi had been a high party functionary (a deputy of the

* The *Chrezvychainaya Komissiya*, which existed from 1918 to 1922: Extraordinary Commission to Combat Counterrevolution, Sabotage and Speculation. (Trans. note)

USSR Supreme Soviet and plenipotentiary of the Central Committee for Latvia, which had recently been seized by the Soviet Union). When war broke out his position gave him the choice of either remaining on the home front in his party post or of becoming commissar of a military division. But Glukhoi chose the hardest lot of all: he requested that he be sent to the front lines as a *politboets*—a soldier in the ranks, with the functions of a party agitator.

He returned from the war with a single modest decoration and three stripes for severe wounds. In accordance with his rights as a veteran, he showed up at his previous place of work, the apparat of the CPSU, where he ought by law to have been offered either his prewar post or its equivalent. But the Central Committee is above the law: Glukhoi found himself jobless. As a professional party functionary he had no profession, and as a no-longer-young man he was not only without a job but without the prospect of finding one. Then he met a friend from the front who was a member of a powerful Jewish underground business clan. When he learned Glukhoi's plight he immediately offered to lend him money with which to buy an artificial-leather workshop. And so this former member of the Supreme Soviet of the USSR became an underground entrepreneur.

Customs governing business and other relations within the underground business world have evolved over the years: there are rules for buying and selling enterprises, for marketing, for settling accounts between debtors and creditors, for relations with business partners, and so forth. Of course, these rules and customs are quite often not observed, but then that is true of the state's laws too, even though the state has at its disposal the entire police-court-prison machinery, while the underground business world, by its very illegal nature, has no recourse to state justice to settle its internal disputes.

"They'd kill you for a thing like that in Siberia!" This was said by a frequent client of mine, a fairly important underground businessman who had recently moved from Siberia to Moscow. He was referring to a retailer who had taken a large shipment of "left-hand" merchandise from him and had paid for only half of it, later alleging that he had paid in full.

I do not know if such unofficial penalties really do exist in Siberia, but in Georgia and Azerbaidzhan underground businessmen really do get murdered for nonfulfillment of their commercial obligations, although not very often. I know that for a fact, for I have read it in court records and it has been related to me by people who were involved in underground business in those areas. I have never heard of such capital punishment in the regions of Central Russia, in the Ukraine, or in the Baltic republics.

In cases of cheating or misrepresentation in underground transactions, the only pressure that can be brought to bear on the violator is the pressure of solidarity within the underground business world, and the only sanction is to ostracize him in that world. The circles in each region are comparatively small, and the regional centers are closely linked with one another, so the word that so-and-so is not to be dealt with spreads widely and quickly, and the violator is almost completely excluded from doing business. When the conflicting parties are hopeful of a mutually agreeable solution, they have recourse to their own arbitration tribunals. Without fail, I turned down all invitations to take part in these tribunals, but I was able to gain firsthand information about their operation from someone who had a long-standing reputation in Moscow as a fine arbitrator of disputes between underground businessmen. I also heard from the businessmen who had made use of these tribunals to resolve their disputes.

These arbitration tribunals sometimes consist of three members, but as a rule the businessmen make use of the services of a single arbitrator—some middle-aged businessman with a reputation as a just and reasonable person, completely to be trusted to settle the dispute impartially. No formal procedure exists for investigating claim and counterclaim. Usually the arbitrators listen first to the principal parties, then to the witnesses they have invited, but it is not always possible to follow such a clear-cut procedure. Often the adversaries become excited and start interrupting each other, and, as the situation heats up, the witnesses begin to break in, and the arbitration proceedings begin to look not like a court but like a free-for-all. If, however, the arbitrator has a good grasp of the essential points at issue and knows all the details of the way in which underground businesses are run, he will be able to maintain his impartiality; a decision he hands down will usually be a just one.

The decisions are generally binding: by and large, the parties abide by them and comply with the orders of the tribunal, either making financial restitution, dropping claims, replacing merchandise, or whatever. Those who do not comply with the decisions of the arbitrators are banished from the world of underground business. The excommunication is effective: people stop doing business with anyone who has been ostracized. If he is a retailer, underground producers will stop supplying him with merchandise; if he is a manufacturer, the retailers will not take his products.

The underground business world should not be idealized, however, and the element of solidarity within it should not be exaggerated. It is easy to find people who do not observe a boycott and who are willing to enter into deals with the violators of the unwritten rules. They exploit the outcast's hopeless situation, imposing crushing terms in any deal they make with him. I know of one case in which a retailer accepted merchandise from an entrepreneur on whom a boycott had been imposed, but only at a 50 percent discount, not the usual one-third.

How to Become a Millionaire in the Soviet Union

The simplest way to become a millionaire is to become the owner of a factory or workshop that produces easily salable merchandise: ladies' underwear, meat *pirozhki,* brooches made of a couple of plastic cherries, or fashionably tailored artificial-leather jackets. But is it possible to become the owner of such an enterprise in a country whose very constitution specifies that all means of production are the monopoly of the people—that is, of the state? It turns out that it is indeed possible; you need one of two things—money or connections in the underground business world.

Even I once had the opportunity to become an underground millionaire. In the difficult wartime year of 1943 I was a graduate student at work on my dissertation in the Institute of Law of Moscow's Academy of Sciences. My wife was studying for the state final examinations for Moscow University. We lived on ration cards, which enabled us to buy sufficient bread, paltry allotments of meat, butter, and sugar, and two bars of soap a month. My only income was my student stipend of 70 rubles a month—and this at a time when the black market price for a kilogram of bread was 10 rubles and for a good pair of stockings 80 rubles.

One day I was in the antique shop that once stood on Stoleshnikov Lane, admiring, with no prospect of buying, the eighteenth-century Russian furniture and china that glutted the antique shops in those hungry years. I was hailed by a friend who had graduated with me from the law department at the university. He was a member of a clan of underground millionaires and had immediately gone into the family business. We exchanged stories on the "How's life?" theme, and he looked at me with regret and said, "Listen, what the hell do you need all this for? So you'll defend your thesis and you'll become a junior research assistant for a hundred twenty rubles a month. You're a Jew, and, besides, not a party member, so you'll stay a junior research assistant for ten years. You'd do better to come and work for us. We're setting up a new operation right now—a soap factory. I know you don't have any money, so I'll ask my father to make you our general legal adviser, and you'll get a twenty-five percent share in the soap business. In three years you'll be able to buy every stick of furniture in this store!" I did not accept his proposition and, alas, never made my million rubles.

The years just after the war saw the creation of many new factories and workshops in the *promkooperatsiya* system and within various voluntary organizations. But both these types of organizations served as a cover for the real organizers, and the future owners, of private enterprises. It was they who shouldered all the expenses involved in setting up the facilities. The first expense was the bribes that must always be given to any state official whose permission was required to establish a new enterprise, and to the heads of the organization under whose auspices the new business was being set up. Once permission to go ahead was secured, the next step was to acquire the premises for the factory or workshop, and again a state official had to be bribed. The prospective owner of the enterprise also had to shoulder the worries and expenses of obtaining equipment—bribes for officials in ministries that authorize orders for machinery, and the cost of purchasing equipment stolen from state facilities.

Such were, and still are, the expenses incurred by the creator of a new private enterprise—quite considerable expenses. Legal cases show that in order to put into operation even a small workshop manufacturing, say, souvenirs, between 150,000 and 200,000 rubles must be spent. A factory made up of four or five workshops will cost approximately one million rubles. But if the product sells well the investment will be recouped in two or three years.

Since the mid 1950s an increasingly popular way of acquiring a private enterprise has been through purchase of an existing one. During one of my first cases involving underground enterprise my client's wife complained that she was short of money and told me that, less than a year before, her husband had bought a workshop for 80 rubles and a small nylon fabrics mill for 4 big rubles. I did not understand her at first; it was only later that I found out that in their jargon a "ruble" meant 1000 rubles and a "big ruble" was equal to 100,000 rubles. I also found out how underground businesses change hands when the owner-sellers have no rights in law.

Once the deal is concluded and the agreed sum handed over, the purchaser has actually bought the following: according to the conventions of the underground business world he has the right to use the equipment and white- and blue-collar labor of the enterprise in order to manufacture goods off the books, and then to sell those goods and profit by the sale. The purchaser also inherits all the established internal and external connections of the previous owner. ("Internal" concerns relations with the employees of the manufacturing facilities producing goods off the books; "external" refers to relations with the staffs of the stores where the goods are sold.)

The prospective purchaser has virtually no way of accurately assessing the enterprise's potential production or sales and, thus, the potential income. Thus, buying and selling underground enterprises can succeed only in an atmosphere of complete trust among all parties and if they all abide by the unwritten laws of the underground business world. In this atmosphere the purchaser hands over to the seller, with no receipt and no witnesses, tens—often hundreds—of thousands of rubles. It is true, however, that if the parties do not completely trust each other, the money is transferred to a third party trusted by both principals, and he passes it on to the seller only when all conditions of the sale have been met.

How Underground Enterprises Function

Let us assume that an underground enterprise has been created or bought. How does the new owner go about conducting business? How does he organize production? Sales? How does he make his millions? The documents of court cases involving such entrepreneurs yield complete answers to all these questions, but it would be hard to find a case providing more material about underground business operations than that of Solomon Silberg, whom I have already mentioned.

During the investigation and trial there was a detailed examination of the ways and means used to run the affairs of the company. Silberg acknowledged partial guilt in the case and told the court something about his private-enterprise activities (but not so much as to harm his brothers and the family company). What he said in court—and what he did not say, but what I was able to find out—makes it possible to reconstruct with fair accuracy a picture of what went on in the Silberg brothers' enterprises, which were similar to all privately held underground enterprises throughout the country.

In the beginning, before the Silberg business expanded, each of the brothers worked as manager of one of the workshops belonging to them, although all workshops were jointly held and all the brothers participated in making important decisions regarding investment of profits, type and quantity of merchandise to be manufactured, and so forth. But when the number of their enterprises grew, the brothers took on the functions of what would be referred to in the West as a board of directors. They made joint decisions, and, in cases of dispute, resorted to majority rule.

In underground businesses with a large number of shareholders linked by ties of kinship or friendship, decisions are also made on the basis of a majority of votes: each co-owner will have one vote, irrespective of the size of his holdings. Of course underground corporations do not hold regular general meetings of shareholders; the co-owners are usually canvassed individually whenever a decision must be made. But there are some underground businessmen in whom the instinct for self-preservation has been blunted; these people are not afraid to hold shareholders meetings—or sometimes to turn them into expensive binges.

In Georgia and Azerbaidzhan, where the underground business world operates more openly than in other parts of the country, these meetings traditionally take the form of banquets lasting several hours, during which decisions are made, business is discussed, and revenues are distributed. In Moscow and in the other republics, where more circumspection is in order, there are only a few who can afford such risks.

But to return to the Silberg brothers. The day-to-day operation of their businesses was left in the hands of trusted managers. A manager usually held an official post at the enterprise in question—foreman, workshop manager, or sometimes technical director of the factory, but never overall director of the factory. The position of those officially in charge of the Silbergs' and other underground businesses was very unusual: they exercised no control over the production and economic activities of the enterprises of which they were the formal heads; those functions were assumed by the owners themselves or the managers they appointed. The directors' functions were purely decorative and boiled down to liaison with party and state organs. Through trusted agents the Silbergs paid a director between 500 and 1000 rubles a month, depending on the scale of activities of the particular enterprise and on how useful the director was to them.

Unlike the directors, the other office staff of the Silberg enterprises earned their second salaries by actively participating in the production and sales of the unofficial merchandise. This was known to the investigators and the court, but there was another aspect of their relations with the Silbergs that was not mentioned at all in the documents of the case.

Seated beside Solomon Silberg in court were twenty-eight codefendants. Only a few of them, even among those who had confessed their guilt, gave evidence about the role of other parties to the crimes, and there was a particular silence about the activities of Silberg himself. Investigators who deal with underground business cases have stated that this situation is typical, and the very good reason for it is known. As accomplices, the several hundred office workers who received salaries from their work in the Silberg organization knew that the brothers would pay their legal expenses and continue to pay their unofficial salaries to their families throughout their prison terms, but only on condition that the employees would betray no one during the investigation and trial and, generally speaking, would not be overly frank with the authorities. Of Solomon Silberg's twenty-eight codefendants, no fewer than seventeen qualified for such aid, as far as I know.

In addition to cooperation from all these office workers, the complicity of many blue-collar workers is also required in the manufacture of left-hand goods, and it is almost impossible to recruit an entire labor force on the basis of total trust. Since such workers are paid by the piece, it cannot be hidden from them that they are producing merchandise off the books as well as officially, and they cannot be paid for the extra work through the regular state payroll. In the Silbergs' enterprises this extra money was paid out through the brothers' trusted agents.

Normally this system is its own justification. The laborers know full well that goods are being produced off the books, but do not inform the authorities because they are interested in the extra money they make, especially as they are paid for left-hand production at higher rates than the official state salaries—and their left-hand wages are not subject to any taxation.

Besides payroll expenses the Silbergs also bore all the costs—for raw materials and equipment—of manufacturing both their own, left-hand goods and the merchandise the factories were officially supposed to be producing.

The Silberg brothers maintained stable contacts with important ministerial officials. They would arrange by telephone to meet in one of the best restaurants in Moscow. Dinner in a private room plus a considerable cash payment were the cost of orders authorizing adequate materials and equipment covering both official and left-hand merchandise.

A second method of acquisition was through purchase. This would sometimes be from ordinary retailers, but as a rule the company's agents would buy materials and equipment that had been stolen from state enterprises, at significant savings over retail prices.

Strange as it may seem, given the illegality of the whole arrangement, the Silberg brothers cooperated with other underground businesses. Clasps for handbags, buttons for leather jackets, and labels were all manufactured to their own specifications by underground enterprises in Moscow, Vilnius, and Riga. But the main source for materials (and in this the Silbergs were no different from the proprietors of other underground enterprises) was the factory itself. Materials "saved" from what the factory received for its official production—that is, materials stolen from the state—went into the production of the Silbergs' products.

It was over the quantity of off-the-books merchandise produced from these "saved" materials that the major quarrels between the prosecution and the defense flared up during the trial. This moot point was of vital importance to the defendants, for the quantity of "saved" materials used in left-hand production would determine the gravity of the charge against them: large-scale misappropriation (maximum punishment, fifteen years in prison) or particularly large-scale misappropriation (maximum punishment, death).

The prosecution was able to prove that reserves were prepared in advance to result in secret surpluses. During the planning stages in the production of a new product the Silbergs would get in touch with the people in laboratories or research institutes who were responsible for setting the factory's norms for use of raw materials per manufactured unit as well as for allowable wastage. In return for large bribes these people deliberately inflated the usage and waste norms, and these exaggerated figures allowed the creation of large secret surpluses for use in the manufacture of merchandise off the books.

Secret economies were made during the manufacturing process as well. Expert witnesses testified in court that they had measured the coats and jackets that were legally manufactured at the factory and that the measurements did not tally with the sizes on the labels, because the factory's cutters had reduced the size of each pattern piece. Chemists testified that they had analyzed the artificial leather legally produced by the Silberg factory and found that the quantities of dyes and other ingredients added to the basic mix fell short of the official specifications.

These procedures were neither unique nor original with the Silbergs; the brothers were merely using practices that are widespread in the underground business world.

When the Silberg brothers were just beginning in business and the only product of their workshop (both on and off the books) was shopping bags, it was easy to solve the problem of how to sell the left-hand bags: employees of the shops that sold the factory's legal output were quite willing to accept for sale a certain quantity of illegally produced bags as well. One-third of the proceeds went to the shop employees and two-thirds to the Silbergs.

As the business grew and the range of their wares broadened, the Silbergs' sales outlets had to grow too. Through friends and family connections they added to their clientele stores that were not supplied with official merchandise from the factories; these included not only little corner shops but also large department stores. In time, however, even this network of retailers, confined as it was to Moscow, proved unable to handle the entire left-hand output of the Silberg empire. At that point a special marketing group was established that traveled all across the country and in short order was able to organize the sale of Silberg goods in sixty-four towns and regions. This is the first instance that I know about of the system of "traveling shops"—which exist for the sale of goods in rural areas—being used to sell left-hand merchandise.

In Soviet conditions, delivering off-the-books merchandise from factory to store is no simple task. All shipments, even within a single town, have to be accompanied by a special document—a bill of lading indicating the nature and size of the shipment, its source, and its destination. The police can stop a truck at any point on the road or on a city street to check its papers against its cargo.

But shipments of Silberg products were always properly documented. This was simple to achieve. Either the accounting departments of the enterprises in question filled in genuine forms with false figures or counterfeit forms, prepared by an obliging printer, were employed. In that way the bootleg merchandise easily crossed the country in trucks and freight trains, even in illegally chartered cargo planes.

From time to time there are articles in the Soviet press covering the trials of underground millionaires. The authors of these articles love to boggle the minds of their readers with descriptions of the fortunes the criminals have amassed. Such stories are very useful to the authorities. The dissatisfaction of the ordinary man, eking out a meager existence on a small salary, and his envy for those who live in luxury are deflected from the ruling elite to all those Jews, Georgians, and Armenians (the Soviet press does not usually write about Russian underground millionaires) who make millions with such ease.

It is no accident that when the ruling elite of Georgia were exposed, the Republic's newspaper *Dawn of the East* (February 3, 1973) wrote with relish of the multimillion-ruble income of the underground entrepreneur Laziashvili while saying not a single word about the enormous fortunes amassed by the secretaries of Georgia's Central Committee in the form of bribes from Laziashvili and other underground millionaires.

The press, the police, and the courts have been unable to establish the real size of the profits made by the big underground businessmen. For example, the investigators came to the conclusion that Laziashvili's income for the period 1968 to 1970 was 836,000 rubles. But it was said in the inner circle of the Georgian Communist party (according to certain members of that group) that Laziashvili used to hand out about a million rubles a year to the highest-ranking functionaries in the Republic. Underground businessmen in Georgia and Moscow who had close business ties with Laziashvili estimated his annual income at somewhere between ten and twelve million rubles.

Comparing data from investigations and trials with that which I received from my clients, I have come to the conclusion that the authorities learn about only one-fifth to one-third of the real income of a large underground enterprise. Using all the information available to me, I can make a rough approximation of the gross and net incomes of an individual enterprise, but there is really no way for me—or the KGB or even the head of an underground clan—to calculate the over-all figures for a family clan of underground millionaires.

Who, for example, can ever know the annual income of

the Liberman family company (not its real name)? And who can imagine the size of that family's fortune? But in the 1960s two members of the younger generation of that clan were seized by the KGB. They had both been involved for about ten years in underground business—independently, but still under the family umbrella. One of them turned about 200 million rubles' worth of valuables over to the authorities, and the other about three-quarters of that amount. If two comparatively young members of the Liberman family were able to have amassed 350 million rubles between them, then what might the whole family's fortune amount to, considering that members of the family had been in business for decades?

The chief investigator of the KGB Central Office asked the 200-million-ruble Liberman, "What did you need two hundred million rubles for? What could you possibly do with such a sum?" Liberman was unable to answer this completely reasonable question. He replied with a show of bravado, "Yes; only two hundred million. I had wanted to make two hundred twenty million: one ruble from each Soviet citizen."

But, then, *is* there any reasonable answer to that question? The incomes of the big underground businessmen are so large that Soviet society hardly provides the scope for spending them. Outlays for expansion, improving production, new technology, advertising, and public relations represent some of the expenses that absorb a considerable proportion of the income of businesses in the free enterprise system of the West. But in a country in which private enterprise is a crime, such expenditures are either completely impossible or so restrained as to consume only a tiny proportion of the income.

It is hard to estimate with any accuracy the percentage of the income of an underground enterprise in the Soviet Union that is spent on expanding production or on technological improvement, but I would imagine that on the average it does not exceed 10 to 15 percent even among the most active businessmen. Among the passive majority who are satisfied with what they have, such expenses would be quite small indeed. The only major ongoing expense that can be connected to underground production costs is the money spent on the bribes without which not a single private factory would last more than a month.

During the trial of the Georgian Laziashvili, one of the biggest underground business figures in the country, the defendant's business agent provided the investigation and the court with a list of the people to whom bribes had been given. The list began with district police officials and went on to name heads of the DCMSP (including the chief of the Republic's DCMSP) and the Ministry for Internal Affairs (including the minister) and public prosecutors from the district level on up to the Public Prosecutor of the Republic. A prominent place on the list was occupied by employees— from the lowest levels right up to the ministers themselves —of ministries on which Laziashvili's enterprises depended. The list of the state officials regularly bribed by Laziashvili was crowned by the names of the Chairman of the Council of Ministers and his deputies. But the largest bribes found their way to party rather than state leaders, among whom were officials ranging from the first secretaries of the Raikoms to the first and second secretaries of the Central Committee.

In other republics (apart from the Transcaucasian and Central Asian republics), in which corruption has not become so all-pervasive, it is rare for underground businessmen to personally hand bribes over to party and state officials of the higher ranks. But as far as we can judge from court documents, even in those republics, underground entrepreneurs expend around 15 to 20 percent of their incomes on bribery.

A good question would be: What can an underground Soviet millionaire spend his fortune on? Luxuries? But the possibilities for that kind of spending in the Soviet Union are extremely limited, even for the few people who enjoy large legal incomes. What can A.A., the dramatist, do with his money—a great deal by Soviet standards? Buy a four-room cooperative apartment (15,000 rubles or so as an initial payment)? A Volga car (10,000 rubles)? Build a dacha to the designs of an Estonian architect and fill it with custom-designed and -crafted Estonian furniture (not more than 150,000 would probably go toward all this)?

But an underground millionaire cannot allow himself even those things. Each expenditure, each purchase is made only with a glance over the shoulder to see if the DCMSP is watching. Whether he is going out to a restaurant or buying a fur coat for his wife, his first thought is always, If they should ask, will I be able to justify these purchases in terms of my legal income?

Thus the Soviet underground millionaire's principal aim is not to spend money but to conceal it. Not all of them, of course, live the life of the family that cooked two dinners. Most of them do try, however, to provide a decent standard of living for themselves and their families and to get at least some pleasure from their riches without standing out from the general mass of ordinary people. The range is enormous: the underground millionaire's life-style in Moscow or Odessa is very different from the underground millionaire's life-style in Georgia.

One client of mine, whom I will call Goglidze, who was tried by the Georgian Supreme Court, openly and legally owned two magnificent houses, one in Tbilisi, the capital of the Republic, and the other in the mountains near Tskhneti, an area considered the preserve of the ruling elite of the Republic. Both houses were luxuriously and expensively furnished with antiques bought from dealers in Moscow and Leningrad. Earthenware jars, called *merani,* containing hundreds of liters of wine, were hidden beneath the floors of their cellars. During their search the authorities confiscated

45,000 rubles in cash (besides his wife's jewelry). Goglidze explained to me that the money was just lying around at home to cover day-to-day expenses.

Goglidze was not afraid of DCMSP agents, for all the higher officials in that organization received monthly bribes from him. Tables would often be set up in the gardens of his houses for dozens of guests, and the traditional Georgian banquets would go on for hours, with a hired orchestra accompanying choral renditions of age-old folk songs; with bucketsful of wine providing countless toasts, drunk from drinking horns; with piles of shashlik made from the flesh of young lambs slaughtered right there in the garden.

In that way Goglidze did not differ from other Georgian underground millionaires: they all shared the same expansive hospitality, the same big spending, and the same open-handed life-style. If there was something that set Goglidze apart, it was probably his generous philanthropy. While not himself an educated man, Goglidze helped several of his young employees get an education; he paid the bribes without which it would be impossible in Georgia to enter an institute, and he granted them five-year leaves of absence while continuing to pay them, in order to permit them to devote themselves fully to their studies.

Underground millionaires in Moscow, the Ukraine, and the Baltic republics do not even remotely approach the Georgian life-style. Forsaking the communal apartment for a separate cooperative apartment, bought under his own name (where he can enjoy expensive foods without having to hide them from the neighbors), buying a modest dacha under a relative's name, dressing well, taking a trip to a Bulgarian resort on the Black Sea—that is about the extent of the visible life-style that a millionaire of the older generation can permit himself.

But a second life goes on beside this visible surface life, a life that is carefully concealed from the eyes of strangers. Yet even in this second life, underground millionaires of the older generation do not dare to do anything involving really big money. Their principal entertainment is getting together with their male colleagues in private. They avoid appearing together in public places for fear of attracting the attention of the DCMSP, so their preference is to gather in private houses. The eternal male need to have a bit of fun outside the family circle is satisfied by several salons maintained by women having connections or business with the world of underground enterprise.

During the 1960s and 1970s the salon of a woman called Sonya enjoyed popularity in Moscow. Sonya's husband had been in the employ of one of the large underground companies and was at the time serving a sentence in the camps. In accordance with the laws of the milieu the husband's partners were providing Sonya with quite a decent sum of money each month, but she also had an income from her salon, which was housed in her small two-room apartment. Middle-aged businessmen liked to assemble at Sonya's place in the evening. Everything there was to their liking: the lady of the house herself, a handsome and very stout woman, both affable and calming; the wonderful meals; and, especially, the card tables and roulette wheel. Ten percent of all winnings at cards, plus the house's winnings at roulette, brought the lady a sizable profit—especially sizable as the guests did not gamble with Soviet rubles, but with dollars and tsarist gold five- and ten-ruble coins—and the stakes were very high.

Games of chance in general occupy a very important place in the life of a wealthy underground Soviet businessman. It is probably only at the card table or the roulette wheel in some private gambling house (such as Sonya's salon) that he is able—if only by risking huge losses—to feel the satisfaction of spending recklessly—to feel rich.

The older generation of millionaires do not allow themselves many pleasures beyond these; they try to shield their children from the underground business world and try to make them into academics, doctors, or lawyers. "I've taken risks and made my pile, and now I want my children to live in peace without the risks of business—I want them to have the benefit of my money.'' That sums up their line of reasoning. Despite this, many children—after acquiring university degrees, even doctorates—continue the family traditions and enter underground businesses. These second- and third-generation underground businessmen are not content with the lives their fathers led; they are habitués of expensive restaurants whose waiters and managers know them by name and treat them as honored guests (and then send reports to the DCMSP about their binges). They are not afraid to make large bets at the races, where DCMSP agents keep an eye on all who make big wagers. They are not afraid to buy cars and dachas, paying prices equivalent to twenty to thirty years' worth of their official salaries. They openly visit the fashionable resorts—which are crawling with DCMSP agents from Moscow, Riga, and other underground business centers—spending five years' salary on a month's vacation.

This does not mean that the whole younger generation of underground businessmen consists of lunatics prepared to trade a year of high living for many years in the prison camp; they all try to be prepared, should the need arise, to justify their expenditures by pointing to some sort of legal income. The most common way is to buy a lottery ticket or government loan bond that has had a big win: they hunt for these with the help of the employees of the savings banks, which pay out all the winnings in the Soviet Union. The majority of the most prominent of the younger businessmen have paid agents among the bank employees who persuade winners who have come to pick up their money to sell the lucky tickets for two or three times the amount of the win. Another subterfuge these businessmen use is to take note of big payouts at the races so that they can claim that it was on this day and on that race that they had won a very large sum of money.

But the main insurance taken out by the younger generation is in the form of bribing DCMSP officials; they are also much more lavish in their bribes than their parents were.

None of this, however, is infallible. Moscow and Riga DCMSP employees have told me, and I have observed for myself, that the businessmen of the older generation land in court far less frequently than their descendants do.

The chronicles of the Soviet family clans of multimillion-aires are still awaiting their Zola. I am sure that the story of the Liberman clan (the name has been changed), for example, would be no less interesting and instructive than that of the Rougon-Macquart clan. The older generation of that highly ramified family passed through all the dangers of the underground business world without suffering any special losses. Only one of them to my knowledge has sat in the defendant's seat in the last twenty-five years, and even he arose from that seat not to be shipped to the camps but to go home. He had succeeded in buying his way out by paying an enormous bribe to the presiding judge. But if the judge was able to discharge Liberman, it was due in part to the prosecution's inability to put forward any evidence that he had "carried on a style of life not in keeping with his income," the phrase usually used in these indictments.

I was a witness to the fall of two representatives of the second Liberman generation. Leonid Liberman and Mikhail Soifer were cousins. Following the family traditions, they were in the knitwear business. Both were well known in the underground business world as big and talented entrepreneurs who did business with daring and panache. The Moscow DCMSP kept constant tabs on them, but it knew about their business lives in only the most general terms. Its agents' reports, however, described every detail of their lives as habitués of expensive restaurants, the racetrack, and fashionable resorts.

As long as they were under the jurisdiction of the Moscow DCMSP, whose heads they were lavishly bribing, the cousins could lead such a life with impunity. But in the 1960s the Central Committee of the CPSU, which had been informed of the corruption that prevailed in the DCMSP, made the decision to entrust the investigations into the biggest underground businessmen to the central office of the KGB.

Leonid Liberman was arrested immediately, but Mikhail Soifer was forewarned by his DCMSP contacts and managed to disappear. He lived as an outlaw for almost a year, hiding from the KGB, which had organized a nationwide search for him. That amounts to a near miracle in the Soviet Union, where each person must carry with him a passport containing his photograph, and where it is illegal to live anywhere for more than three days without showing this passport to the management of a building or hotel and getting a residence permit from the police. It is hard to say how long Soifer could have stayed in hiding had his girl friend not turned him in; one day when he arrived at her Moscow apartment he walked into a KGB ambush.

The investigators were able to discover many—although far from all—of the underground enterprises owned and managed by Liberman and Soifer, but the valuables and money they had accumulated remained hidden. Then they were offered a deal by the head of the investigation department of the KGB central office: if they handed over their wealth to the authorities, the KGB would guarantee that they would remain alive. Leonid was the first to give in, and he told them where, in a forest outside Moscow, his treasures were buried, sealed up in metal pipes and boxes. Within a few months Soifer's nerves also gave way, and he divulged the location of his hiding places.

A KGB investigator who took part in this operation told me that all of them—investigators and accused—stood there silently contemplating the piles of precious stones and jewelry, the heaps of tsarist gold coins, and the stacks of dollars. It was all emptied out onto the floor—there was no table that would hold it. But even this treasure trove, valued by experts at 350 million rubles, was not the extent of the wealth accumulated by the cousins. There are reasons for thinking that they did not tell the investigators about all their hiding places and that they managed to keep quite a bit for their families.

Liberman and Soifer kept their part of the bargain, but the court condemned them to death, and that sentence was carried out.

I was not very well acquainted with Leonid, but I did know Mikhail, as he was a regular client of mine. Behind the unremarkable façade of a reddish-haired Jew lurked an iron will and great determination. He was neither greedy nor miserly. What, then, motivated him? Was he impelled by a blind instinct to amass wealth for its own sake? Up to a point he was, but I think that once he had provided for himself and for his descendants for many generations to come, the main driving force that made him expand his business unceasingly was not greed but a need to use his innate business talents. He was living in a country where such talents carry with them great peril: making use of them in the Soviet Union involves the commission of a serious crime. If you are unlucky, these talents get you sent to the camps; if you are lucky, they bring you a great fortune, which is literally doomed to be buried in the ground or bricked up in a wall.

Because of the profoundly clandestine conditions under which private business must exist in the Soviet Union, accumulated assets cannot even be invested in a savings bank, which is the only way that Soviet citizens can earn interest on their money—2 to 3 percent annually. Deposits made in the name of the underground businessman are absolutely out of the question for reasons of secrecy, because, contrary to the principle of confidentiality enunciated in the law, savings-bank staffs are obliged to inform the DCMSP of all major deposits. But even accounts made out "payable to bearer" are no guarantee of safety. Thus the overwhelming majority of businessmen who make up the criminal world put away everything they have accumulated in secret hiding places. And since they do not believe in the stability of the Soviet ruble, they make every effort to convert all their assets into dollars, precious stones and metals, and tsarist gold coins.

The owners of treasures cache their wealth in various hideaways and secrete it in their homes in places that seem to be secure, but the whole repertory of hiding places is perfectly well known to the DCMSP and the KGB. When they conduct a search they are usually able to find the hidden horde quite easily. Be that as it may, the wealthy entrepreneurs prefer to keep their valuables in their own houses rather than buried somewhere out in the woods.

It may be difficult to find a way to hide valuables in safety, but it is even harder to convert millions of rubles into foreign currencies and gemstones and jewelry in a country where trade in those commodities is prohibited by law and is a serious crime. But even in such a country, demand creates supply, and the 1940s and 1950s saw a burgeoning black market in foreign currency. In those years hundreds of thousands of dollars and tens of thousands of tsarist gold coins (both genuine and counterfeit) were in circulation on the black market. They were brought to the Soviet Union in the suitcases of diplomats and of officers studying in Soviet military academies (mainly from the Arab and African countries). Precious stones were in especially great demand, and it is in them that underground businessmen preferred to invest their capital.

These diamond fanciers soon pushed prices up by five or six times, but the demand still far exceeded the supply. In Moscow at that time there were a number of big speculators in precious stones who managed—in spite of their illegal status—to collect incalculable treasures.

A group of KGB operatives once descended on a dark, damp apartment in the semibasement of an old building. The investigator on the case told me that they were amazed by the poverty—the utter destitution—of the surroundings. But during the search they found boxes bricked up in the walls and concealed under the boards of the stairs. The boxes contained 813 ten-ruble and 308 five-ruble gold coins of the tsarist era, along with 173 precious stones—a 38-carat emerald stood out. Experts later put the total weight of the stones at 546 carats.

Akhmed Akbarov (his real name) was the old Azerbaidzhanian who owned the apartment and the treasure. He was one of the biggest and most popular suppliers of precious stones in the underground business world. Buyers and sellers alike flocked to him from Transcaucasia and Central Asia, from the Ukraine and the Baltic republics. According to the doubtless incomplete information uncovered during the investigation, his turnover in the course of one eighteen-month period was 670,000 rubles.

Akbarov added to his stores of gems from two sources. He had agents planted in all the state *Yuvelirtorg* outlets (the state organization with the monopoly right to buy precious stones and metals from citizens). If someone brought in a good stone for sale, Akbarov's agent would first give the client the official state price (between 5 and 10 percent of the black market price), then immediately offer to put him in contact with someone who would pay twice that official price. In addition, both Akbarov, in Moscow, and his agents in Yakutiya would buy stones stolen from the Yakutiya diamond mines.

Akbarov did not live to see his trial. He died of throat cancer, and he died at home, because the KGB investigators had authorized his release from prison. (This was a rare show of humanity; even the most seriously ill of the people under investigation by the KGB are usually kept in the prison hospital.) Despite the torments that the old man was suffering, he found the strength to see to the disposal of the treasures that the KGB had not been able to find, for he knew full well that his wife, who was also in the hands of the KGB, would sooner or later break down and divulge the remaining hiding places. So he sent trusted people to transfer his valuables from those places to new ones. When a few months later the KGB operatives arrived with Akbarov's widow at the hiding places she had revealed, the repositories were empty, and that was the end of old Akbarov's gemstone business.

There were other dealers in precious stones operating in Moscow, Tashkent, Riga, and other cities, but not all of them shared Akbarov's fate. Some continue to operate to this day and continue to fill the caches of underground millionaires with their wares. Only an insignificant percentage of those caches has fallen into the hands of the DCMSP and the KGB; vast riches, probably greater than the pirate booty hidden away on Caribbean islands, lie there buried in the ground or bricked up in walls. And what about their owners? What are they waiting for? Are they waiting for a future time when they will be able to unearth their treasures and legally make use of them, waiting for the Soviet state to betray its principles and permit this? Are they waiting for the downfall of the Soviet regime and its replacement by a new system?

I fear that they will not live to see that day and that all the treasures, representing an investment of millions—billions —of rubles, the fruits of private enterprise, are fated to lie fallow in the ground for many a decade to come. That fact darkly underscores the senselessness and futility of private underground business in the Soviet Union.

On one hand, private underground enterprise is obviously inconsistent with the whole structure of the Soviet state and Soviet society; it is blatantly out of line in a regimented society that is profoundly hostile to any manifestation of individual initiative. A state-monopolized economy on which the material well-being of all citizens should ideally depend is, you would think, totally incompatible with underground private enterprise that creates opportunities for personal enrichment independent of the state. On the other hand, private enterprise shares with Soviet society and the Soviet state one characteristic that is organically inherent in them all: corruptness.

Underground enterprise is a positive tumor of corruption. Like a drop of water, it reflects the whole world of Soviet improbity. Just as the human body cannot live without air, underground private enterprise could not survive except for the fact that the Soviet state and society alike are rotten with corruption from top to bottom.

No underground enterprise could be created without the venality of the state administration; it would not last a month without the venality both of the organizations charged with combating economic crime and the apparat that rules the country—a venality ranging from the lowest ranks up to the highest elite.

But corruption in the ruling apparat is not the only condition for the survival of underground enterprise. It depends too on the corruption of society itself, on the corruption of the hundreds of thousands of people who have been drawn into its orbit—the hundreds of thousands of white- and blue-collar workers in state factories and salesclerks and managers in state stores, without whose complicity it would be impossible either to manufacture or to sell illegal merchandise.

CHAPTER VII

THE POLICE AND BRIBERY

L ONG-STANDING BELIEF has it that the police in all countries of the world are on the take.

It is from those who depend on them that the police take
bribes. Throughout the world, people whose lives involve
breaking the law—gangsters, thieves, drug pushers, prostitutes, pimps—are dependent on the police. It is the same
everywhere, from the freest of democracies to the most restricted of totalitarian states. Someone not pursuing any illegal activity in a democratic state, on the other hand,
depends very little on the police, but in the Soviet Union the
most honest people, who are careful not to contravene the
law, are made aware at every turn of their dependence on
the police and find it necessary to pay them off.

To what bureaucrat does an American farmer have to
apply if he has decided to leave his farm and move into
town? None, of course. But if a Soviet collective farm
worker wants to become a town dweller, he must first seek
permission from the chairman of the farm (with formal approval to be given only at a general meeting of all collective

farm workers) and then from the chief of the police department of his home district.

Whose permission does a citizen of France or a British
subject need in order to leave one town and go to live in
another? No one's. But a Soviet citizen can become a permanent resident of a town or settlement only by getting special permission from the police department of the place
where he wishes to live.

Without the sanction of the Soviet police, a person is not
allowed to move from one apartment to another, nor is he
even permitted to let his closest relatives or friends stay in
his home for more than three days. This is the kernel of the
system of residence permits. It was established in 1932,
along with the passport system, and has provided an abundant and inexhaustible source of income for all police officials who have anything to do with it. Basically, the way the
system works is that any Soviet citizen, in order to be permitted to live in a given town and in a given house for more
than three days, is required to obtain special permission in
the form of a "right-to-residence" permit from the passport
section of the district or municipal police.

In small towns and villages there are no official restrictions
on residence permits. According to the law, residence permits are issued to anyone who wants one, irrespective of
whether he has a permanent job or close relatives in that
particular town or whether he has a criminal record. The
only condition is the availability of what in the Soviet Union
is called "living space"—that is, an apartment, a room, or
even part of a room in which a person can live.

Despite the favorable conditions for obtaining residence
permits, the people in charge of the passport sections of the
police still contrive to elicit bribes.

Tens of millions of Soviet people wish to move to the large
cities. However, residence permits in those cities are not
given out as easily as they are in the small towns. The big
cities all belong to the "restricted" category of localities,

and the granting of residence permits to new inhabitants is generally prohibited and is allowed only as an exception, with special permission from the municipal police department. In effect, all major cities in the country are "restricted," and the most restricted of all, the one with the most stringent rules governing the issuance of residence permits, is Moscow.

According to the regulations, a residence permit for Moscow can be granted only to someone who has been summoned for employment by an institution or enterprise that has obtained special permission from the Ispolkom (Moscow Municipal Executive Committee) or to the prospective spouse of an inhabitant of the city who already has a residence permit.

But even these very strict regulations cannot stem the flow of illegal "immigrants." Each year the Ispolkom takes note of this alarming situation and each year adopts new resolutions demanding in the most categorical terms that the police "take immediate steps" or "tighten control." But all these efforts are futile, for they are negated by the corruption that pervades the Moscow police department. In real life all the restrictions and prohibitions are disregarded and violated every day—usually, of course, in return for a bribe.

And this goes on in Moscow! (We're not speaking of the provinces, where surveillance of police activities is not so strict and where local customs are much more rough-and-ready.) Such bribery is never mentioned in Soviet newspapers. Nevertheless, the fact that bribes of this sort are offered and accepted—and very often too—is borne out by court cases. A familiarity with these cases and various private conversations with people who have had to hand out bribes for residence permits make it possible to draw a few well founded conclusions.

In large regional towns in Russia the bribe to obtain a residence permit fluctuates around the 500-ruble mark. A residence permit for Moscow costs considerably more, and there has been a marked tendency over the years for it to increase. At the beginning of the 1970s a Moscow permit could be acquired for an average bribe of approximately a thousand rubles—with small fluctuations up and down. As far as I know, by the end of the decade the price was between 2500 and 3000 rubles, and in some cases even more.

The Soviet driver, whether he drives a vehicle belonging to the state or owns a private car, is completely at the mercy of the police, or, more precisely, of the division known as the State Automobile Inspectorate, usually referred to as GAI (Gosudarstvennaya Avtomobilnaya Inspektsiya).

Some sections of GAI are in charge of issuing drivers' licenses, some are responsible for carrying out the required annual mechanical inspection and issuing inspection certificates, and others enforce traffic regulations on the streets and highways throughout the country.

In cities and rural areas alike the practice of getting a driver's license by means of bribery has become very widespread, for both professional and private licenses. There are two patterns of bribery in this area. More often than not the person taking the driving test does not know the GAI examiner and has no information about what he will be like. That, however, does not prevent the applicant, once in the car beside the inspector, from offering him a few banknotes. In such cases the bribe is fairly small as a rule, usually no more than a hundred rubles.

In the second pattern, the candidate takes the test with a GAI inspector whom he already knows and whom he or a middleman has previously approached to settle the amount of the bribe required for a surefire result. One might say that in such cases the license is simply bought; the applicant may not know how to drive a car at all and may not even show up for the test. Such candidates hand over the payment and then simply call in at the GAI office to pick up their licenses.

The aforementioned middlemen do not necessarily act out of greed. They may have obtained their own licenses by bribery and want to do their friends a good turn by fixing them up with a "helpful" inspector. However, over the last ten or fifteen years a category of professional middlemen has emerged who systematically and by no means selflessly deal in passing on bribes to GAI employees on behalf of people who want drivers' licenses. A series of court cases has shown that these people are usually instructors who train people for the test in the special state driving schools.

Bribes given within the framework of this arrangement are much larger than the spontaneous ones mentioned above, which have not been negotiated in advance. And not only are they large, they are also stable. Quite some time ago a fairly fixed rate was established in Moscow, well known to all people concerned—150 rubles for a third-class (the lowest category) professional license, 200 rubles for an ordinary private license, and 300 rubles for an international license. But fairly substantial increases in these tariffs occurred from 1977 to 1979, according to information I obtained privately from Moscow.

From time to time GAI employees are charged with accepting bribes to deliver drivers' licenses. Now and then these cases are the results of complaints lodged with the public prosecutor's office by people from whom bribes have been solicited, but mostly they are initiated on the basis of information from secret agents. In Moscow and other cities throughout the country, trials of GAI staff are not unusual. The latest series of such trials took place in the district people's courts of Moscow in 1976 and 1977; and in 1979 almost all the GAI bosses found themselves in the dock of the Moscow City Court. This series of trials demonstrated just how commonplace the trade in drivers' licenses had become in the Soviet Union.

Once a year all vehicles—private and state-owned—have to undergo a mechanical inspection, and the owners are issued a certificate stating that the vehicle is in working order. Both the inspection of the vehicles and the issuance of the certificates fall within the purview of the GAI and have become reliable sources of income for its employees.

Any owner of a private car is very well aware that the GAI inspector can always find some tiny problem even if the vehicle is really in perfect shape. Therefore car owners prefer not to tempt fate and are resigned to handing over the sacred 10 rubles, the going rate for the inspector—not only in Moscow but, as far as I know, in all regional cities in the Russian Republic. In Georgia, Azerbaidzhan, and Armenia the rate fluctuates between 25 and 50 rubles.

The required mechanical inspection takes place in the springtime throughout the whole country. In April and May tens of thousands of vehicles are inspected in each GAI district department. Consequently the amount of money collected by the inspectors of each department is on the order of 150,000 to 200,000 rubles. The sacrosanct 10- (or 25-) ruble bills are handed over directly to the inspectors when the vehicle is being tested, but they wind up being shared out among all the district police department chiefs, and, as far as one can judge from certain case documents, some of them go even higher up, to the municipal central offices.

When a car owner arrives at the inspection center he simply holds out a 10-ruble bill along with the necessary documents. In cases in which the inspection is carried out in the garage complexes where private cars are kept, someone from among the owners goes around with a checklist of the other owners collecting 10 rubles from each, and, when the inspector arrives, gives him the amount collected. The enormous apartment building I lived in in Moscow had just such a complex, consisting of fifty-two parking spaces. Each year in April my neighbor would collect 520 rubles for the GAI inspector. Each year I added my 10 rubles to the pile, and my car passed the test without any complications, along with those of the other lucky car owners.

A corps of tens of thousands of GAI inspectors is responsible for enforcing traffic regulations throughout the country. They are authorized to stop offenders and, depending on the gravity of the crime, may either demand an on-the-spot fine or enter the infraction on the offender's driver's license (after three such penalties the license is withdrawn). Or they may revoke the violator's license then and there as a preliminary to settling the matter at a GAI office.

In the large cities GAI inspectors are not in the habit of stopping bus or trolley drivers if they have violated the regulations. It is also fairly rare for an inspector to stop a truck driver, and then only for serious offenses. Usually those professional drivers do not have any spare cash on hand and are not inclined to part with their money easily; they are therefore not of much interest to GAI inspectors. On the other hand, the latter show no mercy to taxi drivers or the owners of private cars. At the slightest infraction—and even for no reason at all—the GAI inspector will flag down a private car with a grandiose gesture of his police baton and will adopt a monumental pose, not moving from his spot, waiting for the driver to come up to him at an obsequious trot.

The balance of power between the almighty GAI officer and the offending driver is absolutely clear. The violator will already have slipped a precautionary banknote into his license before handing it over—one ruble if he has no previous violations, 3 to 5 rubles if his license is already penalized, and 50 rubles if his breath smells of alcohol (for which his license may be suspended for a year).

GAI inspectors have another source of illegal earnings on the long-distance highways: bribes from people transporting produce—meat, fruit, vegetables, whether their own or from state or collective farms—to sell in the city marketplaces.

Since the law forbids anyone to own a private truck, bus,

or minibus, and since the collective and state farms never can get enough of them for their needs, these organizations all make under-the-counter deals with drivers of trucks or buses belonging to some state institution in order to get the produce from the country into the towns. But as soon as the loaded truck is on the road, both the driver and the owner of the goods become easy prey for the GAI patrols.

Trucks and buses are obliged to carry official documents specifying what route the vehicles are to take and what is being transported and in what quantity. Naturally these ''un-official'' trucks and buses travel either without any documentation at all or with fictitious documents that the driver can always procure from his boss (also for a bribe, needless to say).

And so, if the driver and the cargo owner are stopped by an inspector along the road, they are completely in his power. If they have no route authorization, the inspector can forbid them to drive any farther or even arrest them. Even if they do have an authorization, the inspector may quibble about some inaccuracy or other and detain the vehicle for one or two days under the pretext of having to make sure the documents are in order. Since, in the Soviet Union, produce such as meat and fruit is not usually carried in a special refrigerated compartment but is just piled into an ordinary truck, holding it up for two days is tantamount to destroying the shipment. Therefore the only recourse for the owner of the merchandise is the cure-all bribe. Without even attempting to argue, he simply gives the inspector 10, 25, 50, even 100 rubles, depending on the value of the cargo.

Regrettably, no police force in any country whatsoever can manage without the services of secret informers. They are an inescapable evil, and somebody has to do the work of an informer, just as some police official must keep in contact with the informer, give him assignments and collect information from him. (This is referred to by the police and KGB as having an agent "in tow.")

Both the Soviet and criminal police and the KGB have to give their agents permission to commit crimes so that they can infiltrate the criminal world, gain the trust of its members, and thus acquire the information they need. This basically immoral situation results in the crooked police official making it possible for his agent to push the bounds of his criminal activities far beyond the requirements of verisimilitude. Often the relationship between official and agent grows into a relationship between accomplices, each of whom gets his cut from the criminal gains. And, needless to say, even if an agent fails in his primary mission he is protected from prosecution by the police authorities.

There never is—nor can there ever be—any mention of this topic either in the mass media or in the specialized professional literature. The subject of undercover agents and informers is absolutely taboo in the Soviet press, and everyone pretends that the state does not employ their services at all. However, in my own legal practice I came across many cases involving secret informers and their police patrons bound together by a relationship of bribery and corruption.

It happens that I had dealings on three separate occasions with an organization of professional women shoplifters who operated in the big Moscow department stores. In all three cases it turned out that they were informers for the Moscow criminal investigation department and that they regularly paid off their contacts in the police. My connection with them began when a young man called Alexei came to see me one day. His face did not leave a strong impression on me, but I do recall that he was exceptionally well dressed, suspiciously so in fact, even by Moscow standards.

He carried references from former clients of mine, and when he asked me to defend a "friend of his," a woman who had been charged with rifling a customer's purse in the shoe department of GUM, the country's main department store, I agreed without giving the matter a second thought. The defendant, Varyagina (I have changed her name), impressed me favorably. She had a pretty face, light, fluffy hair—not fashionably cut but rather braided into two thick plaits wrapped round her head in the old-fashioned coronet style —and calm, light-blue eyes. She looked like a young, naïve provincial girl, but Varyagina was neither naïve nor a provincial. She was a professional Moscow thief, thirty-four years old, with thirteen previous convictions (the first at age thirteen) for pickpocketing and shoplifting. She had done a total of about fourteen years' time in the camps and in prison, although there had been no arrests or legal proceedings for the previous two years.

This decently but modestly dressed "yokel" attracted no attention in the women's shoe departments of GUM and TSUM, the large Moscow department stores, and was able to mingle with the crowd of shoppers. With a deft movement, unseen by those around her, she would slip her hand into the purse or bag of a woman who was trying on shoes and extract from it the sheaf of bills put there in readiness for the purchase. She committed several of these thefts a day, her average daily take totaling 300 to 500 rubles.

Varyagina told me about all this quite calmly, without any feeling of shame—even with a touch of professional pride in her skill. She explained the reason for her good luck over the past two years and why she had not once been arrested. When I studied the documents relating to her case I was immediately struck by certain incongruous points that I could not understand. The file contained three or four reports of Varyagina's having been caught red-handed by the victims or some bystanders at the scenes of the crimes. Plainclothes agents of the criminal investigation department (who carry on constant surveillance in all the large department stores) had taken her and her victim to the police room (these also exist in all large stores), drawn up a report, and then—simply allowed Varyagina to go free.

The secret of her invulnerability was extremely simple: she worked as an undercover agent/informer for the Moscow criminal investigation department. According to her, she never gave any real information, but twice a month signed a report that was written for her by someone else. These reports contained information either about nonexistent, invented people or about real-life thieves who, like herself, were secret informers, whom her reports could not harm. Occasionally, at meetings in prearranged apartments, she used to hand these reports over to her contact, a major in the criminal investigation department. In addition to the reports, Varyagina gave the major five hundred rubles a month, in return for which fee the major would protect her; whenever she was caught stealing in the stores she would immediately inform the officers that she was an informer and give them the major's telephone number. After a short talk with him the officers would release her without further ado. Eventually the officers got to know her by sight and did not stop her even when they saw her going for someone's purse.

On that fateful day in August when, instead of releasing her, they sent her to jail, the machinery had not functioned properly. The officers on duty that day in GUM were not the usual ones and did not know her, and the major was away on leave and the captain who was deputizing for him knew nothing of Varyagina's existence, for, according to the rules, a secret informer is known only to the person who is his "handle" or contact and to the section chief.

On two other occasions Alexei came to ask me to defend "a friend of his," and both times the women turned out to be professional shoplifters who were also secret informers for the Moscow criminal investigation department. They were being "run" by two captains whom they paid off punctually each month so as to be able to work in peace, as they put it.

I shall be writing about prostitution in the final chapter of this book. For the moment I shall talk only about those prostitutes who solicit foreigners exclusively—not just *any* foreigners, but only those who can pay in hard convertible currency—and who are hence called "hard-currency prostitutes."

In view of the fact that foreigners from Western countries are closely followed as a matter of routine, absolutely all prostitutes who regularly meet with them very soon come under police or KGB surveillance. Their meetings with clients are recorded on film, in reports of agents who observe from outside on the street, and in the reports of informers. When sufficient compromising material has been collected, the women are requested to go to the police, or more often to the KGB, where they are presented with a choice: either they agree to give information about the foreigners they meet with or they will be expelled from the town in disgrace.

Sometimes women who have been confronted with such a choice categorically refuse to collaborate with the police or the KGB and at the same time give up prostitution. Most often, however, they go along with the offer to collaborate and begin to have regular meetings with the police and the KGB.

From that moment the prostitute-informer is able to solicit clients in restaurants, theaters, and near hotels without any interference, and to meet with them freely. In return for this freedom she passes on information about her clients to the police and the KGB.

Usually another kind of business relationship develops between the "hard-currency prostitutes" and their police bosses in addition to the official one. As a rule, police officials who have "hard-currency prostitutes" in tow obtain bribes from them in the form of Soviet and foreign currency, goods from abroad (American jeans, current recordings, tape recorders, and so forth), and sometimes sex (the meetings in "safe" houses provide ideal conditions for this).

However, it is neither thieves nor prostitutes that are the main source of income for the police. The people who have lined the purses of more than one generation of police officers are the foreign-currency speculators on the black market.

The late 1950s and early 1960s were a time when the foreign-currency market was absolutely flourishing in the Soviet Union. It is difficult to believe nowadays, but that is exactly how it was—in the Soviet Union, a country with extremely tight police surveillance, where the Soviet ruble is the only legal unit of currency and where any exchange into other currencies is prohibited. In that country tens of thousands of people were dealing in foreign currency on the black market, day after day buying and selling dollars, English pounds sterling, tsarist-era gold coins, gold, platinum, and precious stones.

The smart young dealers would be there in the morning near the Moscow hotels or at the docks, scurrying about, cornering the foreign tourists and sailors to see if they had any foreign currency to sell. They did not sniff even at five dollars, but when the opportunity arose they would buy several hundred dollars' worth at a suitable price of two to three rubles to the dollar (while the official rate at the time was seventy-two kopecks). By evening these smart young people (the slang word for them is *fartsovshchiki*) had disappeared from the streets of the city. They had gone to their bosses, the people who financed their activities, to turn in the day's take.

But even if he was lucky, a *fartsovshchik* would make only a couple of hundred dollars a day, obviously not enough for a big operation. The main sources of the foreign currency that suddenly appeared on the black market were the diplomats and the officers from Arab and African countries who were studying in Soviet military academies. Without fear of arrest they brazenly and lavishly flooded the black market with hundreds of thousands of dollars, pounds sterling, and ten-ruble tsarist gold coins—manufactured in special workshops set up in Cairo and Alexandria.

How was such an orgy of speculation possible in a country that has the most highly perfected system of police surveillance in the world? The black market in foreign currency thrived so well because its existence happened to be useful and necessary to the very organs whose job it was to combat it—the police and the KGB.

During this period of prosperity the black market was, to use the jargon of undercover agents, "under a glass dome": all black market personalities of the slightest degree of importance and all the more or less important deals were perfectly well known to the police and the KGB. This was possible because the people who were combating currency speculation made skillful use of the means at their disposal to saturate the black market with their agents.

The situation reached fantastic proportions. A client of mine, a black marketeer (not one of the big wheels, but no mere *fartsovshchik* either) who was himself a secret informer for the police, once told me of the following episode. One evening two of his speculator friends came to see him in order to meet with an old man from Kiev who had brought with him several thousand dollars that he had inherited from his father, who had died in the 1920s. It turned out that the dollars, which had lain in their hiding place for thirty years, had been issued at the beginning of the century. Since the speculators were uncertain about the market value of old dollars, they decided not to buy them.

My client did not inform his police boss about this incident because he felt sorry for the old man and thought that the matter was of no importance. However, when he next went to see his boss he was reprimanded for insufficient zeal: one of the two other speculators who had been present at the meeting (perhaps even both of them!) turned out to be an informer, like himself.

The process for recruiting these agents presents no difficulties. A currency speculator's activities are such that for days on end he has to seek opportunities to get in touch with foreigners. It is only natural that after a short while the police and the KGB get to know the currency speculators. So when they are arrested they are given the choice of either becoming secret agent/informers or being arrested and sent to the camps for eight years.

Because of this it was quite easy for the police and the KGB to use their speculator-agents to reach their bosses and the big wheels. By using the same primitive, though effective and reliable, blackmailing method they were able to recruit agents even from among the uncrowned kings of the black market.

Hence these organs, which were responsible on behalf of the state for combating the trade in foreign currency and precious stones, had in their hands all the accumulated information that would have made it possible for them to wipe out the black market in the space of a few months. But this they did not do. For both the police foreign-currency department and the KGB—although for different reasons—found the existence of the black market useful.

The police were not anxious to have the black market completely wiped out for two reasons. According to the laws governing bureaucracy, *no* institution strives toward its own obsolescence, and the police department was not exempt from that law; the existing state of affairs suited them perfectly. Using the information they regularly received from their informers, they could always arrest any one of the black marketeers, easily compile the necessary evidence against him, and hand the case over to the courts. In this way the police in the department to combat foreign-currency speculation gave their superiors the impression that the fight against the black market was being waged skillfully and effectively. Thus at one and the same time they made sure of a quiet life for themselves and gained kudos for their successful fight against crime.

There was, however, another, no less important, factor: bribes. In the 1960s a series of trials took place throughout the country marking the end of the boom period in the foreign-currency black market. It was these trials—held in Moscow, Leningrad, Baku, Tbilisi, and Riga—that established beyond the shadow of a doubt that hundreds of foreign-currency speculators, former undercover agents, had paid regular bribes to their police contacts and, through them, to the entire leadership of the currency division of the DCMSP (the police). It transpired that the bribes were given not only by the small-time speculators and the low-level currency dealers, but also by the big-time black market magnates themselves.

There were three Moscow black market syndicates that were probably the biggest of any operating in the country at that time. It was revealed that the leaders of two of these syndicates were important police and KGB informers who passed on enormous sums of money in rubles and foreign currency—through their police contacts or directly—to the heads of the police foreign-currency division and to the top people in the over-all leadership of the Moscow DCSMP.

And so for the DCSMP the black market in foreign currency turned out to be the goose that laid the golden eggs. Naturally it was in no one's interest to wring that goose's neck.

Neither did the KGB want to paralyze the black market completely, although the reasons for this were different. KGB officials did not need their informers among the foreign-currency speculators to line their own pockets. In fact, their services were not needed at all by the division responsible for fighting the black market, but rather by the departments in charge of spy recruitment and counterespionage.

In the KGB the undercover agent/foreign-currency dealer would be used to contact a foreigner the KGB was interested in, entrap him into agreeing to sell foreign currency (which is a heinous crime under Soviet law), and set a time and place for concluding the deal so that the KGB might catch the foreigner red-handed. As the result of such an operation the KGB would be able either to recruit their victim as a full-time spy or to obtain specific information from him by threatening him with scandalous exposure and expulsion from the country (if he had diplomatic immunity) or with arrest and many years of imprisonment in the camps.

So it happened that the currency-speculation divisions of both the KGB and the police were anxious for the criminal activities of their informers on the black market to spread far and wide, and were not in the least interested in seeing that market totally eliminated. The currency speculators naturally had the same interests at heart.

As a result a system of organized crime developed that operated successfully for many years. It consisted of two interrelated and symbiotic elements: the state organs responsible for fighting crime (the police and the KGB) on one hand, and several criminal syndicates operating on the black market in foreign currency on the other hand. The criminal syndicates, headed in fact by the secret agents, were able to buy up and sell foreign currency and gemstones without any concern for surveillance or arrest. That is the precise reason why they paid off their police and KGB bosses, whether in bribes or services. With the backing of the police and the KGB, such syndicates easily cornered the black market and eliminated any dangerous competitors.

A picture of organized crime and corruption in the black market world can be reconstructed from the documents relating to the wave of trials that brought that stage in the foreign-currency boom to a close. Among the trials one case occupies a special place. The documents of the case show very clearly indeed, and in great detail, how the formation and activities of the organized-crime system may be traced. The defendant in this case was Lieutenant Valentin D——, an officer in the Moscow DCMSP's department for combating speculation in foreign currency, who was charged with taking bribes from one of his informers, Yan Rokotov, nick-named "Cross-Eyes" by the police and KGB as well as in black market circles.

In the summer of 1966, when Lieutenant D—— appeared before the Moscow Municipal Court, the black market in foreign currency had already been smashed. The small-time speculators were waiting out their sentences in the camps and the uncrowned kings of the currency business had been shot. The most celebrated of these kings, Yan "Cross-Eyes" Rokotov, who, besides working for D—— was also his accuser, had been executed in 1961. D—— pleaded not guilty. In order to prove his guilt, the KGB investigators on the case included in his dossier top-secret material usually available only to police officers directly responsible for the organization and day-to-day running of the network of agents and informers.

For example, the dossier contained the *Instruction Manual for Operatives in the Service,* which specifies and de-scribes in great detail: how to recruit agents and informers by using compromising material (in the case of criminals) or ideological convictions (for young Komsomol or Communist party members); the relationship between an agent and his "handler"; methods for indoor and outdoor surveillance; procedures for the remuneration of agents; and much else besides.

The dossier also included top-secret decisions by the Council of Ministers of the USSR authorizing the KGB to conduct searches of private apartments in the absence of the occupants by breaking down front doors (the code name for this was "Operation E") and to tap private telephones, called "hanging Marusya" in agent jargon (code name, "Operation M").

Finally there was the *Log of Secret Agent Rokotov,* even though the logs of agents are the holy of holies in the secret service. A log such as this mentions only the agent's code name, never his real name. The police or KGB official running the agent writes down with his own hand the agent's assignments and mentions a specific victim who is to be "cultivated" (the *Instruction Manual* refers to the victim as a *figurant*). What the manual calls the "legend" is set forth in detail: in what way, under what pretext, and under what name the agent is to establish contact with the *figurant* and gain his trust.

The log also records all sums of money paid to the agent as expenses incurred in conducting the operation (in some cases quite large sums) and as remuneration (always paltry amounts—15 to 20 rubles, 50 in exceptional cases). Particular facts are noted, such as when an agent is given a special disguise (such as an officer's uniform) from the wardrobe department of the police or KGB for performing the "legend." It goes without saying that the log also keeps a record of all the agent's reports.

Rokotov's history is that of a man who, in the space of a few years, was transformed from a small-time speculator in hard-to-find books into a dealer who controlled millions and was at the same time an important *agent provocateur* for the police and the KGB, responsible for the arrest of dozens of people. This man's story—although it sounds fantastic—is to some extent very typically and intrinsically Soviet.

In the late 1940s Rokotov was arrested and sent to the camps, along with millions of other Soviet citizens. After 1956, during the period of mass rehabilitation of the victims of the Stalinist terror, Rokotov returned to Moscow. He was no longer a youth and had acquired neither an education nor a profession in the camps. He was averse to starting life over again from scratch, so turned his hand to making a living by speculating in hard-to-find books.

Things went quite well for him, but he soon became known in the black marketplace, in the alleyway by the Moscow Art Theater, not only to book lovers but also to DCMSP agents. He was arrested and taken to the Moscow Municipal Police Department to undergo what the *Instruction Manual* calls "recruitment of a secret agent on the basis of compromising material."

Without a moment's hesitation or reflection Rokotov accepted their offer. He began as an ordinary small-time informer, since to the Moscow police the black market in books was a subject of no great importance. But it turned out that Rokotov excelled in the secret-investigation line, and he was soon promoted to the post of secret agent in the department to combat foreign-currency speculation in the Moscow DCMSP.

It did not take Rokotov long to achieve prominence in Moscow's foreign-currency market and become one of the biggest dealers in the country. The initial capital for his first ventures on the black market—twenty-five hundred rubles —was given to him by his police bosses from the state coffers, a fact that was also duly recorded in the log. The same bosses guaranteed him a free hand in his business and safety from arrest. But to give Rokotov his due, he demonstrated outstanding commercial and organizational abilities and successfully increased the working capital given him by the state.

Rokotov did not tarry long on the lowest levels of the black market; very soon he worked up to a position of having several currency speculators working for him. He probably had every reason to consider himself invulnerable and not to fear arrest, since even at that early stage he was not only an active and useful agent who provided his bosses with invaluable information, but in a certain sense it was he who was their boss: he was the one who paid them, and not the other way around. Each month the entire administration of the currency-speculation department and the top management of the Moscow DCMSP received quite sizable payments from him.

At this point the scale of Rokotov's operations was already fairly large, although it was only by chance that he was able to make contact with foreigners who had large amounts of currency to sell. But by now he was not satisfied with what his *fartsovshchiki* were able to provide. With his growing flair for business, he needed other, more stable and abundant sources of foreign currency—and he got them. But this happened after his next promotion—from police informer to KGB agent.

Having received KGB sanction to buy currency from foreigners, Rokotov established stable contacts with a few foreigners who were permanently resident in the Soviet Union and bought up tens and even hundreds of thousands of dollars' worth of currency from them.

He conducted all his criminal operations with the connivance and even the protection of the police, and later with that of the KGB. Beyond this, however, when he was working for the KGB he committed a number of crimes on their direct orders. This is not a guess or a conclusion drawn from circumstantial evidence; it is a fact, recorded in an official document that I was able to study.

Throughout the entire investigation and at his trial, Lieutenant D—— categorically denied his guilt and said that he was a victim of slander. In order to prove the truth of D——'s defense, I had to have access to Rokotov's official KGB log (which was not included in the case documents). A KGB log of an agent's activities is an incomparably more secret document than its police equivalent, for the log of a KGB secret agent contains information about entrapment of foreigners and recruitment of spies. As D——'s defense attorney, I had almost no hope of seeing that document. Nevertheless I petitioned the court to request Rokotov's log for examination. I was refused. I submitted my petition three times more, and each time the judges retired for consultations and each time they refused me (of course after having spoken on the telephone with the appropriate KGB officials). Just as the investigation was drawing to a close I petitioned once more, without any real hope of success. This time the judges spent about two hours in their consultation room, and then the miracle happened: the court decided to request Rokotov's log from the KGB.

Under the vigilant eyes of a pair of KGB couriers I spent more than two hours studying the log and copying out excerpts. The log of secret agent Rokotov contained the assignments given to him by the KGB captain who was running him. It made explicit mention of the selected victim of entrapment—the *figurant* (who was sometimes a foreign diplomat)—and also described the "legend." In such cases Rokotov assumed the role of a solid merchant from Riga who wanted to get hold of a large consignment of foreign currency and was willing to pay any price without haggling.

The task assigned to Rokotov by the KGB captain was spelled out quite clearly in the log: to get in touch with *figurant* N——, entrap him into agreeing to sell foreign currency, and arrange a time and place for the deal so that the ambush could be set up. The log did not mention what happened to the foreign currency that Rokotov acquired if the deal went through successfully: Rokotov was allowed to keep it as payment for services rendered.

This went on for three or four years until Rokotov's connection with the police and the KGB was no longer a secret to anyone involved in the black market. He then lost his value as an agent and the KGB decided to remove him from the scene.

Rokotov was not the first or the last police or KGB agent who was removed when his usefulness ended. A special procedure has been formulated for such cases. The agent who has lost his value is arrested and charged with crimes that he has indeed committed, albeit with the authorization or at the behest of the very departments that are now his accusers. At the same time they come to an arrangement with their former agent that he will keep quiet at the trial about their relationship: in return for his discretion they guarantee him a comparatively short term of imprisonment, a privileged position in the camp (the post of librarian or stockroom manager), and, halfway through his term, if he does a good job as a "brood hen" (camp slang for a prisoner who secretly informs on his fellow inmates), a pardon from the Presidium of the Supreme Soviet. According to an unwritten rule, the "collective president" of the country grants such pardons to all "brood hens" at the request of the police or the KGB. (I could name several people who certainly followed this route.)

These were the conditions submitted to Rokotov, and he obediently accepted them. During his first trial in the Moscow Municipal Court, Rokotov said not a word about being a secret agent, let alone about his having given bribes to his bosses in the DCMSP. And he was sentenced to fifteen years in a severe-regime camp.

But by the personal order of the General Secretary of the Communist Party, Khrushchev, this sentence was rescinded. Rokotov was retried and got the death sentence. Only *then,* after the sentencing, when he found himself on death row, did Rokotov begin writing. He hurled himself into a frenzied fight for his life. In his desperate attempt to avoid execution, and hanging onto each day of respite, he sent a whole string of statements addressed to the General Secretary of the Central Committee of the Communist Party of the Soviet Union—Khrushchev—in which he named officials in the Moscow DCMSP to whom he had paid bribes, giving the dates and the amounts paid. Virtually the entire top leadership of the foreign-currency department was named, but particular viciousness was reserved for Colonel N. A. Averin (his real name).

Colonel Averin had played a special role in Rokotov's life. He was in charge of the department to combat speculation in foreign currency when Rokotov was working as a secret agent for the Moscow DCMSP. From the letters Rokotov wrote in prison and from notes in the log we know that Colonel Averin met with his agent several times at "safe" apartments, where he gave Rokotov assignments, collected denunciations from him, and, according to Rokotov, accepted money and expensive gifts as well.

Of all the police officers mentioned by Rokotov in his statements only Lieutenant D——, his direct superior, was convicted in the end. But for the other officials in the department to combat foreign-currency speculation everything turned out well. Colonel Averin and several other officers were eventually dismissed from their jobs, but they retained their freedom and indeed their Communist party membership cards.

At that time people such as Rokotov were not at all rare on the foreign-currency black market. Every so often evidence about their double lives as criminals and agents who paid bribes to their police bosses would be revealed to me in documents of criminal cases in which I was participating or about which I heard from my colleagues.

The black market in foreign currency may have been smashed in the early 1960s, but it reemerged at full strength at the beginning of the 1970s. It showed new characteristics distinguishing it from the black market of the 1950s, which were engendered by a new phenomenon in Soviet life: mass emigration. In this new black market the "merchants" are in the main not underground millionaires buying up foreign currency and gemstones to bury in hiding places but people planning to emigrate to the West or to Israel.

When the Soviet state gives someone permission to emigrate, it does not allow him to take out of the USSR any valuables that might be sold abroad. The prospective emigrant therefore tries to sell whatever cannot be taken out of the country and to convert the rubles, which are now useless, into dollars or gemstones that he can then attempt to smuggle out.

Not only has the type of customer changed but the variety of goods bought and sold on the black market is different. Whereas previously, foreign currency (especially dollars) and precious stones had pride of place, now new types of goods have begun to appear—icons, paintings by famous artists, antiques; in other words, anything that might fetch a high price at auction sales in London and New York.

Businessmen with dealings in the millions have already cropped up on this new black market. Not much is known about them yet since they do not show themselves quite as openly as their predecessors of the 1960s, but by 1975 or 1976 cases were being tried involving the owners of collections that included original works by Rembrandt, Veláz-quez, Rubens, Manet, Kandinsky, and Chagall or dozens of fourteenth- and fifteenth-century Russian icons, all ready for shipment to the West.

The 1970s black market in foreign currency has not yet been smashed. As yet no trials have been held that would provide information about the methods being used either by the dealers on this market or by the organs fighting it. Nor has any reliable information yet emerged about cases of corruption. But it will—the abscess is still festering and has yet to burst.

CHAPTER VIII

CORRUPTION IN EVERYDAY LIFE

I ONCE visited a lawyer friend on business and found him at his writing desk. Before him lay a piece of paper covered with writing.

"Just look at this," he said. "It's a list of the chores I had to get through last week." And he showed me this list:

1. Food—Lyubov Lazarevna
2. Dry cleaning—Big Lyuda
3. Toilet paper—Little Lyuda
4. Dostoevski—Olga Nikolaevna (candy)
5. Concert tickets—Irina Mikhailovna (candy)
6. Flowers—Ivan Kirillovich (bottle)

For an old Muscovite like me there was nothing cryptic about this list and I could easily make sense out of it: the left column was the list of chores to be accomplished and on the right were the names of the people who helped my friend to circumvent the immense complexities presented in Moscow by each one.

205

"You know," continued my friend, "I looked through the list and was horrified. I did manage to get hold of everything I needed and to do everything I'd planned, but in every case —and I mean *every* case—I had to behave with something less than complete honesty."

He then went on to give me a detailed account of his week. "First of all I had to get hold of some decent food as I had guests coming, so I went to the special-orders department of GUM." (The *G*lavny *U*niversalny *M*agazin—"main department store"—has a special-orders department that offers an assortment of foods usually to be found only in the private Kremlin stores or in the *Beryozka*—"Birch"—food shop, where everything is sold for foreign currency and only to foreigners.)

"As you can imagine," my friend went on, "I didn't even go to the woman on duty—I went straight to the manager's office. She greeted me like an old friend, asked me what I needed, and told me what was available: caviar, fresh and smoked sturgeon, smoked eel, fruit, cucumbers and tomatoes. [And these were all to be had in winter.]

"The lady asked me kindly to take a stroll around the store for fifteen minutes or so, and on my return to her office I received a neatly tied box. At the cash desk I paid for my order and then gave the nice lady fifteen percent of the amount. It never occurs to her—let alone to me, a lawyer— that we've just committed a crime: I'd offered a bribe and the friendly lady had accepted it from me.

"Anyway, to continue. The next day was dry cleaning. I use only the American process. [Some dry-cleaning services in Moscow have installed American equipment.] There are always long lines of people who wait many hours to hand in their clothes, only to have to go back again two or three days later to collect them.

"So I called up the cleaner's," my friend continued, "and asked to speak to Lyuda. 'Lyudochka, it's Boris Petrovich speaking. Can I come round now?'

"I arrived and walked through the room, which was crammed with people waiting their turns. I went straight into the back room with a suitcase full of clothes. Lyuda, a large and beautiful young woman, was expecting me. She picked up my case and called out, 'Come back in an hour.'

"She wasn't at all afraid that someone would catch us in the act; all her fellow workers have their own customers, and each month they all pay the management not to notice anything.

"An hour later Lyuda gave me back my case and I paid the bill, and not a kopeck more than the official price— except that my money goes straight into Lyuda's pocket instead of into the state's cash register.

"I had another thing marked down on my list for that day: toilet paper. I called in at a large paper-goods store, and, naturally, there was no toilet paper for sale. This didn't bother me; I went up to the counter and called to the salesgirl I know, also Lyuda. This Lyuda, unlike her namesake at the dry cleaner's, is very small, a young kid almost. She didn't even ask me what I wanted, but just whispered to me quietly, so that the other customers wouldn't hear, 'Meet me out in the courtyard.'

"I went outside and Lyuda was already waiting for me at the employees' entrance holding a package of ten rolls of toilet paper. The official price for ten rolls is two rubles eighty kopecks, so I gave Lyuda a five-ruble bill. She thanked me and I thanked her."

My friend and colleague went on. "After corporal needs had been taken care of, it was time to worry about the spiritual ones: getting tickets to a concert by a well known foreign chamber orchestra that is on tour in Moscow, and finding a copy of the latest volume in the new edition of the complete works of Dostoevski, which I wasn't able to subscribe to.

"This was a bit trickier than the toilet paper, but here too I have my ins. I got the concert tickets from Irina Mikhailovna, the box office manager of the Philharmonic Society, and the Dostoevski from Olga Nikolaevna, a saleswoman in the special-subscription publications shop. I paid exact official prices both for the tickets and for the book. I didn't push any rubles in anyone's direction, and in any case they wouldn't have been accepted. But several times a year on special occasions I go over to wish them both all the best and take them quite expensive gifts—French perfume or magnificent boxes of chocolates that you cannot buy in ordinary stores.

"You think that's all? No. I had another errand that week —the flowers. You know how very difficult it is—practically impossible—to buy flowers in Moscow shops in winter. But I know the manager of a flower shop on Kutuzovsky Prospekt—a lovely fellow: a retired military officer and a drunk. About two years ago I just happened to drop by his shop and ask him to help me find a bouquet of flowers. He did, and I handed him a quarter-liter bottle of brandy. And that's how things continued: he gives me the flowers and I give him the quarter liter."

Having concluded this tale of his adventures, my friend raised his hands in a helpless and perplexed gesture and said, sighing, "You'd think I was some kind of procurement specialist—and an amoral one at that—wouldn't you?"

No. My lawyer friend is no artful dodger, nor is he without morals. He is merely a normal representative of the educated establishment. The connections he used had been built up gradually over the years. Sometimes he had sought them out specially, but most often they had just evolved spontaneously through clients, who readily offer their services to a lawyer, or through friends—likewise respectable members of the establishment—who are willing to share their own connections and, if need be, take advantage of those of their friends.

Those who are not willing to accept corruption and who prefer to wage an open battle with it are doomed to failure.

Of course, when they encounter corruption they can complain about the people who would not serve them without their showing "gratitude." However, if, after sacrificing time and energy on the matter, they do manage to have the culprits punished, their only reward is moral satisfaction. The suit will still be uncleaned, the patient will still not have a hospital bed, and the airplane ticket will still not be bought. The state can punish the guilty, but even the mighty administrative apparat of the Soviet state is incapable of making them work properly and conscientiously. In obtaining goods and services in real life a ten-ruble bill is sometimes more powerful than the KGB. And I am not being rhetorical or hyperbolic when I say this: this proved to be precisely the case in my own experience.

Once a Soviet citizen has received permission to emigrate, he has to perform a multitude of the most varied tasks before he can leave the country, and the majority of those tasks can be accomplished only after he has his exit visa in hand. But in order to be issued that visa in the first place, he has to surrender his apartment to the Housing Administration Office. But he can surrender his apartment only after the District Repairs Office has drawn up an estimate of the cost of refurbishing the apartment and after the prospective emigrant has paid that estimated cost to the repairs office.

It is practically impossible to get through this entire predeparture schedule in less than three or four weeks, and the authorities usually give would-be emigrants a month for their preparations. But my wife and I were in a special position. We were to be thrown out of the country immediately, and were to be given only ten days for all our preparations.

Colonel Zotov was the deputy director of the Visa and Registration Department and, as far as I know, the KGB's representative in that department. He welcomed me like a long-lost friend: "Konstantin Mikhailovich! Why didn't you come straight to me? You don't have many days for your preparations—I understand perfectly. Let's see now—you make a list of the things you need to do, write down the offices that handle them, and I promise to help you. Give me the list, and if there are any problems, do not hesitate to call me at any time and I'll get things sorted out."

Then it started. Every office I visited gave me the same answer: "Come back in two [sometimes three!] weeks." Back I'd go to Colonel Zotov, who would call the office concerned, and everything would be sorted out in a matter of hours as if at the wave of a magic wand.

But the first thing on the list I prepared for Colonel Zotov was "District Repairs Office to send assessor urgently," and this presented problems. The first time I went to the repairs office, they assured me that no assessor could be sent out in less than two weeks. I rang my colonel, and fifteen minutes later I received the reassuring reply, "The assessor will be at your apartment by tomorrow."

Tomorrow arrived and no one showed up. I called Zotov again, and again he reassured me. "They will be there tomorrow without fail; the boss himself has given me his word of honor."

The next day the same thing happened, and each day my deadline was drawing nearer. I went back to the repairs office and impressed upon the dispatcher that the KGB had called her boss, who in turn had promised to send me an assessor. No assessor had come, so I was going to complain to the KGB. She answered me with perfect calm, "Don't try to scare us; we have nothing to fear from the KGB—we don't get involved with politics here. I told you I'd send an assessor in two weeks, and two weeks it will be."

At that point I surrendered. I placed a ten-ruble bill on the desk in front of her and begged her in an agonized voice, "Put yourself in my position; help me—send the assessors. I'll show my gratitude to them too."

The money vanished from the desk and immediately I heard, "Okay, they'll be there today."

Corruption permeates the life of *Homo sovieticus,* and the

situations in which he is compelled to have recourse to corruption are as varied as life itself. Neither the almighty ruling apparat nor the victims of corruption themselves are able to do anything about this situation.

TRADE AND CORRUPTION

A day almost never goes by without a Soviet man or woman needing to turn to the services of state stores, restaurants, and cafeterias. (After all, other, nongovernmental stores simply don't exist in the country.) Because of this, someone is always falling a victim to corruption, which permeates the whole system of Soviet trade from top to bottom.

The Soviet Union is a country in which there are permanent shortages of consumer goods. For the Soviet shopper, buying an article of clothing is not merely a money problem —it is a problem of finding the article he needs. Naturally, under such circumstances the buyer becomes an easy victim to the department store workers, to whom he has to pay more than the official cost in order to get what he wants. But even when the buyer doesn't pay more than the official cost, he still becomes a victim of corruption. In the food stores he is cheated, in the restaurants and cafeterias he receives smaller portions than those he paid for, and in the manufactured-goods stores he is sold goods of inferior quality for superior prices.

But don't hurry to condemn mercilessly all these salesmen and cooks who trick the consumer. After all, they're not only taking from their clients; they still "give" supplies from their wares to the director of the store or restaurant or the manager of the wholesale depots. And, in his turn, the recipient must give to someone even higher, who must turn around and give to someone on an even higher rung of the ladder.

Here are two sketches, both of them strictly accurate and

both based on documentation drawn from criminal cases, illustrating how the Soviet system of trade works in practice.

SKETCH 1.   SCENE: *Food Shop Number Five, in a central district of Moscow.*

The day begins very early in a large food store. Long before the store opens, goods are distributed to the various departments from the basement storerooms. The assistant manager is in charge; she issues carcasses to the butchers and items such as broiler-ready steaks and chops and salami to the salesclerks in the delicatessen. The salespeople pay the assistant manager on receipt of their merchandise—not the retail price, for that is what is paid by the customer to the cashier to form part of the official receipts of the store, but what is called "extra," the sum paid to store managers in return for merchandise.

The store has opened, and long lines of people (an inevitable feature of Soviet stores) have formed at the counters. The line is especially long in the meat department, for meat is scarce even in Moscow, with its privileged supply status. The butchers work as hard as they can, for over and above the official cost of the merchandise, they have to make up the money they have paid the store managers for the carcasses plus getting a bit extra for themselves as well.

The official rule is that carcasses are butchered into cuts of three grades, but in practice virtually every shopper among the hordes that crowd the meat counter pays top-grade prices, no matter what part of the animal is purchased. That is not the sole source of illegal income. The counter-weights on the butchers' scales do not look in any way remarkable, but they have been drilled out, and each one-kilogram weight in fact weighs about 870 to 900 grams. The drill holes are covered over and painted black to match the weight, and the customer is never the wiser.

The clerks in the delicatessen must also recover the money they have to pay the store managers for the scarce merchandise. In fact, scarce items such as salami and ready-to-cook meat products are not visible on the counter; they are kept hidden under the counters and are sold only to regular customers who know the conditions of sale and who, when they come from the cashier to pick up their merchandise, hand over not only the chit for the official price paid but also additional money, carefully folded small enough to be concealed underneath the chit.

The line also contains many people who have traveled to Moscow from the provinces, where it is impossible to buy any sort of sausage in the stores. To these customers a second-rate sausage is sold as first rate. Furthermore, the provincial customer willingly hands over a tip of two or three rubles in gratitude for being allowed to buy four or five kilograms of sausage instead of the two kilograms per person allowed by the regulations in Moscow stores.

There are similar goings-on in all departments, with the customer being cheated in each one.

The management too has its own worries, its own expenses—and, of course, its own sources of income. There has just been a delivery from a meat-packing plant, whose manager will already have been given his bribe for the merchandise. But a few rubles must be given to the clerks who arranged the shipment, as well as to the loaders who are hired off the books. The management does not have official money at its disposal for such expenditures, so the loaders must be paid out of the manager's own pocket.

While the manager is busy with the delivery and unloading of his merchandise, his assistant is dealing with regular customers, the representatives of a large factory located about 350–400 miles from Moscow, where such things as meat, sausages, and eggs are not available in the stores. They bring a truck into Moscow twice a month to stock up on food for their employees. These visitors are interested in "wholesale" purchases. Stores, of course, are categorically prohibited from engaging in wholesale operations by a strict rule, so these customers pay over and above the official price in return for this "favor." When accounts have been settled and the customers have gone on their way the assistant manager notes in her "black" ledger: "Goods sold—1800 rubles. Received—2580 rubles."

The illegal profits extracted from customers' pockets by the salesclerks are very large indeed compared with their official wages. The average salary for a salesclerk in a Moscow food store is 120–130 rubles a month, but the illegal earnings could range from 500 to 700 rubles for someone working in the delicatessen or another department to 1500 or 2000 rubles for a butcher. The store managers' illegal earnings totaled an average of 40,000–50,000 rubles a month. But we are not speaking here of clear profit, since the manager and his assistant also had their expenses, and quite sizable ones at that.

Since the assistant manager kept her "black" ledger with great accuracy, the investigation and trial turned up detailed facts about both illegal income and illegal expenses. First of all, there were the overheads, without which the normal functioning of the store would not have been possible. The managers had to pay the loaders, as well as skilled workmen hired off the books to repair all the minor breakages that are inevitable in any large store. In addition, the store management had another kind of expense: there were thirty-six salesclerks working in the store, and each of them took food home each day without paying for it. The resulting shortages had to be made up by the manager and his assistant. This amounted to the quite sizable sum of 4,000–5,000 rubles a month.

But it was not these overheads, part of the store's day-to-day operation, that were the main drain on the managers' incomes. In Chapter III I noted that Food Shop Number Five supplied the district elite with food at less than full price. I also said that the store's management made regular tribute payments, in cash and merchandise, to all the various inspectors, auditors, and police employees. Eighty-five hundred to 9000 rubles were spent each month on these gifts.

But the expenses did not stop there. For the store to fulfill its sales plan and make sufficient illegal income besides, it needed good and scarce products. In order to get such items from the wholesale depots, the cold-storage outlets, and the meat and fish processing plants, the managers of Food Shop Number Five had to pay regular bribes, and quite sizable ones at that. The assistant manager's ledger recorded 9000–11,000 rubles a month for bribes.

Finally, the assistant manager paid a monthly visit to the municipal administration of the chain of food stores to deliver a package of money—10,000–12,000 rubles—which she handed to the administration head or one of his deputies. The documents of the case gave certain indications that a portion of that money had a higher destination than the municipal administration—the Department of Trade of the Moscow Committee of the Communist Party and the Trade Department of the Moscow Municipal Executive Committee.

Thus the great bulk of the illegal income received by the managers of Food Shop Number Five—35,000–40,000 rubles per month—went for business expenses and various kinds of bribes. Even after that, however, there was still a profit of 5000–10,000 rubles a month left over for them.

SKETCH 2.   SCENE: *A large department store in one of the recently built-up suburbs of Moscow.*

A large Moscow department store is a complex and highly developed organism consisting of many departments, each of which enjoys considerable independence. While each department has its own characteristics, the basic ways in which they make their illegal profits are similar.

In the mornings, before the store opened, there were always large crowds of customers waiting outside. When the doors were flung open, the crowds would dash inside and flow through the store. But there is a privileged category of customers. They did not need to mill around outside the closed doors or spend hours and hours waiting in line near the various counters. These customers had connections with salesclerks or department managers and got what they wanted by paying a premium over and above the regular price.

Each department led a double life. Alongside the trade in items displayed on the counters, for which people paid normal prices to the cashiers, another trade was going on, to which the staff devoted most of its attention and which provided most of their income, an income that was three to five times their official salaries (or, in the case of department managers, fifty to a hundred times).

Here is the scenario for a normal working day for some of the departments in the store, reconstructed from the documents of the case. Before the store opens, the manager of the fabrics department has distributed hard-to-find materials among his salesclerks. In order to get hold of them the manager has already paid a bribe to the manager of the wholesale depot, so he passes the material on to the sales staff on the following terms: they will pay him two to three rubles per meter of suiting sold. But he keeps a large percentage of the fabrics in the storeroom for his own purposes.

The clerks conceal these scarce goods under the counters and sell them for a premium of three to five rubles per meter to their regular customers, or to new customers who ask in a confidential whisper whether there might be any hard-to-find fabrics and promise to "express their thanks" for them. Meanwhile the department manager greets his regular wholesale customers in his office. These are the professional retailers (mainly from the provinces) who buy whole bales of fabrics, several hundred meters at a time, and who also, of course, pay a premium of three to five rubles a meter.

In a back room of another department, work is in full

swing: salesclerks and cleaning women are busy ripping the labels out of undershorts, labels indicating that these are second-grade undershorts and cost a certain price. In their place they are sewing labels marked "first grade" and showing a correspondingly higher price. (The manager bought these labels illegally from the same factory that made the shorts.) Thus the customer will pay first-grade prices for second-grade shorts, and the department manager will pocket the difference, distributing a portion of it to the salesclerks and the cleaning ladies.

In the ready-to-wear clothing department are rows upon rows of racks containing drab, badly sewn men's suits made in the Soviet Union, ugly women's winter coats with expensive mink collars, and sundry other merchandise for which there is very little demand except among the least discriminating of customers, mainly those visiting Moscow from the country. To be sure, the department does have other merchandise: men's suits from England and Yugoslavia, elegant knit suits for women made in France and England, Italian raincoats, and many other items much sought after by customers. But those things are not on the sales floor; they are in the storerooms, the keys to which are in the possession of the department manager and his assistant. *Le tout Moscou* knows Monya and Fima by name. They are two young, personable lads from whom you can always get something "from abroad" by paying a premium of between ten and thirty rubles. They have a lucrative and large clientele and well established connections with the wholesalers. Naturally their customers also include professional retailers who buy clothing in wholesale lots.

The department store management leads the same double life; there is an illegal side to the operation that exists in parallel with the official side. It is the management's responsibility to maintain the building and the furnishings of the store and to keep it all running smoothly. In this particular department store the average expenses fluctuated between

100 and 150 rubles a day. Tips to officials and policemen also added up to quite a sum.

Keeping the store supplied with merchandise cost the management a considerable amount. When they procured authorizations for orders from the Ministry of Trade or the Ministry of Light Industry, bribes would always change hands, which ranged from 1000 to 3000 rubles per authorization for a large order of scarce merchandise. An average of 200,000 rubles annually went for such bribes.

Finally, there were the bribes paid to high officials in the Department of Trade of the Moscow Municipal Executive Committee and the Trade Department of the Moscow Committee of the Communist Party. The two assistant store managers as well as the department managers alleged that the manager handed over 25,000 to 30,000 rubles a month to some top official in the Department of Trade and to the Moscow Party Committee.

Perhaps everything that happened in these stores was a result of the managers being swindlers, and if these posts had been held by honest persons, everything might have gone normally—bribes would not have been paid or buyers tricked.

But everything we know tells us that any manager who tries to act strictly in accordance with the law, without resorting to bribery, cheating his customers, or speculating, is either brought into line by the system and compelled to play by its rules or else is expelled by that system. This fact has been verified many times experimentally, but probably the most graphic of these experiments—at least of the ones I know about—was conducted by the Moscow Committee of the CPSU.

In the 1960s, "in order to improve the situation in Moscow's commercial network" (as the Moscow Committee's decree put it), several dozen retired officers, all members of the Communist party, with irreproachable reputations, were sent out to work as managers of shops, restaurants, and cafés. I was able to follow the course of this experiment.

One of the officers was Lieutenant Colonel Boris Adamov, who was assigned the post of manager of Food Shop Number Five, which I have already discussed. Adamov was an honest officer, educated by military concepts of discipline and obedience, and when he arrived at his new post he could not at all accept the fact that the normal functions of a state enterprise could be carried out only with the help of bribes and by cheating the customers. He started out by operating in strict compliance with the law of the land: he took no money from his sales personnel, sold nothing at speculative prices to professional retailers, and categorically refused to pay bribes to top people in the municipal administration of the chain responsible for the shop or to the managers of the wholesale depots, cold-storage facilities, and meat-packing plants that supplied the store with merchandise. It did not take long for the results to make themselves felt.

Since the municipal administration officials were not receiving their monthly payments from the new manager, they began to carp at any petty blunder made by an inexperienced employee. A hail of reprimands fell on Adamov, and he ran the clear risk of being fired in scandalous circumstances. At the same time, the managers of the various supply facilities —since they too were going without their regular bribes— stopped providing the store with goods that were in short supply, and even made great difficulties about supplying things that were available in abundance. Consequently Food Shop Number Five did not fulfill its sales plan, and the incomes of the sales help fell sharply. (Even the official wages fell, as they are not paid in full unless the plan is met.)

Adamov could not stand the pressure and accepted a compromise: he remained an honest man and took no money for himself, but he permitted his highly experienced assistant to run the business according to the unwritten rules of Soviet trade—to take money from the salesclerks, sell goods at inflated prices, cheat the customers, and, of course, bribe the top people in the municipal administration and all the store's suppliers.

That was the initial result of the Moscow Party Committee's experiment. During Adamov's trial I met his friend M——, a retired colonel, who had been appointed manager of a large fabrics store around the same time as Adamov. When he arrived on the job, he paid no bribes either to the heads of Tekstiltorg, to which the store was subordinate, or to the managers of the wholesale depots on which the store depended for its supplies. Not only would he himself not sell goods at inflated prices to professional retailers but he was ruthless with his assistant and the sales staff who tried to cheat their customers. He fired them and informed the public prosecutor's office about their abuses. Unlike Adamov, M—— turned out to be a man with an iron character; he would accept no compromises.

Meanwhile the wholesale depots were not supplying the store with any scarce merchandise, and month after month M——'s shop was falling short of meeting its sales plan. The sales staff, bitter at the consequent reduction in their official wages and at the loss of their illegal earnings, declared war against the new manager. M—— was presented with a bald ultimatum: he would either leave the store "of his own accord" or the faked evidence of his wrongdoing would be transmitted to the courts.

Retired Colonel M——, the holder of numerous wartime military decorations, preferred capitulation to the prospect of waging a long battle in the offices of investigators and in courtrooms.

That is the second result of the experiment which came to my attention; neither result was in any way out of the ordinary. Judging by what Adamov and M—— told me, the stories of all the other retired officers sent out into the commercial world by the Moscow Party Committee conformed with one of the two models: either subordination to the laws of corruption governing the Soviet trade system or expulsion from that system.

There was nothing exceptional or out of the ordinary about what went on in Food Shop Number Five or in the department store. Similar criminal setups exist in all stores throughout the country, and everywhere the mechanics of the illegal operations follow the picture I have sketched. Within certain limits, of course, the details may vary, depending on circumstances, but in the main the method is typical and universal.

The reason for its universality lies in the fact that it reflects the laws that govern the functioning of the Soviet system; it reflects in particular the inevitability of that system's corruption. There are two factors that underlie the inability of the Soviet trade system to function without corruption. The first (which is at the root of the whole phenomenon to some extent) is the necessity of bribing the ruling party-state apparat, which is corrupt on every level. The second (which creates an environment favorable to crime) is the never-ending shortage of goods that exists in the Soviet Union.

FREE MEDICAL CARE AND CORRUPTION

Man's life begins with birth, and it is from the moment of birth that corruption enters his life.

Of course a woman about to go into labor will be taken to her local maternity home without any bribery, but if she wants to give birth in a hospital known for its high standards of service and its qualified staff, or if she wants specific midwives and anesthetists to perform the delivery, then a bribe will be required. In most segments of the state medical system, which is a part of the lives of all Soviet citizens without exception, corruption has become an everyday mass phenomenon over the past quarter of a century.

On January 8, 1980, *Pravda* published a letter from a young woman that said in part: "My husband and I are doctors and our joint earnings are 220 rubles a month. We have a son who earns nothing: he is four years old. Two hundred and twenty rubles for three people—it's a bit tight . . ." The woman described her family budget: 60 rubles a month for rent, 40 rubles for the baby sitter, without whom the writer would not be able to go out and earn her 110 rubles a month; that leaves 120 rubles (or rather 98 rubles after taxes) for everything else—food, clothing, transportation, books, and entertainment. (A family of three must spend at least 150 rubles a month on food alone—and this is eating very modestly.)

Later on, the writer of the letter informs us with defiant candor that she and her husband have "begun taking bribes." But since, regrettably, they are not surgeons or gynecologists, who are paid off by patients in cash, and are only general practitioners, they are given "candy, perfume, caviar, sausages, meat and anything else the patients can think of." But the anonymous *Pravda* correspondent is not downcast: she states that by taking bribes she and her husband reckoned on being able to save up 30,000 rubles and buy a house in five years.

This letter is striking in its outspoken openness and for its reflection of the bitter facts of life that give rise to corruption in the medical service.

All medical services are provided completely without charge to all Soviet citizens. The patient gets everything free: hospitalization (including general medical care, operations, treatments, drugs, examinations, and food), visits to doctors in local clinics, and house calls.

The bulk of free medical services is provided through the network of district polyclinics that covers the entire country.

Anyone in any district can visit his polyclinic and be seen by a doctor, or if his state of health does not permit this, can request to be visited in his home.

This network of polyclinics is the weakest link in the medical system. It is weak because of the medical staff and because of what they can reasonably accomplish. The number of patients each doctor must see in a day is so large that a doctor is able to devote only seven to ten minutes to each patient, and a patient must often wait an hour or more to be seen. The situation is about the same for house calls. Only about fifteen minutes can be spent on most visits—hardly enough time for the doctor to take off his coat, wash his hands, ask the patient how he feels, examine him, give him the necessary instructions, write out the prescriptions, and make whatever notes he needs to make.

It is not possible for a patient to correct all these defects by means of bribery. But money or gifts can ensure more attentive care and more time being spent on one patient than on another. Almost all people—even the very poorest—seek to do this whenever they have to use the services of the local polyclinic doctors, and the desire for more and better attention has resulted in this kind of corruption really becoming nationwide in scope.

It is relatively rare for doctors to be offered money in such relationships: most often, thanks for better care is expressed by small gifts and services.

This form of payment is particularly widespread. In a country of permanent shortages—food, decent clothing, and high-quality services—the chance of obtaining all these things without having to pay black market prices is much sought after.

There exists one more way of avoiding the shortcomings of free medicine, and that is not to make use of it at all. But we know that the entire Soviet medical service is run by the state. Therefore, can you get away from it? And if so, where do you go?

In the summer of 1976 my wife was in Brest, Belorussia,

where she was to appear in court. However, one morning on her way to the courthouse she fell down and suffered a very bad multiple fracture of the collarbone. She was taken, semiconscious, to the surgical department of the nearest polyclinic. When she arrived in the X-ray room, the surgeon, the radiologist, and the nurses (all women) were busily occupied in a lively discussion about the merits of a knitted cardigan from abroad which a patient had brought in to sell to one of them. They paid no attention to my wife, and only after they had exhausted their topic of conversation—about ten minutes later—did the radiologist tell her, without even asking how she felt, to climb up onto the high X-ray table. Then the surgeon put her arm and shoulder into a cast that was as heavy as medieval armor. (Back in Moscow our doctor could only shake his head as he removed the cast—together with the skin of her shoulder—and say, "Another week in that cast and you'd never have moved that arm again.")

As soon as my wife returned home we called the doctor from the local polyclinic. She did not even look at the arm, which was still confined in its plaster armor, nor did she ask how my wife felt. The only thing she was interested in was when and in what circumstances the injury was sustained (facts determining how much insurance would be paid). After these questions were answered to her satisfaction she wrote out a doctor's certificate for three days' sick leave and told my wife to have the permission extended when the three days were up.

We realized immediately that free medical care was not going to get us anywhere, and so the very same day we arranged through friends who had the necessary entrée that my wife should be treated at one of the best hospitals in town by experienced surgeons, physiotherapists, specialists in therapeutic gymnastics, and masseuses, all experts in their fields and all thoughtful and considerate people. They saved my wife's arm, and we remember them to this day with feelings of profound gratitude. The total cost in cash and in gifts for all their work was probably not more than two hundred rubles.

Meanwhile, what did the free medical service do for us during this time? The treatment went on for more than three months, and throughout this time I would go every week to the polyclinic doctor who had originally called on us and every week she would extend the doctor's certificate. Throughout those months she never once asked me how the patient was or whether the cast had been removed.

The only way, then, to avoid free medical care is to go to the same free, state-run institutions—not, however, as a normal nonpaying patient but, rather, privately, by visiting a specific doctor by prior agreement and for a fee.

The number of hospitals in the Soviet Union is obviously insufficient to cover the needs of the population. No amount of bribery can increase the number of hospital beds, but people willing and able to pay can have those beds redistributed in their favor; by the same token, those who will not or cannot give bribes are at a disadvantage.

There is great injustice and immorality here, since while the person giving a bribe to get into the hospital is genuinely ill, he is still occupying the bed of someone who is not only sick but also has more right to it than he, since he has been patiently waiting his turn for several weeks.

Bribing one's way into the hospital can take various forms, depending on where one lives. In a humble rural hospital, where patriarchal customs are still observed in matters of corruption, a person who requires hospitalization will simply go to the doctor without making any prior arrangements and give him some modest offering, usually produce from his peasant plot.

Corruption in a district hospital is more "civilized." The bribe here is paid in cash—even if not very much—rather than in kind. In the Russian provinces, the Ukraine and Belorussia, the bribes are not very large: 25 to 50 rubles is considered adequate.

Moscow, Leningrad, Kiev, and other major cities contain the famous hospitals and specialized clinics that are sought after by patients from all corners of the country. Friends or bribes help out here. A bribe is given to whoever has the power to authorize a patient's admission, either the chief doctor or his deputy or a departmental chief—or even the doctor on duty in the admissions ward. The size of the bribe will be in proportion to the prestige of the hospital or clinic and the official position of the bribe taker.

It is incredibly difficult to get into the Herzen Oncological Clinic in Moscow in the normal way; even a very large bribe does not make it easy. Several years ago a rank-and-file doctor of that clinic was tried in the Leningradsky district people's court and the following came out in the course of his trial. If a doctor on duty in the admissions room determines that a patient's state of health requires urgent medical attention he can send him immediately to one of the standby beds, which may be set up in hospital corridors or squeezed into the overcrowded wards in emergencies. It was by exercising that right that the defendant used to hospitalize his "clients" on days when he was on admissions duty, for bribes of between 100 and 200 rubles. To be admitted to a first-class specialized clinic, people usually pay between 300 and 500 rubles.

Even when the patient has finally gotten into the hospital he is not spared the need to resort to corrupt practices.

When it became clear that a close member of my family had cancer, we needed to negotiate with a competent surgeon for an operation. Our close relative—a professor and doctor of sciences—belonged to a privileged category of the population that was served not in the local clinics for ordinary Soviet citizens but in special clinics and hospitals of the USSR Academy of Sciences. Nevertheless the surgeon on duty, whose qualifications were not known, would have operated on him. For this reason we attempted to find a specific surgeon to operate on our relative, a surgeon renowned for his skill. We found such a surgeon, negotiated with him, and he performed the operation successfully. It goes without saying that in our negotiations with the doctor before the operation we handed over the stipulated fee.

As little as twenty years ago, operations for fees were rare in the Soviet Union. Today, however, there is every justification for stating that they have become a very widespread phenomenon, which has even come to encompass members of the surgical elite—the most celebrated professors and academicians.

The rates can vary from 100 (or even 50) rubles to 1000 or 1200 rubles, depending on the location (a provincial hospital versus a clinic in a capital city) and on the fame and rank of the surgeon (a provincial doctor with a decent reputation versus a member of the Academy of Medical Sciences).

While not so clear-cut as it is in patient-surgeon relations, corruption also plays a part in a patient's relationship with his other doctors. The most common way of repaying a physician is with a fairly expensive gift, such as French cosmetics or perfume, French cognac, dinner services, or movie cameras. More rarely, but still often enough, patients pay doctors a predetermined amount of money for a course of treatment in the hospital. My sources stated that corruption of that kind is becoming ever more widespread each year. They also told me that more and more hospital doctors are taking money from patients for drugs.

Soviet hospitals are supplied with a wide range of drugs, especially imported ones, in quantities that fall far short of their needs. Quite often, when a doctor gives a patient a drug that is in short supply, the patient will have to pay for it. These transactions are never conducted in a straightforward, open manner; that would simply be too risky for the doctors. Rather, they inform their patients that the necessary drug is not available in the hospital but that they can obtain it privately elsewhere. (In the 1960s in Riga a criminal case against a group of doctors charged with such a scheme was heard in the Latvian Supreme Court.)

A close friend of mine, a doctor in Botkin Hospital, used to complain about growing corruption among her colleagues there. She spoke with indignation and disgust about her fellow doctors, some of whom extorted money or expensive gifts from patients and their relatives and would give serious and careful treatment only to "grateful" patients.

My friend was a specialist in her field and a person of irreproachable honesty, who never took anything from patients apart from flowers and candy. But when I asked her why she did not expose her unworthy colleagues, she answered me in a way that fully summed up the social and psychological factors hampering the fight against corruption in medicine: "Well, you know, writing denunciations to the authorities is not at all in my line. Besides, even if I did overcome my aversion to denunciations, they would simply persecute the life out of me. Even if I went to work in another hospital, my reputation as an informer and a violator of the 'professional guarantee' would follow me."

Although there has been a massive spread of corruption in Soviet medicine, very few doctors have been taken to court on charges of receiving payment for hospitalizing or treating a patient. To some extent the paucity of court cases is due to the fact that under Soviet law bribery is an indictable crime only when money is taken by an "official person," not an ordinary doctor. So when an ordinary doctor receives money from a patient he is treating, he is not brought to trial. The main reason, however, lies elsewhere.

With rare exceptions, all Soviet doctors accept money,

presents, or some kind of service from their patients. It is virtually impossible for doctors to keep their bribe-taking a secret, nor do they see any need to, since to their minds there is nothing immoral about it and it cannot impair their professional reputation or standards. Thus a "professional guarantee" has emerged making it highly improbable that cases of corruption will be exposed from inside the profession.

Free Education and Corruption

Like health care, education in the Soviet Union is free. The state provides all education from kindergarten to postgraduate studies, and most students in higher and special secondary colleges (that is, technical colleges) receive a small expense grant in addition.

Corruption enters the life of the Soviet citizen at a very early age, even before he or she is old enough to be aware of it. The five-year-old granddaughter of some friends of mine, who was a pupil in kindergarten, showed a full grasp of the situation when she told her parents that one girl's mother had given Antonina Ivanovna some fabric to make a jacket for International Women's Day and that now Antonina Ivanovna was always praising the girl and had given her the leading role in the First of May show. Antonina Ivanovna had already informed all the mothers that her birthday fell in May, so now they were each giving five rubles to buy her a present. Then everything would be just great: Antonina Ivanovna would praise all the children in the kindergarten.

My five-year-old "informant's" experience turned out to be absolutely representative. A journalist writing in *Pravda* on January 8, 1980, drew his conclusions from a number of letters to the editor when he stated that "giving presents has become some kind of epidemic." Lengths of fabric, dinner services, fashionable shoes, sheer drapes—these, according to the author's information, are the most common offerings. The journalist goes on to say that even in kindergartens voluntary gifts gradually turn into obligatory ones and, "When they get to know the children's parents, the administrators and teachers make no bones about quite brazenly telling them their birthdays. The parents deferentially write down these dates in their notebooks so as not to forget to bring gifts on the appointed day."

What a clear depiction of mass corruption, all-pervasive but somehow ordinary—for what is going on in the kindergartens is not real bribery. These are small-scale gifts, little sops to curry favor in a general way, to make sure the child gets more attention. The real corruption enters the child's life when he starts school. It is here, in the primary and secondary schools, that the line of demarcation between little gifts and bribery becomes more and more blurred.

According to a tradition that has evolved over recent decades, the parents of the children in a class contribute money to buy the teacher a present—usually an expensive one. Is this a bribe? Not yet. But what happens to a pupil whose parents refuse to participate in the collective gift for reasons of principle or because they are reluctant to waste their money?

I know of several cases in which such pupils became the class pariahs, relentlessly persecuted by their teachers, who gave them undeserved bad marks, found fault with every trifling thing, and held them up to ridicule in front of the whole class. In these cases the parents usually capitulated and went crawling back with a present for the teacher; sometimes they transferred the child to another school, at which, having by now learned their lesson, they scrupulously observed the gift tradition.

But there is corruption in Soviet schools that comes closer to real bribery: paying for high marks. This kind of corruption is gaining more and more ground in Russia and in other Soviet republics. Nowadays many teachers do not merely accept these bribes—they often extort them. I was told about this by many informants with firsthand knowledge of the facts or who had reliable sources of information. Details also came from articles on the subject appearing in Soviet newspapers from time to time. One such article was published on March 24, 1976, in *The Literary Gazette;* it related that one teacher had demanded a crystal vase from the parents of a pupil about to graduate from secondary school in exchange for putting a good grade on his diploma records. Another teacher demanded an imported umbrella for the same service.

As they climb higher and higher up the pyramid of the education system, boys and girls approach the threshold of higher education. By now they are psychologically prepared for this moment and they expect to encounter corruption at this stage as well.

In the dock of Moscow City Court, there were nine defendants, all of them employees of one of the most prestigious institutes of Moscow. Sitting in the dock were the assistant dean of the institute, Professor B——, Assistant Professor L——, and a few teachers. All were accused of taking bribes from the parents of a number of candidates. In return they would arrange for candidates to be accepted at the school by giving them high marks on entrance examinations.

In the Soviet Union the system for entering higher educational institutions is by competitive examination; all candidates have to take written and oral examinations, each marked on a scale of one to five. The students with the highest total number of points on the various parts of the examination are accepted.

The *modus operandi* of the illegal organization was fully revealed during the course of the trial. The most active role in the group belonged to the secretary of the selection committee, Assistant Professor L——. This young woman was given information about those with whom an agreement had been reached. She informed the teachers in the illegal group whom to give a passing mark to. If there were too many candidates to remember, a discreet sign—such as a dot in a previously decided-on color—was placed next to their names. It was L——'s duty to draw up the list of those who were to be admitted into the institute as a result of the exams. Naturally she included those students for whom bribes had been paid. And then this list was forwarded for the approval of another member of the illegal group, the assistant dean, who had to make it final with his signature.

Each new crop of students brought the illegal group 50,000–60,000 rubles. The tariff varied in the range of 3000–5000 rubles, but the number of clients at every admission was between ten and fifteen. Among the participants of the organization, the lion's share of the bribe would go to the assistant dean and the secretary of the admissions committee. The teachers giving the exam were given 50–100 rubles for every applicant illegally pushed through.

This illegal group functioned with impunity during a period of seven years, though more than once statements reached the office of the president, exposing the bribe takers. But the assistant dean of the institute, Professor B——, and the assistant professor of the chair of Marxism-Leninism, L——, took full advantage of the support of the dean and the party bureau. Besides this, they were both honorary members in the regional committee of the Communist party, the first secretary of which unfalteringly supported them even in the most complicated situations.

But there was one more circumstance favoring the prosperity of bribe taking at the institute, a circumstance applicable to all the universities, institutes, and technical schools of the country. The ruling party-state apparatus steadfastly and openly conducted a policy of favoritism for socially privileged applicants and discrimination against Jews.

Court evidence, given by teachers and school administrators appearing as defendants and witnesses, as well as private conversations with people who worked as executive secretaries on selection boards and with teachers who administered various entrance examinations in Moscow, Leningrad, and Tbilisi make it possible to assert that in the universities, institutes, and technical schools of the Soviet Union, a system of far-flung and imposed favoritism was practiced. The children of the ruling apparatus and those whom the apparat favor were accepted whether or not they did well on the entrance exams.

Ethnic discrimination is the lot of Soviet Jews. Quite a number of schools do not admit them at all: the institutions that train the upcoming ruling elite (the party schools, the Academy of Social Sciences, the Institute of International Relations) and also some institutes and university departments that train key nuclear scientists and electron physicists. Then there is another category that accepts Jews according to a strict quota system similar to that used in tsarist Russia. (This includes all humanities departments of the prestigious universities, the leading institutes of technology, medical schools, foreign-language institutes, and certain others.)

At the time of the trial I am talking about, all of the teachers, having been interrogated both as defendants and as witnesses, openly told how they received from the top officials of the institute the names of applicants for whom influential people had petitioned and the order to provide these applicants with entrance numbers independently of their qualifications.

Less willingly, some of the teachers talked about the discrimination against Jews. Answering the question of the defense attorneys, witnesses and several defendants told the court that Jewish names in particular were not reported to them. Usually, typically Jewish looks and surnames speak for themselves, so the examiners are not especially informed about any individuals. A directive is simply issued to give

Jewish candidates the right sort of marks—marks ensuring that not a single one, or almost no one, obtains the number of points needed to be accepted for admission.

The majority of witnesses and defendants talked about the methods for discriminating against Jews as though discussing something unpleasant but necessary. There were even some who discussed the affair with shame and bitterness. One of the witnesses not involved in the bribe taking told the court that her conscience was tormented every time she failed Jews who had answered well on the entrance examinations.

At this point the chairman asked her a question with feigned bewilderment: "If your conscience was bothered, why, then, did you carry out these illegal orders?"

The witness, a mature woman with forty years' teaching experience, answered him bitterly: "Why are you such a hypocrite? You know full well that if I had refused to carry out these orders you have called illegal, they would have retired me next year. And my pension is only seventy-two rubles. Can one live on that?"

The reader may be wondering whether it is really possible that all Soviet teachers are prepared to obey the demands of the school administration and pass ignorant dolts because strings are being pulled for them or deny access to a talented, well prepared candidate just because he is a Jew. There are not many teachers who are indeed prepared to do this, but the process of natural selection ensures that it is they who sit on the selection boards. It invariably happens that any teacher who does not do as the administration tells him during an entrance examination is never again asked to sit on the board. So within a fairly short time a stable group of teachers is formed that will shrink from no moral compromise and no unlawful action. Though there are not many of them in the country as a whole, there is never any shortage.

Thus selection at the whim of the administration has become the rule in these examinations—with favoritism on the one hand and anti-Semitism on the other—and so an auspicious climate is created for corruption. Thus bribery becomes, if not a routine matter, at least not an extraordinary occurrence or a rare exception in hundreds of technical colleges, institutes, and universities.

In Moscow, Leningrad, and large cities in Russia, the Ukraine, and Belorussia the size of the bribe varies on the average from 3000 to 5000 rubles, although in the fall of 1979 I received information from Moscow indicating that the rate was on the rise, and in some departments of Moscow University had at times reached 6000 rubles.

Much larger bribes are paid in the Transcaucasian and Central Asian republics. In Georgia the price for getting into the Medical Institute is 15,000 rubles, and for the Teachers Training and Polytechnical Institutes 10,000 rubles, according to my own data. In Azerbaidzhan, according to I. Zemtsov's information,* which on the whole tallies with that I collected in Baku, admission to the Medical Institute costs 30,000 rubles, to the Economics Institute 35,000, to Baku University 20,000–25,000, and to the Foreign Languages Institute 10,000 rubles.

That corruption in admissions to educational institutions is so integral a part of Soviet society is underscored by the fact that the average person with children about to apply to an institution of higher education has a firmly entrenched belief that you can get into any place you like for a bribe, and that everyone takes bribes. To try and convince such a person that by no means every staff member of every school takes bribes is not merely difficult, it is often impossible.

A young assistant professor, who had for several years been executive secretary of the admissions board of a department of Moscow University, described to me how every year at entrance-examination time he would be subjected to the importunities of parents eager to get him to take their

* I. Zemtsov, *La Corruption en l'Union Soviétique* (Paris, 1976).

bribes. They would follow him and accost him on the street; they would trail him to his home, even though he lived in the suburbs and commuted by train; in the morning when he left his house several silent figures would always be waiting for him nearby. They would follow him to the station, promising him thousands and trying to slip packets of money into his hands and pockets in an effort to sway him.

My informant was a discreet and shy person who gently but categorically rejected all these solicitations. Although such scenes might be repeated more than once, the parents refused to believe that the executive secretary of an admissions board would not accept bribes. But my informant was an honest person who did not take bribes, and had no dealings with the criminal ring that existed in his department, although his position made him aware of its activities.

The commonly held conviction that bribery is an effective tool in the fight for admission to schools has created a psychological atmosphere in the country that makes it quite an easy matter to find clients willing to offer a bribe in order to get into an institute or university. What happens most of the time is that the clients—that is, the candidates' parents—use their own acquaintances to seek out contacts with likely go-betweens to pass along the bribes.

Court case material has shown that as corruption spreads among the staff of an educational institution, a character who deals specifically in locating suitable clients appears with increasing frequency: the professional middleman. This phenomenon has become so widespread that it has engendered a new type of swindle: the fake middleman. In the 1970s there were several cases tried in Moscow involving swindlers who passed themselves off as bribery middlemen and wheedled money from their victims. I am particularly familiar with one of these cases.

A seemingly highly respectable middle-aged retired man chose the corridors of Moscow University for his area of operations. He was a clever psychologist—an indispensable skill for any professional swindler—and, as he stated at his trial, he hardly ever erred in his choice of victims.

He was an "honest" swindler: he did not take down payments. "Once your boy's been accepted, then you can settle up with me. I can see that you're a decent person and that you won't cheat me," he would tell his clients.

On the day the lists of successful candidates were to be posted he would be at his place early in the morning. If the name of the candidate "under his care" did not appear on the list he would disappear, and the hoodwinked parents would never see him again. If the outcome was successful, he would turn up for his money. Typically enough, in only one out of fourteen cases was the swindler himself cheated: only once did the parents of a successful candidate refuse to pay up and even threatened to take him to the police station.

Legendary tales of corruption in Tbilisi Medical Institute had reached me before I ever set foot in Georgia, but what I discovered for myself in Tbilisi surpassed what had seemed in Moscow to be wild exaggeration.

When Professor Gelbakhiani became rector of the Tbilisi Medical Institute he made it clear from the outset that favoritism in all its aspects was the name of his game. Soon he became "our man" for the highest strata of the republic's ruling elite; this enabled him to become one of the biggest and most brazen bribe takers in Georgia during the 1960s.

Each new crop of students netted the rector and his accomplices about one and a half million rubles. The whole of Georgia knew that the only way to get into Tbilisi Medical Institute was either to have very high patronage or to pay fifteen thousand rubles; and all were equal before this law.

The mafia, headed by the rector and the secretary of the party committee, held absolute sway in the institute. Everyone was unquestioningly subservient to them, both their accomplices and those staff members who were not involved in the corruption. There was nothing surprising about that, for the rector enjoyed the patronage not only of the First

Secretary of the Central Committee but also that of his all-powerful spouse, Tamara, to whom Gelbakhiani would give the presents she loved so much: antiques and large jewels.

Nor was it surprising that one of the first actions of the new administration, which undertook to purge the Republic, was to break up the medical institute mafia, which, over the years, had become a kind of symbol of the corruption that had rotted Georgia. The investigation and trial managed to establish only about two hundred instances of selling places in the medical institute; the amount received by Gelbakhiani in bribes was calculated as around three million rubles.

Seven years have passed since Gelbakhiani was expelled. The new rector of the Tbilisi Medical Institute is Professor Virsaladze—a man of unimpeachable honesty and a true representative of the remarkable Georgian intelligentsia. He has done everything in his power to drive out corruption from the institute. But all these efforts have been futile. Although it may not flourish on the same blatant scale as it did before 1973, corruption still lurks within the Tbilisi Medical Institute.

I regret that I was unable to bring with me from the Soviet Union a copy of the order issued in the early 1970s by Academician Rem Khokhlov, rector of Moscow University. It was notable for its statement that a number of teachers in the Marxism-Leninism Department were taking bribes of three or four rubles to pass students in their examinations. (I don't know where he got his figures. According to available information, students were paying eight to ten rubles for the Marxism exam at that time.) Further on it listed the names of several teachers who had been found guilty and fired from the university. Finally the rector ordered that "these degenerate practices be terminated forthwith."

And that happened in Moscow, in the nation's top university. You can imagine, then, what goes on in the provinces, where the bonds forged by the "collective guarantee" system are much tighter and where procedures are more patriarchal.

Once he has crossed the threshold of his university, institute, or technical college, there is no guarantee whatsoever that the fledgling student will not come across the need for bribery again. And no longer will the comparatively innocent gifts his parents would give his school teachers suffice; we are talking here about real criminal bribes in final exams, tests, thesis evaluations. The bribes will no longer be paid by his parents but by the student himself, a boy or girl who has just barely turned eighteen or nineteen.

The following is one of many cases, typical both in its events and in the psychology of the participants.

Of the two D—— brothers who were on trial, the elder was an assistant professor in physics at one of Moscow's big technical institutes, and the younger was a graduate student at another, even more prestigious Moscow institute. Since, as far back as the students who testified could recall, it was difficult—well-nigh impossible—to pass assistant professor D——'s examinations without first paying a bribe, a custom had evolved: the leader of the group taking an examination or test would collect money beforehand—four or five rubles from each student for a routine test and eight to ten for a final examination. The money, together with a list of who had contributed to the bribe, was handed either to Assistant Professor D—— or to his brother, who, while he did not work there, was almost a part of the family at the institute and would sometimes even administer the exams with his brother.

The envelope stuffed full of money was handed over without making any show of secrecy. Afterward, in court, the students who appeared as witnesses testified that the group leader would give D—— or his brother the envelope in full view of everyone in the corridor or auditorium where the examinations were held. During the exam the D—— brothers would have before them the register issued by the director of studies and, next to it, the list of students who had paid up.

What happened to the ones not on that second list? As one student witness testified: "I didn't have any money, and, as I'd done all the work for the physics exam and felt that I knew all the material, I decided there was no point in paying. When the group leader came to me before the exam and asked me for my ten, I asked him, 'What the hell for?' "

This witness made three attempts to pass the exam, and three times Assistant Professor D—— gave her a grade of 2, or "unsatisfactory." The examination period was coming to an end, and a 2 in physics meant losing her state grant, so she surrendered and handed over her ten rubles to the group leader.

It was this witness who decided to expose the D—— brothers. She went to the Moscow office of the Department to Combat the Misappropriation of Socialist Property (DCMSP), where she was listened to with interest. They suggested that she write out a statement complete with names and descriptions of specific episodes in which bribes had been paid. Then they summoned the student group leader for questioning and made it clear to him that since he had collected the money and passed it on to D——, he was an accessory to the crime and would be held criminally responsible. This, however, was merely a tactical ploy, and the investigator immediately told the thoroughly frightened student that there was a way out. If he would write out a "voluntary statement of the events," help the investigation expose the bribe takers and then appear in court as a witness for the prosecution, he would be given a guarantee of immunity from prosecution.

A few weeks went by, and when examination time came round again the group leader collected money from the students as usual. But before handing it over to Assistant Professor D——, he took it to the DCMSP, where the numbers of all the banknotes were recorded on an official document. In addition, each bill was electronically imprinted with the word *Vzyatka*—bribe—invisible to the naked eye but clearly legible with special apparatus.

When the D—— brothers emerged from the auditorium at the end of the examination two young men politely requested them to report to the rector's office. There was no need for a very thorough search to find the marked bills, as they were right there in their envelope together with the list of students who had paid up. The searchers merely had to remove the envelope from the pocket of the younger D——'s jacket.

Even on the Moscow court calendar, such cases of corruption are by no means isolated. And if over a six-month period the principal newspaper in the country, *Pravda* (which consists of a total of six pages) publishes three reports on corruption among teachers in high schools and in higher education, this fact alone shows that corruption is quite widespread in the educational systems of all fifteen republics of the Soviet Union.

In talking about corruption in education it is impossible not to highlight the situation in Georgia and Azerbaidzhan. During the great purge in the early 1970s the District Party Committee of the Ordzhonikidzevsky district of Tbilisi, Georgia (where most of the city's institutions of higher learning are located), came to the conclusion as stated in a special decree, that bribery, extortion, and forgery were flourishing not only in the medical institute but in all the district's schools. This was written up in *Dawn of the East* on December 12, 1973.

The decree gave no details and mentioned no names, but according to a teacher from one of the institutes who was present at the committee's plenary meeting, the people who took the floor—including the First Secretary of the District Committee and the Public Prosecutor of the Republic—stated openly that the overwhelming majority of teachers charged from 25 to 100 rubles for a final examination mark to be entered into the records.

In Azerbaidzhan the scandalous dominion of corruption in higher education had surfaced even before the purge of the ruling apparat connected with the exposure of Vali Akhundov, the First Secretary of the Central Committee of the Communist Party of the Republic. This occurred after an extraordinary and tragic event: a student at Baku Medical Institute, driven to despair by the faculty's extortion, murdered the assistant dean of the institute. During the subsequent investigation it was established that each student had to pay the teachers between 50 and 100 rubles at the time of each usual test or final examination. (This fact was reported by I. Zemtsov.)

Ten years have passed since the assistant dean of Baku Medical Institute was slain, and since then there has been a wholesale purge of the ruling apparat in which top Central Committee people and the heads of practically all the Republic's institutions of higher learning were replaced. Then, on June 11, 1978, *Pravda* reported that students at the Azerbaidzhan Polytechnical Institute still had to bribe their teachers at each exam; the same sum of 100 rubles was quoted.

BRIBES FOR SERVICES

In the Soviet Union there is only one category of the population that is not required to overpay or to give bribes and that still gets all the high-quality goods and services it needs, and gets them punctually—the ruling party-state apparat, from its lowliest district stratum right up to the Kremlin elite.

The lowest stratum obtains all this not merely without paying anything extra but generally without paying anything at all. The middle and the highest strata—especially the latter—are served by a special network of stores, repair shops, and tailoring workshops. And, if tipping does occur, it is only because a customer is generous and not because it is required.

In the early 1960s a trial was held in the Moscow Municipal Court involving employees of the tailoring workshop used by the Central Committee of the Communist Party of the Soviet Union and the Council of Ministers. On trial were the workshop managers and some cutter-designers. They were accused of having used the workshop to make dresses, coats, and furs for ordinary mortals—that is, for their own private customers, who paid them fairly substantial sums—out of the fabrics and pelts earmarked for the most privileged members of the elite.

During the examination of one witness, a famous Moscow designer of women's clothing called Lebedev (I am using real names here), who was always swamped with orders from clients ranging from famous film stars to the wives of Politburo members, the judge reprimanded him: "Aren't you ashamed of yourself? The state pays you a salary, but it's not enough for you—you have to go begging for five-ruble handouts from your own customers. Your salary's too small for you, is it?"

Lebedev was not afraid of him and answered in an off-hand, even somewhat impudent, manner. "Don't you try to tear me down—you know as well as I do that you cannot feed a family on a hundred eighty rubles a month. Anyway, I ask no one for money; people force it on me—and no one ever gives me less than fifty rubles."

"Well, who gives you that kind of money? An honest person living on his salary can't throw fifty rubles around!"

"Who?" replied Lebedev. "Well, just last week, for example, I finished a coat for one customer who gave me fifty rubles—Nina Petrovna Khrushcheva."

Nina Petrovna Khrushcheva, of course, was the wife of the then all-powerful General Secretary of the Central Committee and Chairman of the Council of Ministers. The judge's face showed both fright at having offended the wife of Khrushchev himself and impotent anger as he could not parry the witness's lunge.

The wife of the Secretary of the Central Committee of the CPSU was able to get the necessary services and did not give away who offered her these services "on the sly" or "under the table." These slang expressions are widely used in the country. They mean that a client who pays for professional services must also give some money "on the sly" for whatever the service.

There are no sociological studies published reflecting that aspect of Soviet society, despite the fact that the lives of ordinary people are dominated by their daily grind and with satisfying their everyday needs.

A legal practice is not a good vantage point from which to study everyday corruption. When ordinary salespeople, order clerks, plumbers or drivers of state cars take money over and above official state prices, they are not perpetrating any indictable crime. They are not officials, and the tips they take from customers for accepting their clothes for dry cleaning out of turn or for fixing a leaky faucet quickly and properly are not, legally speaking, bribes. Thus I can back up my statement that all service industries are riddled with corruption with a not very scientific piece of evidence: that every urban adult in the country knows it.

Because of a number of circumstances I was able during my nearly sixty years in the Soviet Union to observe at quite close quarters the lives of the workers and engineers in a large Moscow factory as well as the lives of Moscow professional people. And so it is with full knowledge of the facts that I am able to offer an evaluation and to repeat that the entire sphere of services in the Soviet Union is affected by mass corruption.

The daily routine of a Soviet family consists of a mass of petty chores that, while insignificant in themselves, are an absolutely essential part of life. Food must be bought to feed the family, the ever-leaky faucet must be fixed, the clothes must be taken to the cleaners, or, if one is about to leave on vacation, a pass to a "house of rest" or a hotel room must be seen to and airplane or railway tickets booked. Then there are the less regular needs connected with occasional events, both happy and sad. A close friend may die, and the only consolation for the bereaved is to fulfill the last wishes of the deceased and bury him beside his ancestors or his nearest and dearest. These needs are not so vital as the daily needs for food and clothing, but a Soviet citizen, like anyone in any society, does not live by bread alone.

I began this chapter with a list of the services my lawyer friend had to overpay for. I could expand that list ad infinitum with examples of situations in which a service is unattainable without recourse to corruption.

Earlier I discussed the corruption attendant on giving birth to a child. I want to conclude it with corruption bound up with the death of a man or a woman.

It is not proper to mention "cemetery trials" in the Soviet press, although such trials are held regularly in the large cities of the Soviet Union.

A sociologist friend of mine in Moscow counted twelve ways in which a Soviet citizen may be buried. I do not know whether there really are twelve forms of burial, but judging by the cases that pass through Soviet law offices, I can say that however many categories there are, they are all—apart from a place in the Kremlin Wall—available for a bribe. It is even possible to "arrange" for burial in the cemetery of Novodevichy Monastery (which is second only to the Kremlin Wall) by payment of a sizable sum of around 2000 to 2500 rubles—even though approval for burial there is required from one of the secretaries of the Moscow Party Committee and the Deputy Chairman of the Moscow Municipal Executive Committee.

It is simpler—and, of course, cheaper—to make arrangements for a burial plot in old, less officially prestigious cemeteries situated within the boundaries of old Moscow.

These cemeteries have long since been almost completely filled up. But "almost" is the operative word here; there is still some reserve space at the disposal of the cemetery administration. Moreover, a legal provision exists whereby the administration of a cemetery can permit what is blasphemously referred to in officialese as "burial in a relative's grave." In more explicit language this means that a person may be buried alongside deceased family members—a spouse or parents. These reserve spaces are used by cemetery administrators and officials of the Moscow Municipal Executive Committee departments to which cemeteries are subordinate as a basis for extorting bribes.

From time immemorial, burial of the dead has been a sacred duty for all peoples, with the rituals varying from culture to culture. Duty to the memory of the deceased and grief at the loss of a relative make the bereaved easy and pliant prey for corrupt officials.

During "cemetery trials" I was always struck by the polarity of attitudes in the bribe givers and the bribe takers. For the latter a grave was just another scarce commodity for which they could receive money "into the paw." Their behavior and testimony in court cannot even be called cynical. They simply did not see how what they did was any different from what an official in a district housing office did when he accepted a bribe for giving a petitioner not a grave but an apartment. I do not know what struck me most in one of the most notorious "cemetery trials"—the one involving employees of the Moscow Crematorium; there is no end to the astounding details and facts contained in the documents of this case.

A group of crematorium employees, headed by the administrator, were on trial not only for taking bribes for allocating interment for ashes but also for thefts of a kind that caused even the lawyers—who are inured to all sorts of crimes—to feel at a loss when faced with choosing a defense strategy.

When a coffin was lowered down the hatchway to the

tones of a funeral dirge, the crematorium staff would be there awaiting its arrival. Their individual duties were strictly defined. Some would open the lid of the coffin with a few quick movements and toss the body onto a nearby table. While they set the coffin and the wreaths to one side, deft fingers would strip the clothes and underclothes from the corpse while others set to work with special dental instruments, ripping out gold teeth and crowns. After that they would dispatch the stripped, coffinless remains into the blazing oven.

Everything in this business generated profit. The coffins and wreaths were returned to the funeral supplier, who would resell them twice or even three times. The proceeds were divided thus: two-thirds to the crematorium employees and one-third to the funeral supplier. The clothing and underclothing would be sent on consignment to a secondhand shop, and the gold was sold to one of several black market currency dealers with whom they did business regularly. Hearing all these details, one was struck by the callous efficiency and matter-of-factness prevalent in the grave trade.

It is impossible in one book to write about all facets of the life of a Soviet citizen and all the situations in which he is compelled to resort to corrupt practices. I have not discussed many aspects of mass and ubiquitous corruption: bribes given for apartments, airplanes, railway and boat tickets, bribes for having a telephone installed, bribes for a disability certificate (which entitles one to a state pension), and much, much else besides. But what I have written is, I hope, sufficient to demonstrate that bribery permeates every aspect of Soviet life.

Chapter IX

THE CORRUPTED PEOPLE

W E ARE approaching the end of our tale of the land of kleptocracy, in which corruption is rife among the country's rulers at all levels from the very lowest to the very highest.

But how do things stand with those they govern, the people who do not occupy the positions of power that make it possible for them to obtain bribes and gifts? How do things stand with what they call "the people"—ordinary Soviet citizens?

The corruption that has rotted the ruling apparat of the country has had the terrible effect of eating away the morals not only of the people who give or receive bribes but also of the innocent, those who have not been party to corruption but who have merely been living in an atmosphere of corruption and have been forced to breathe its tainted air.

The atmosphere of corruption has bred the conviction in the minds of the people that everything can be attained by bribery: a good job, a university diploma, or an undeserved judicial verdict. And although that conviction is far from

248

justified in all cases, it has led to the climate of tolerance toward corruption that holds sway in Soviet society.

Apart from these moral preconditions for corruption, there is an absolutely fundamental material precondition as well: the need to find additional means to ensure a minimum living standard for one's family. The majority of Soviet people are faced by that need, since they are wage slaves, hired by the country's one monopoly employer, the state, which does not even provide them with the barest of living wages.

The average income of a wage earner in the Soviet Union may be stated with fair certainty. According to official Soviet statistics the average monthly wage for manual and office workers in the first half of 1979 was 163 rubles, or about $230 (my source for this is the issue of *Pravda* dated June 21, 1979). But it is impossible to obtain official statistics about the minimum subsistence requirements of an average Soviet family. Such information is simply not published; it is a state secret.

We do, however, have one official indicator, which was published in the Soviet press: the decree passed by the Central Committee of the Communist Party of the Soviet Union and the Council of Ministers regarding allowances for families with many children. In this decision the poverty line was set at 50 rubles per month per person, or 150 rubles for a family of three.

That is the poverty line as officially recognized by the state; but official statistics have to be disregarded when calculating the true minimum needs of an average Soviet family, which most typically consists of three people—mother, father, and child. I am able to calculate these figures because I lived in the USSR for almost sixty years, thirty-five of them in a large apartment building full of factory workers and engineers, and I have my own experience and my observations of my neighbors to go by. I also have a body of information collected during a special survey I conducted in Moscow during the three years when I had gone into isolation, even from close friends, in order to work on this book.

The technique I used was very simple. Throughout those years I traveled three times a week to the Institute where I worked, taking a taxi or a "left-hand"* state car there and back. I would ask each driver the same questions:

> 1. *What is your official salary?*
>
> Everyone without exception answered this question.
>
> 2. *How much do you make in tips* (for taxi drivers) or *in your "left-hand" work* (for state chauffeurs working privately on the side)?
>
> By no means was everyone willing to answer this question, and the answers I did get were for the most part vague.
>
> 3. *How many members are there in your family and how much do you spend each month on food, alcohol, clothes, local transportation, and entertainment?*
>
> These questions were answered readily and in great detail.

In this way I polled at least eight hundred drivers over the three years, thinking that I was risking nothing by doing so. Moscow drivers readily enter into conversation with their passengers, and my curiosity aroused no suspicion.

On the basis of this information and by being careful to discount exaggerated replies, I am able to project the budget for a three-person household of a Moscow manual or office worker or an average engineer. It is about 250–300 rubles a month. According to the statistics, the average monthly wage of a manual or office worker is 163 rubles. (One hundred sixty-three rubles is not a real figure but an average,

* See pp. 261–266 ff. below. (Trans. note)

since among "manual and office workers" Soviet statisti-
cians include both the highly paid functionaries of the party-
state apparat and academics and university professors.)
Moreover, the state deducts between 10 and 13 percent in
taxes, so that people actually end up with 147 rubles a
month, not 163.

This means that the average wage of a manual or office
worker in the Soviet Union is below even the poverty line
fixed by the state itself at 150 rubles. The average wage of
147 rubles covers less than 60 percent of the 250 rubles
needed by a family of three as a more realistic subsistence
minimum; the remainder—more than 40 percent—of 103 rubles has to be met from other sources.

One should bear in mind here that these are the calculations for a Moscow family that is able to buy produce in
state shops and at state prices (although with difficulty and
only by waiting on long lines). What, then, about a family
living in any city or town in the country apart from the few,
like Moscow, that enjoy special supply privileges? In these
other places practically no basic staples are to be found in
the stores, so people have to buy them at the markets for
prices three to five times the state prices. In such cases the
subsistence minimum must be increased by 150 rubles even
by the most conservative estimates; it thus climbs to 400
rubles. Accordingly, the deficit that must somehow be made
up rises to 253 rubles.

Does the average Soviet family really live on 147 rubles a
month, by half starving and denying itself the very basic
necessities, or does such a family make up the shortage of
funds from other sources? It does indeed supplement its
basic income, and it not only covers the deficit in the family
budget—it does much more than that. According to official
data the people of the Soviet Union keep more than 140
billion rubles in savings accounts. This is money that is
clearly not being spent on current expenses. Where do these
billions come from?

To begin with, they come from legal sources: from the

wages of the second working member in a family. For, according to sociological samplings, both husband and wife work in one family out of two. This is how the problem of the subsistence minimum is solved in families in which the wife is able to leave her child with someone and go out to work. There are, however, other sources of additional income—moonlighting, pilfering from employers, private trade, and many other semilegal or totally illegal activities.

There is no way of saying exactly the extent to which each of these two types of source supplement the family budget, as there have not yet been any studies published on this matter. On the basis of my own observations I would say that both legal and illegal sources are used to approximately the same extent. That illegal earnings account for such a large proportion of the additional income is not due exclusively or even largely to a family's need to meet its subsistence minimum. It is more the result of human nature, which the Soviet regime has not been able to change despite all its futile efforts over the last sixty-three years to eradicate from people's minds the desire for gain, the desire to have not only the essentials but the nonessentials as well. And this battle has even less chance of being won in a society in which stratification in material well-being has gone very far. There are indeed rich and poor in the Soviet Union, and there is quite a wide gap between them.

The need to be assured of a subsistence minimum income and the desire for not just this minimum but also the things that more privileged people may clearly be seen to possess have led to a pervasive determination to get hold of money by any means, whether legal and moral (such as moonlighting) or illegal and immoral (such as theft and prostitution).

ON-THE-JOB STEALING

I think I am right in stating that among the illegal ways of supplementing the Soviet family budget the most common is to steal from one's workplace. Over the sixty-three years of its existence the Soviet economic system has failed to meet the needs of the population for food and good clothing, both of which are constantly in short supply. It is natural, then, that these are the most popular items to steal from wherever they are produced, processed, or stored.

I have every justification for asserting that food and alcoholic beverages are stolen from all such enterprises without exception. This rule is unfailingly observed, for example, in the small provincial dairy plant, whose employees would never dream of buying butter or sour cream in a shop or at the marketplace when they can simply carry it home without charge. And the same rule operates just as unswervingly in a place such as the gigantic Mikoyan meat-packing plant in Moscow; the workers never buy sausage or meat in the stores, but simply take the factory produce home with them.

It is amazing how widespread this phenomenon is. Millions of workers have been caught on their way out of a tobacco factory or a meat-packing plant with a couple of packs of cigarettes or a few pounds of sausage, and have been let off with a reprimand from their bosses or a "public censure" from the trade union organization. However, it is not because of any humane considerations that the Soviet state shows such leniency. The present Soviet leaders simply cannot afford to send millions of citizens to the camps, thereby removing them from their jobs.

A reader unfamiliar with Soviet society might deduce from this that the Soviet people are dishonest and immoral, that they are a people for whom thievery has become a way of life. Such a deduction would be misleading; it is simply that the mass of the population does not look upon theft from the state as real theft, as stealing someone else's property.

Of the tens of millions of people who do not think twice about lifting nails, light bulbs, and equipment from their factories, construction sites, or offices, the overwhelming majority would never steal a kopeck from another person. They would, indeed, consider such a theft immoral and would roundly condemn anyone committing the most paltry pilfering of that kind—but only if the victim of the theft is an individual and not some state enterprise. Such are the paradoxical ethics of a Soviet citizen. This demonstrates the complete alienation of the Soviet citizen from the state, his total indifference and even hostility toward it. Without such feelings, factory thefts on such a scale would be impossible.

A fair amount of detail is available regarding the ways of getting stolen goods off the factory grounds. It comes from court case documents as well as from questioning people who have engaged in these activities. In all food, wine, and vodka factories, as well as in those producing things that are easily sold, there are special checkpoints manned by guards who monitor all people entering or leaving the premises. The job of these guards is mainly to ensure that employees do not remove merchandise from the factory; to do this they are authorized to check the contents of purses and briefcases and even to carry out body searches.

In places where the guards are not open to bribery the workers have to resort to various ruses. They carry hard, loose, and dry objects in specially fitted bags that hang under their skirts or inside their trouser legs. Things that can be laid flat, such as stockings, furs, underwear, and so forth, are wrapped around the chest or the stomach. If the factory manufactures clothes, they are worn under the workers' street clothing. For liquids they use flat rubber or metal hot-water bottles, attaching them to their stomachs, legs, chests, or backs—a trick also used by American bootleggers during Prohibition.

Controls on people working in jewelry factories are especially strict, and these employees are usually subjected to meticulous body searches. But even so, they find ways of walking out with quite large amounts of gold, platinum, and gems. Court cases involving thefts from jewelry factories crop up fairly regularly, and the case evidence reveals which smuggling methods have been used. Men usually carry the loot in special hollowed-out belt buckles or in hollow shoe soles, and women use either the heels of their shoes or their genitals as hiding places.

These ways of getting stolen goods out of the factory grounds are routine. But now and then the court calendar reveals cases of theft whose inventiveness and technical skill are amazing.

Probably the most nearly perfect mechanical contraption for stealing that I ever heard about was the one installed in Moscow's Cold-Storage Plant Number Two. Late one evening someone who lived on the street facing the back wall of the plant chanced to glance up at the sky and discerned in the darkness some object resembling a coffin floating through the air. The object glided across the street and disappeared into the darkness. The person immediately informed the police of what he had seen.

The criminals turned out to be two electricians from the cold-storage plant who had rigged up an overhead cable-car system about 110 yards long, which they used to convey boxloads of sausage, butter, and meat from the top floor of the plant to the deserted courtyard next door. During the daytime they would fasten the coffin-sized box, filled with about a hundred pounds of produce, onto special automatic-release hooks. In the late evening they would go to their deserted "cable-car terminus" and switch on the engine that set the system in motion; the box, suspended by the hooks, would sail smoothly across the street. When it reached the deserted courtyard and hit the post to which the cable was attached, the hooks would open and the box would drop at the feet of the inventive crooks.

The workers of the Gorky automobile factory, which manufactures the popular Volga model, operated with real panache, which would have been impossible without the complicity of the security guards. They carried out—by hand or even in trucks—two major assemblies of an automobile: a completely assembled body and an engine. They then completed the cars in a garage that had been especially adapted for the purpose and sold them. These cars had been assembled from stolen parts and had no documents or license plates, so anyone purchasing one ran the risk of being caught by the first policeman who took it into his head to check the driver's papers. But still this didn't prevent the customers from buying, especially those from the Transcaucasian republics.

As one such customer, a man I was defending, explained to me, it made sense to pay 3000 or 4000 rubles for a car that would cost 9600 rubles if bought through a state dealer (from whom it would be practically impossible to buy anyway) and 20,000 to 25,000 rubles on the black market—even if it meant running the risk of having to abandon it right there on the road from Gorky to the Caucasus to escape the police.

The cooperation of security guards is quite usual; in cases that have gone to court it has been shown to be an inevitable concomitant of all large-scale factory misappropriation. When I say large, I mean stealing not by the pound but by the ton, not by the quart but by the barrel, stockings not by the dozen but by the bale.

The bond between security guards and factory thieves really has become a matter of routine, so that it crops up all the time in any court case involving on-the-job theft. And even in all circumstances of daily life it is known that bribing security guards, whose job it is to protect state property, is a commonplace occurrence. I shall cite only two examples of this.

In the courtyard of the building that houses one of Moscow's legal-advice offices is a brandy-bottling plant belonging to one of the small North Caucasian republics. Its exits and entrances were watched over with such vigilance by so many guards and special inspectors that it looked as if they were manufacturing some top secret bacteriological weaponry, not pouring liquor from casks into bottles. And even so, after a day of court sessions, when the lawyers would be gathered together in the office in the evening to meet with their clients or simply to chat with one another, once or twice a week the office secretary would announce, "Aunt Dusya's here. Any takers?"

That announcement meant that the cleaning woman from the brandy plant had arrived with a large basket piled with bottles that were unlabeled but were filled with fine brandy that had been maturing for eight to ten years. Aunt Dusya would calmly carry her basket past the massive military fortifications of the security guards, who naturally did not let her by through the goodness of their hearts. Trade was brisk: Aunt Dusya charged 4 or 5 rubles for a bottle of brandy that would cost 15 to 18 in the stores, and the lawyers, who, unlike Aunt Dusya, were perfectly well aware that buying goods known to be stolen was a crime, were always her eager customers.

Incidentally, the security guards and inspectors who work in really secret weapons factories are no different from the ones who guard brandy plants. Once, the day before my wife and I were due to set off on a boating trip on the remote rivers of northern Russia, I discovered that the keelson, an essential wooden component of my collapsible kayak, was broken. The situation was desperate—train tickets had been purchased, our vacations from work had already started—come what might, I had to get hold of that wretched keelson in the space of a single day.

I was sufficiently familiar with the Soviet commercial system not to rush out to the stores to hunt for the part. I set off for the factory in which my kayak had been manufactured. The factory actually builds military airplanes, but it also has a small workshop that makes collapsible kayaks from leftover production materials. Like all aircraft factories in the Soviet Union, it is a hush-hush place, surrounded by a tall fence topped with rows of barbed wire, behind which one could see guard dogs running about. A special pass is required for admittance to a factory of this kind, but it was not my intention to penetrate into the factory grounds.

I called up the kayak workshop from the security office and asked one of the employees I had had dealings with before to come out and see me. When I explained what I needed, my acquaintance said that it could not be done, that a large wooden part could not be carried past the guards and inspectors.

"I have to have it, my friend. I need it *this* badly," I said, making the usual Russian gesture indicating a matter of life and death—slitting my throat with the edge of my hand.

He looked at me pensively and asked, "Will it be good for a ten-spot?"

Twenty minutes later my contact brought out a brand-new keelson gleaming with a fresh coat of pale-blue paint and measuring about forty-five inches long and a foot wide.

SHABASHNIKI

Another source of income for Soviet citizens which is not controlled by the state is "freelance" work, referred to in Russia by the strange word *shabashnichestvo*. *Shabashniki* are people who, having completed their main jobs on schedule (or indeed having walked away from their jobs at a state institution or on a farm), engage in freelance work.

The Soviet regime is based on its monopoly power over its people, a monopoly that comprises all spheres of life—political, economic, and ideological. The *shabashniki*—people who earn their living from sources that are not controlled by the state—infringe on this monopoly power (and not only in the economic sphere) and also undermine the very principle of state monopoly.

Clients are attracted to *shabashniki* because of their diligence and the high quality of their work, and it is these same characteristics that bolster their reputations and win new jobs for them. Of late, it is true, more and more teams of *shabashniki* have appeared on the scene who attract clients not only by the quality and intensiveness of their work but also because of their ability to get hold of scarce building materials. In these cases "clean" *shabashnichestvo* is complicated by indictable offenses.

I came in contact with the activities of an "unclean" team of *shabashniki* that serviced the rich collective and state farms of the Stavropol region in southern Russia when I defended the chief accountant of one of the collective farms there. The investigation established that the team had its own permanent representative at a state lumber procurement station in the Arkhangelsk region whose duties included obtaining lumber and having it shipped to the Stavropol region. He bribed the managers of the lumber yards to give him the timber, and he bribed the railway officials to give him the freight cars to transport it in.

The team leader did not work on the construction site himself; he was busy maintaining his contacts—by means of bribes—with factories manufacturing slate, water pipes, and cement, as well as with gravel quarries. Basically, he was the manager of an enterprise and was responsible for all the work of the organization. Apart from obtaining building materials, he was also engaged in getting contracts and in keeping in touch with the clients. In this respect the activities of the team leader went far beyond what is permitted by law. Out of each construction contract he negotiated, he would always give the client's representatives a bribe of, on the average, 10 percent of the value of the order—and these contracts ran to tens of thousands of rubles each. In the process of obtaining materials he would regularly bribe factory directors, and would also buy large consignments of stolen materials from construction-site managers.

Over the years the income of this team amounted to hundreds of thousands of rubles, and the annual earnings of each team member were as much as 20,000 to 24,000 rubles. The team leader's income, which the investigation could only guess at, was about 50,000 rubles a year. (It is worth while reminding the reader here that the average yearly wage of a state construction worker is 2400 rubles, and that of the supervisor of a large construction site about 5000.)

There are tens of thousands of teams of *shabashniki* operating throughout the country—both the small "clean" teams and the large-scale "unclean" ones. It is impossible to make an approximate estimate of the proportion of construction work they account for in the rural areas, although it may be said with certainty that it is very high.

One should be cautious in drawing conclusions, and I think it hardly proper to extend to the whole country the data quoted by the director of one *Mezhkolkhozstroi* (a state organization responsible for construction work in a rural area), who alleged in an interview with a *Literary Gazette* journalist (No. 24, 1978) that almost 100 percent of all construction work in his district (costing a total of a million rubles a year) was done by *shabashniki*.

But if one takes into account the same journalist's statement that the services of *shabashniki* are used not only by collective and state farms but also by state construction contractors, then the assertion that *shabashnichestvo* has become a serious factor in the country's economy and that about two-thirds of all rural construction work is carried out by *shabashniki* does not sound like an exaggeration.

Of course activities on such a scale necessitate new forms of organization. As far as one can judge from the lawyer's vantage point and from the findings of the journalist who published a special study of the problem in *The Literary Gazette,* the *shabashniki* teams have not been confining themselves to sending out representatives to hunt for orders every winter before the building season begins; in recent years they have been trying to coordinate their activities. By the mid 1970s unofficial offices acting as intermediaries between prospective clients and teams of *shabashniki* had come into being in many towns throughout the country, coordinating the operations of the teams and dividing up the orders equally among them. These agencies are paid a percentage of the value of the contract (5 percent from the client and a like amount from the team) as a fee for their services.

LEFT-HAND WORK

It is difficult to draw a clear-cut distinction between *shabashnichestvo* and what in the Soviet Union they call "left-hand" work. As a general rule, *shabashnichestvo* is work done by people outside of their working hours or by people who have no full-time jobs at all; in short, it is work done on the *shabashnik*'s own time and with his own equipment. "Left-hand" work, on the other hand, is usually done during working hours, using state tools, equipment, and means of transport.

It is difficult to name a profession whose members have not engaged in left-hand work. It would not be an exaggeration to say that an enormous part of the population of the country, from manual workers to famous actors, was involved in such work.

There are many other professions in the Soviet Union whose members regularly engage in left-hand work, about whom I am unable to write. But I cannot pass in silence the left-hand work of transport workers: taxi, bus, and trolleybus drivers in the cities.

The very conditions under which taxi drivers work force them to seek left-hand earnings. If you ask a Moscow taxi driver, "Well, how's life? Things okay down at the depot?"

you are sure to get the answer, "Just about tolerable—if you remember to pay off the right people." And "the right people" are everyone at the taxi depot, from the woman who cleans the cars up to the manager.

Cases of bribery in the taxi depots are periodically tried in Moscow courts, and the material is published in the press. The picture of this kind of corruption is therefore a very well known one.

The first bribe a taxi driver has to pay is to the depot manager in order to be assigned a decent, new vehicle. Anyone who omits doing this will be given an old wreck that will wind up spending more time in the repair shop than on the road. Court cases have shown the amount of this bribe to be in the 100- to 500-ruble range.

Next in line is the mechanic. Even if a vehicle does not need any repair work, the mechanic still has to look it over and certify it for service, in return for which the driver has to hand over three rubles or suffer endless faultfinding and delays. If the vehicle does in fact require repair work, the driver will come to an agreement with the mechanic as to how much he is to be paid for doing the job. In addition to that, any parts that are needed must be "bought" from the manager of the spare-parts storeroom.

Then comes a small tip of two or three rubles to the controller to get him to put the driver down for a convenient shift (some drivers prefer to work nights while others prefer morning shifts) and to mark down the time he leaves the depot and the time he returns, not by the clock but by mutual agreement.

After that there is a trifling matter of 50 kopecks for the car washer. Then we come to the exit gate and the person on duty there, whose job it is to give the car a final inspection before it leaves the depot. He is referred to in taxi driver jargon as the goalkeeper, or "Yashin" (the name of a very popular soccer goalkeeper of the 1950s). And he really does defend the exit like a goalkeeper; not a single car gets past him until he gets his "rightful" ruble.

Depending on the number of cars going out on the road on any given day, a goalkeeper can collect from 300 to 500 rubles per shift, although he keeps only about 100 of this for himself. Part of the rest is divided among the depot manager, the chief engineer, the chief mechanic, the party Committee Secretary and the Chairman of the Trade Union Committee, and another portion continues its ascent to the main Automobile Transport Administration of the Moscow Executive Committee and to the transport division of the Moscow Communist Party Committee.

Where does a taxi driver come by all this money?

In a good month, when he has fulfilled his plan, his official earnings will be about 200 rubles. He makes about as much again in tips, particularly if he is not too fussy or if he can pick up a few naïve provincials (called *pidzhaki*—"jackets"—in taxi driver jargon) or drunks at railway stations or the airport. It is easy to wheedle money out of passengers like that and they are easy to cheat. But even this is insufficient to live on and to pay bribes with. And so the taxi driver looks for ways to make left-hand earnings, and life in a big city, especially the country's capital, provides many opportunities for this. It is possible to find a multitude of customers on the streets who do not simply want to get from point A to point B.

One might find someone in the late evening who is desperate to get hold of a bottle of vodka—which is on sale in the stores only until 7:00 P.M. A resourceful taxi driver might be able to oblige such a passenger by offering a bottle for six or seven rubles (as opposed to the normal price of four).

Another passenger might be a provincial who has arrived in Moscow on a two- or three-day shopping spree with a great deal of money and needs someone to guide him round the capital's stores. He could find no better guide than an experienced taxi driver, who not only knows where the large department stores are but also knows how to find other stores on the outskirts of the city which sell scarce merchandise. He will often put his passenger in touch with a salesclerk who might bring something really scarce and tempting out from behind the counter in return for payment over and above the state price.

Different passengers pay different prices for these services. A visitor from the Russian provinces or from the Ukraine or Belorussia will usually pay a driver 10 rubles for a day's transportation, while someone arriving from the far north or a professional speculator from Transcaucasia might pay 25 to 30 rubles for the same services.

Then there are the passengers who require prostitutes. Taxi drivers can sometimes help out here too, although by no means always, since not many drivers have ongoing connections with prostitutes. But they often know where to find them—which lonely streets or parking lots they have to drive their passengers through to find sex. Payment for this service plus a thirty-minute trip can range from 10 to 15 rubles.

This, then, is how taxi drivers make their money: by dashing about town, by being resourceful, and by rendering any kind of service, sometimes including fairly dubious ones. They can thus make enough to pay their regular bribes and to leave themselves not badly off either, with a three- or fourfold increase of their official earnings.

The drivers of city trolleybuses, trams, or buses have no such opportunities for left-hand work. They are tied to their allotted routes and to a schedule that is monitored by a traffic controller. The only possible way they can make anything extra is by stealing the ticket money. Throughout the country this is usually the only source of profit possible for a city transport driver—throughout the country, that is, apart from the cities of Transcaucasia.

When I boarded a trolleybus in Tbilisi for the first time in my life, I naturally made for the coin box and put in my four kopecks. But there was no roll of tickets, either there or near the other coin box. I pointed this out to the driver and asked him for a ticket; he gave me a look of disgust before tearing off a ticket from the roll lying nearby and handing it to me in silent indignation. I took a seat beside a middle-aged Georgian man, who looked at me in tacit criticism, as one might look at an outsider who had tactlessly violated the native customs.

"Why'd you bother him?" he asked me in his strongly accented Russian.

In my defense I said that the ticket inspector might get on and fine me for not having a ticket.

"Ticket inspector? But it's his own bus!" answered my neighbor, motioning with his head in the direction of the driver.

Later my Tbilisi friends explained to me where I had made my mistake. It seems that in the 1960s and early 1970s Tbilisi had "private" buses and trolleybuses that "belonged" to their drivers. A driver would "buy" his vehicle from the manager of the bus depot for between eight and ten thousand rubles and then would pay a series of bribes: to the depot's traffic controller, to give him a good route on which he would always be assured of lots of passengers; to the ticket inspectors, so that they would not board his bus to check his passengers' tickets; and to the mechanics, so that his vehicle would be maintained in good order. In return for all this the driver would then be able to keep almost all the passengers' fares—almost, but not all, because the reel of tickets could not be left completely untouched; an insignificant number of tickets would have to be entered each day in the ledger as sold. Then, in order to ensure that the chief accountant and the depot auditor would shut their eyes to the fact that the sums entered on the books were improbably low, the "owner" of the bus or trolleybus would give them a share too.

Consequently, when I visited the capitals of Armenia and Azerbaidzhan I was no longer surprised at their private modes of urban transport, and I dropped my coins into the box without even looking for a roll of tickets.

Tens of thousands of trucks and buses belonging to state organizations charge about the country in all directions on business that bears no relation to the owners' nominal activities. What they are doing is transporting left-hand consignments. No nationwide studies have ever been carried out to prove the truth of that statement, but the results of a sample survey conducted by a journalist in collaboration with the police fully confirm my assumptions.

During this survey, which was described in *The Literary Gazette* (No. 27, 1979), the travel documents of thirty trucks and buses were checked; the sample included both vehicles leaving Moscow and those traveling within the city itself. These checks established that not one of the trucks or buses was engaged on a trip consistent with the economic interests or even the nature of the institution or enterprise to which it belonged. Thirty journeys out of thirty had no purpose from the standpoint of the state organizations. In these circumstances there is ample opportunity for making left-hand use of the vehicles.

PRIVATE COMMERCE

What is commerce?

Since the day that first saw the appearance of the commercial middleman, whose aim it was to supply people with what they needed, buying something and reselling it at a profit has been known as commerce. For many thousands of years mankind has considered that making a commercial profit is legitimate and natural.

However, in the Soviet Union, buying merchandise and reselling it to make a profit is called commerce only if it is engaged in by the state. When this activity is carried out by a private individual it is called "speculation" and is a criminal offense. From the very first years of its existence the Soviet state has concerned itself with the fight against speculators. This fight has been waged through punishment—sometimes even the death penalty—and propaganda.

Newspaper and magazine articles, novels and short stories, movies and plays sang paeans of praise to the glorious Cheka officers who mercilessly annihilated enemies of the Revolution, and were full of bombastic scorn for "petty entrepreneurs" and "speculators." In a memoir written in the 1920s I happened upon an accurate but sad observation: the author expressed surprise at how quickly the Soviet regime had inculcated in its citizens the notion that executing people is an honorable thing, whereas engaging in commerce is ignominious.

But this, while reflecting exactly the feeling of the 1920s, did not turn out to be prophetic. Illegal private commerce in the Soviet Union never disappeared; indeed, during—and especially after—the Second World War it became a huge, everyday and all-pervasive phenomenon. There is in essence a second market operating in the country parallel to the legal state market. The second market deals in goods which the state is not able to supply the consumer because of permanent nationwide and local shortages.

The distribution of goods throughout the country does not occur spontaneously or according to the laws that govern a free market but is the result of an administrative directive from the state authorities. In the Soviet Union there are cities, such as Moscow and Leningrad, that enjoy a special supply status. Then there are towns, such as the capitals of the Union republics and the famous resorts, that are allocated goods as Category I localities, and, finally, there are all the remaining towns, which are supplied under Category II.

Naturally, people do everything possible to make this uneven distribution more equitable, and goods available in some towns and not in others tend, like water seeking its own level, to trickle from well supplied to poorly supplied places. In part this process occurs spontaneously: people visiting towns other than their own buy things there for themselves and their families and friends which they are unable to acquire at home. However, an important role in the process of the redistribution of goods is played by professional middlemen, who buy up goods wherever they are available and try to sell them in localities where they are scarce. Or, alternatively, they sell them in the very same places they buy them, to people who do not have the time, the inclination, or the strength to spend many hours on line.

These professional retailers spend their own money on transportation as well as their own time and effort in traveling and in acquiring the goods, therefore it is absolutely normal for them to try to make a profit by selling the goods for higher prices than they paid for them. In the Soviet Union these retailers are called speculators and are hauled into courts of law.

But as long as there are items that are in demand and that cannot easily be bought in the stores, speculation will be ineradicable. Therefore, notwithstanding persecution by the police and the threat of heavy prison sentences of up to seven years, speculation is so much a part of Soviet life that it is inseparable from it. It is difficult to name any sector of the population that does not have recourse to speculators, whether in the country or in the urban areas.

It is usual for professional speculators to have a more or less stable clientele, people they sell to either at their homes or at their workplaces. Thus the concept of "one's own regular speculator" has come about. Some, for example, might service apartment buildings whose tenants are writers, artists, and film-industry employees. Such buildings are all located within a small area of Moscow, and the regular speculators know many of the residents and are familiar with their tastes and requirements.

Speculators who regularly service entire institutions have also become firmly established as a part of Soviet life. They go to a polyclinic, academic institute, or ministry during working hours, ensconce themselves in some office or other and await their customers—mainly women—who drop by to see what is for sale in the way of blouses, shoes, dresses, and so forth.

Society at large does not share the state's negative attitude toward speculators. People in all strata of society see them not as criminals but as a useful and necessary part of daily life. This attitude has been so wholeheartedly adopted by people that speculators even make regular rounds of the people's courts in Moscow. This is viewed as absolutely natural. Like the doctors in a polyclinic, for example, the women judges and prosecutors buy boots or dresses from their speculators without any twinges of conscience. When these very same speculators are brought before them on criminal charges, they have no qualms about sending them off to the camps.

Many times in the breaks between sessions I have seen the court secretary lead a speculator with her wares into the judge's chambers. Everyone present, including the public prosecutor, would examine the merchandise with interest and discuss the items' relative merits and prices.

Speculation has become part and parcel of life in the Soviet Union because it supplies people with daily needs. To realize this fully it is sufficient to go down the lists of items that the police confiscate from speculators they have arrested.

The February 11, 1979, issue of *Pravda* informs us that the suitcase of an engineer who had returned home to Kaunas, Lithuania, from Moscow yielded: 1400 rubles' worth of medicines, tape recorders, American jeans and shirts, imported records, and chewing gum. It was reported in *Dawn of the East* on December 24, 1972, that when three women, who regularly traveled between their native Georgia and Moscow, were arrested, the police found—and of course confiscated—a large quantity of overcoats and fur coats, more than 50 imported raincoats, men's suits, 103 pairs of shoes, 123 children's outfits, 269 yards of fabric, and dozens of pairs of imported jeans.

Then we learn from the February 10, 1980, issue of *Pravda* what the police confiscated from a woman who headed a tentacular organization of speculators: a mass of gold articles (40 rings, 4 pairs of earrings, 5 pendants, 3 bracelets, 7 signet rings and 4 wristwatches), 40 ladies' wigs, boxes of imported cosmetics, a large quantity of imported jeans, velveteen suits, women's and men's jackets, fur coats, fur hats, dozens of pairs of shoes, bolts of fabric, 10 cameras, a pile of imported umbrellas, purses, sunglasses, scarves, rugs, mohair yarn, and, finally, 500 plastic bags of the sort that are found hanging in rolls in any American supermarket.

Even this extensive list does not give a full idea of what items are scarce in the Soviet Union, and are, accordingly, the objects of speculation. A complete list could be culled from the case material of tens of thousands of trials of speculators; it would include most things that people need in everyday life, such as food and clothing, and would also include items that could certainly not be called absolute necessities, such as popular records and American jeans. Later in this chapter I will discuss the professional speculators who deal in each of these items.

When in the summer of 1977 I was in Yerevan, the capital of Armenia, on court business, I stopped by one of the district courts to meet with two colleagues from Moscow who were arguing a case. The small courtroom looked unusual—it was cluttered with television cameras and lighting equipment, around which camera operators and lighting technicians, brought in from Moscow, were shuffling. In the dock I saw an old, unshaven man and a woman who was just as old. I was amazed to see this hullabaloo. Why should a group from

Central television travel here to shoot a trial of an old man and woman? Then my colleagues told me about the case, for which they had come from Moscow.

The K——s, brother and sister, were put on trial for dealing in flowers. They were both elderly by then and owned a house with a small garden in which they grew carnations. In addition, they bought up other people's flowers, which the brother would take to Moscow and Leningrad to sell along with his own. There are quite a few flower dealers of this kind in Yerevan, and they all lead a fairly peaceful existence, since they protect themselves from the police with regular bribes.

The arrest and trial of the K——s was in itself extraordinary. Even more amazing was the sensation caused by the case in the press and on television—which not only broadcast the court hearings but even showed the defendants' home and the belongings that had been confiscated from it. The secret of all the K——s' troubles lay precisely in the nature of these belongings. The confiscated items eventually took up four rooms of the local museum and included historical relics—furniture and works of art that had belonged to Napoleon himself—seventeenth- and eighteenth-century French furniture, a collection of porcelain valued by experts at many tens of thousands of rubles, and, finally, a collection of paintings, among which were fine examples by great Western masters of the sixteenth to the eighteenth centuries.

K—— was a passionate, maniacal collector. All his not inconsiderable funds went toward enriching his collections. The people he would stay with in Moscow and Leningrad when he came to sell his flowers testified in court that this man, who made 1300 to 1500 rubles a day from his merchandise, would deny himself everything; he would not even allow himself to spend a ruble on lunch in a canteen, but would make do with five *pirozhki* at 10 kopecks apiece purchased from a street vendor. His collection became his sole interest in life.

Rumors about this collection circulated ever more widely around town, until finally people in Armenia's Ministry of Culture became interested in it.

When K—— was summoned to the DCMSP, "advised to donate" his collection to the state, and told that unwillingness to do so could lead to extremely unpleasant consequences for him, he categorically refused. K—— stated defiantly that he had used the money from his own labors to build up his collection over a period of fifty years, that he had denied himself everything for it, and that he did not intend to donate it to anyone.

I left Yerevan before sentencing, but before long, sitting at home in front of the television set, I saw the familiar hall at the Yerevan local court and the same old people sitting in the dock. It was a broadcast from the series "Man and the Law" and reported the K—— affair fully.

The narrator branded the K——s "dangerous criminals," emphasizing the harm to the Soviet state in what they had done, and, with an obvious feeling of satisfaction, reported to the TV viewers that "the criminals received their just deserts." The brother was condemned to ten years in the camps of "strict regime" and the sister to five years, with everything belonging to them confiscated, including of course the collection.

All this anger, this indignation, was heaped on these two old people, whose entire guilt rested in the fact that they had traded in flowers.

Private trade in imported clothing, recordings of popular music, radios, and tape recorders—which have always been much in demand in the Soviet Union—has attained a particularly large scale in recent years. A great deal of merchandise imported from Western countries is sold on the black markets of Moscow, Odessa, Riga, and Leningrad, but American jeans—indeed anything in denim—and records and cassettes of popular and rock music are in especial demand.

The fashion for jeans has spread like an epidemic among Soviet young people. But not just any jeans will do—only American jeans: Levi's, Wranglers, and Montanas. These are the jeans that have become status symbols, a necessary component of youthful fashion. It is not so much the quality of the jeans that is important as the label, and therefore people deal more in the labels from the jeans than in the jeans themselves. People will pay up to 50 rubles for an American jeans label, while the Soviet-made variety (with the garments attached) or those imported from Poland or Bulgaria—which can be purchased for 8 to 10 rubles—gather dust in the shops. The prices of American jeans have reached a level that is completely out of line with their real value, and yet they continue to rise. In 1977 American jeans had already risen to 160–170 rubles on the Soviet black market, but by 1979 people were paying 225–250 rubles (about $330) for a pair of Levi's or Wranglers.

The Soviet authorities adopt a very serious stance toward the fashion for American jeans, as if it were a kind of ideological sabotage, an attempt to inculcate a fondness for the American way of life among Soviet youth. Articles regularly appear in Soviet newspapers, especially those aimed at young people, deriding the fashion, with writers and famous clothing designers holding the jeans fans up to ridicule. However, the author of one of these articles, which appeared in *Izvestiya* on December 8, 1979, quite rightly admitted that "Of course, it is a hopeless matter to struggle against the whims of fashion."

And still the Soviet authorities persist in their futile battle and use not only propagandistic methods but administrative and punitive ones as well. First and foremost, the authorities have tried to restrict the importation of American jeans into the country, and to that end have substantially increased the customs duty on jeans either carried into the country or received through the mail. Second, anyone entering the country—whether a Soviet citizen or a foreigner—is allowed to bring in with him only one pair of jeans.

But notwithstanding all these restrictions, the quantity of American jeans secretly brought into the country is increasing all the time. A great number of specialized criminal organizations deal specifically in this commodity. Many such criminal groups boast well oiled machinery for smuggling in large consignments of these items and marketing them. The usual suppliers of the goods are either Soviet sailors who sail foreign routes or foreign sailors who have docked in the Soviet Union. Both categories manage to conceal whole bales of jeans from the customs inspectors by hiding them in the deepest recesses of their ships. They bring them through the customs checkpoints ashore by using the method, by now familiar to us, of giving the customs officer a pair of jeans for himself if he agrees "not to notice" the bale of contraband.

In addition to this, an ever-increasing number of diplomats accredited in the USSR are being drawn into contraband operations and are becoming accomplices of criminal organizations on a regular basis.

At the head of the group, uncovered by KGB agents in Moscow in 1976, was a former law student at the University of Moscow who had abandoned his studies to go into illegal business. Having started his activity with the sale of a few pairs of jeans, which had fallen into his hands by chance, he managed, with outstanding skill, to create a far-flung organization dealing in smuggled goods, with an annual turnover of three hundred thousand rubles.

He obtained American jeans, denim skirts, and sunglasses largely from the diplomats of several African countries. (Neither during the preliminary investigation nor the trial in court were the diplomats or the countries named.) All of these goods were sold primarily to young workers and students in dormitories and on the streets near the department stores of Moscow and of many provincial cities. As the defendants demonstrated, in one night it was possible to sell the students or workers of a single dormitory 30 to 40 pairs of jeans at 225 to 250 rubles a pair. (The student allowance is 25-50 rubles a month, and the average monthly salary of workers and laborers is 169 rubles.)

For the sale of these goods the head of the organization created thirteen small groups (with five to six people in each), composed of students and young workers. Four groups were continuously in action in Moscow, seven in the provincial centers, while two mobile groups traveled with their wares to various towns and cities throughout the country. But the head of the whole organization was known only to the leaders of each group. Only they came in contact with him and received the goods for sale, and only they settled the accounts for the completed transactions. Neither the sources of supply nor the extent of the operation was known. This organization was so well concealed that it was able to function illegally for three years regardless of the fact that, after the arrest of several of its second-rank members, the KGB came on its tracks. Only when the KGB had succeeded in planting a number of its secret agents in the upper levels of one of the groups, to whose leadership the head of the organization had become well known, was the latter finally arrested and the whole operation broken up.

The types of income-generating activities not dependent on the state are so numerous and varied that to enumerate them would take up too much space. There is one profession that I cannot omit mentioning in this book, and that is the oldest profession in the world. I feel compelled to do so not because prostitution is particularly rampant in the Soviet Union but because official Soviet sociology and propaganda would have it that there is simply no such thing in the Soviet

Union. Because of that, not a single word may be read about the subject in any Soviet newspaper or book.

PROSTITUTION

In the Soviet Union there are many trades that people are forbidden to work at, and they are prosecuted if they do. The list of these trades, which is annexed to the Criminal Code, includes, for example, the production of church candles, icons, and religious appurtenances and the manufacture of copying machines. Prostitution, however, does not appear on this list of forbidden trades, and the reason for this lacuna in the Criminal Code is not that the Soviet state has adopted a lenient attitude toward prostitution and does not deem it necessary to prosecute prostitutes. It is simply a manifestation of the state's hypocrisy: the state pretends that there is no prostitution in the country. But prostitution does exist in the Soviet Union and the state does fight it, although not really consistently or harshly.

Once, during a trial I was attending, a recess of several hours was called, and, as I had nothing to do and nowhere to go, I looked in at the courtroom next door, where another case was in progress. A prostitute was on trial, but not for prostitution; she had been charged with robbing her clients. She would bring them home with her, and, at the height of the sexual fun and games, a man would appear in the room. The irate "husband" would raise hell and use physical violence to chase out the terrified client, having first removed his money, valuables, and sometimes even some of his clothes.

I got into a conversation with an employee of the Moscow Criminal Investigation Department who was appearing in this case as a witness for the prosecution. He worked in the department's special section to combat prostitution, which had been set up in the 1940s. He was a lively talker and knew a lot of things that practically no one in the country knows apart from the Criminal Investigation Department employees and the prostitutes themselves. I had already had the idea of writing this book, and the problem interested me, so I suggested to this man that we meet again over a meal in a restaurant. I met him and a colleague of his several times more, and they provided me with a wealth of accurate information.

My informants told me about many things: the card index that keeps several thousand registered professional prostitutes on file, the yearly increase in the number of fourteen- and fifteen-year-old girls working as professional prostitutes, and much else besides, all of which made it possible for me to write this section of my book with such relative thoroughness.

Just as in all countries of the world, prostitution flourishes in the Soviet Union in large cities and in ports where foreign ships dock. Even so, prostitution is incomparably less widespread in the Soviet Union than it is in the West, and the forms it takes are somewhat different.

First and foremost, prostitution in the Soviet Union cannot be the organized business it is in the West, owing mainly to the very strict surveillance imposed upon all Soviet adults without exception. In the Soviet Union a professional prostitute who does not have some kind of legal screen—a husband who officially supports her or a legal job—becomes easy prey for the police; for, according to Soviet law, any able-bodied citizen who is without a permanent job for a period of more than four months in a year can be charged with leading a "parasitical style of life." Therefore, with rare exceptions, professionals try to have a legitimate cover: housewife status or a permanent job of some kind. Hence in the Soviet Union even the real professionals, for whom prostitution is the main source of income, usually hold down some sort of regular job.

There are also a large number of semiprofessionals working in the Soviet Union for whom a legal job provides the main means of existence and for whom prostitution brings in regular side earnings. This semiprofessional prostitution is particularly common among waitresses (especially in hotel restaurants), hotel chambermaids, and salesclerks in the large department stores.

Street prostitution is not nearly as common in Soviet cities as it is in their Western counterparts. There is nothing to compare with Paris' Place Pigalle or New York's Times Square, either in Moscow or in the port cities of Leningrad and Odessa. The reason for this is not only the strict surveillance kept by uniformed and plainclothes police on the main streets and in the vicinity of the hotels; prostitutes can usually come to some sort of agreement with them. The overriding reason is that it is rare for any prostitute to have a room to which she can take her clients.

It goes without saying that a prostitute with a family cannot bring men home with her, and there are very few single women living in their own apartments in the Soviet Union; they are particularly rare among street prostitutes. Hotels are off limits; if the client himself is staying in a hotel, he cannot have anyone in his room after eleven o'clock at night. Even before that hour it is virtually impossible for him to bring a woman up to his room. In Soviet hotels there are women known as *dezhurnaya,* always on duty on each floor, who make absolutely sure that the rooms are not used for sexual encounters.

Having decided with her trained eye that the hotel guest's companion is a prostitute, the *dezhurnaya* will simply not allow her to enter the room and will have her ejected from the hotel forthwith. If the *dezhurnaya* sees a woman about whom she has any misgivings, she will allow her into the room, but after five or ten minutes will always find an excuse for trying to get into the room to check. If the occupants do not let her in, she will call someone from the management and make a fuss outside the closed door.

Generally, a *dezhurnaya* can be won over with a ten-ruble bill, but the clients of a streetwalker will rarely agree to such additional expenses. There are, of course, quite a few prostitutes plying their trade in hotels, but these are the professionals or semiprofessionals of a higher category, about whom more later. This higher category includes the few lucky women who have their own apartments and, as a rule, their own personal clientele and who do not usually lurk about the streets looking for men.

And so the street prostitutes are left with the dark, deserted doorways and the neglected basements for their unfastidious clients to make do with—the ones who are willing to pay five or ten rubles for a session of squalid pleasure.

There is yet another, not very comfortable possibility—to take the client to the home of "an old woman friend of mine." Quite often these *babushki,* who live in semibasements or in *dvornik*'s* lodges with a separate entrance from the street, will readily agree to sit out in the kitchen or with a neighbor for half an hour in return for a couple of rubles. This phenomenon has given rise to a peculiar kind of swindle.

A few years ago a series of trials of street prostitutes was held in people's courts in Moscow (in particular in the Sverdlovsky Central and Timiryazevsky districts). Behind each of these cases was an identical story: After the prostitute had brought her client to a building with a central courtyard or a through passageway, she would inform him that she had to go ahead to get her "old woman friend" to vacate the room. Explaining that the *babushka* had to be paid in advance for her hospitality, the prostitute would take the client's money and disappear for good.

* A *dvornik* is a cross between a concierge and a building superintendent. (Trans. note)

The women were brought to trial not for engaging in prostitution but for fraud—for having taken money on the basis of a certain agreement and not having discharged the obligations thus assumed. The defense lawyers in the trials quite reasonably put the question to the court and the prosecution: What if, having accepted the money, the defendant had honored her agreement and had perpetrated what would have constituted an act of prostitution? Could she not then have been brought to trial? Therefore she was being prosecuted for not being a prostitute, and it followed from that that one is better off being a prostitute than a swindler in the Soviet Union.

However, despite all the obstacles, there are streets and squares in Moscow and in other large cities where prostitutes can traditionally be found strolling up and down in the evening. In Moscow streetwalkers generally congregate in a small area on Sverdlov Square and at the beginning of Gorky Street, where the theaters, restaurants, and hotels are concentrated. To the innocent observer there do not seem to be many of them strolling about in this *pyatachok,* or "five-kopeck piece," as Muscovites call it. However, that impression is deceptive, as I once found out for myself.

A few years ago my wife and I were walking with some friends late one night along Gorky Street when we were attacked by some hooligans. We got into a fight, as a result of which all of us—attackers and victims alike—ended up at the Fiftieth Police Station, not far from Sverdlov Square and the place where the police take arrested prostitutes. (In prostitute's slang this police station is known as the *poltinnik,* or fifty-kopeck piece.)

A large section of the room in which the officer on duty was sitting had been partitioned off by a wooden barrier, and it was literally packed full of women. There were at least thirty of them there, and their profession left no room for any doubt, especially when the arrival of our wives was met by gleeful cries of "Look! They've brought in some clean ones!"

In contrast with the situation in the West, the pimp is rarely encountered in Soviet street prostitution. This fact was mentioned by my informant from the Moscow Criminal Investigation Department and also by my informants in Leningrad and Arkhangelsk. The only attempt I know of to exploit street prostitutes was made not by a pimp but by one of the prostitutes herself.

A few years ago a case was tried in the Moscow Municipal Court which at first sight had a hackneyed plot. A young woman and seven young men who were her accomplices were charged with having brutally beaten three women (they "inflicted grievous, life-threatening bodily harm," to quote the Criminal Code) and having attempted to murder a fourth. But there was something very unusual about the case: no one involved in the trial—not the defendants, not the victims, not the attorneys for the prosecution or the defense— ever mentioned the motives for the crime.

The prosecution confined itself to the set formula "from motives of hooliganism" (that is, without apparent motive), and the word "prostitution" was not even mentioned in the prosecution's summing up. And yet the whole case had to do precisely with street prostitution.

The principal defendant was a street prostitute who stood out from the rest of the prostitutes milling around the sidewalks near the restaurants and hotels in the evening by virtue not only of her striking appearance (which in itself gave her an advantage over her competitors) but also of her intelligence and forthright character. Very soon she had become the center of a group of prostitutes to whom she passed on the clients she herself could not serve; she also advised them about the best spots for drumming up trade. In addition, she maintained contacts with the police and with the agents who monitored that district and gave them regular bribes on behalf of her group.

In return for all this—for the clients and for her mediation with the police—she demanded money and subordination from her friends. However, some of the prostitutes did not need to rely on her and refused to knuckle under. Then she hit upon a method by which she hoped to make all the professionals operating in that area answerable to her: she set up an organization that would allow her to exact regular tribute from any professional who appeared in the evenings on the *pyatachok*.

To help her carry out her plans, the heroine of the trial, known by the nickname of Klavka Komendant* in the Criminal Investigation Department and among the prostitutes, organized a punitive force of ten strapping lads who were devoted to her and were ready to carry out her orders. They began terrorizing all the prostitutes working in that area by chasing them away from Sverdlov Square and Gorky Street and preventing them from soliciting clients. They threw ink at their faces and clothes and beat up the most obstinate ones.

For a while the police, to whom Klavka Komendant paid a regular daily tribute from her earnings, shut their eyes to the whole thing and even helped her in certain ways in her struggle for power: on her instructions they arrested insubordinate rivals and took them off to the *poltinnik*. However, when one woman was found with broken ribs and a fractured skull in the basement of a building not far from the Metropol Hotel, another section of the Criminal Investigation Department became involved—the homicide division. The victim found in the basement in fact survived her injuries and supplied the necessary evidence.

At this point the attempt to set up organized prostitution in Moscow was abandoned. I never heard of other, similar attempts involving professional pimps who tried to exploit street prostitutes, nor have I seen any mention of them in court annals.

* Commandant (Trans. note)

Male homosexual prostitution is not at all widespread in the Soviet Union, the main reason being the harsh punishment that awaits any man found guilty of homosexual practices. Even sexual relations between consenting male adults are punished by terms of imprisonment of up to five years. Relations involving violence or threats and relations with minors entail terms of up to eight years.

Notwithstanding these harsh sentences, homosexuals have, of course, not disappeared in the Soviet Union. They carefully conceal their proclivities and their activities, but nevertheless it is known (from, among other things, the court calendar) that there are very many of them in the country, and among the most varied sections of the population. They include world-famous musicians and dancers, artists and writers, whose fame protects them from prosecution to some extent. Then there are the thousands of unknown ordinary people whose tormented lives are haunted by the abiding fear of exposure, the law, and the camps.

Even given all these factors, male homosexual prostitution does exist in large cities. In Moscow and other principal cities male prostitutes solicit their clients in the places where homosexuals gather to seek out partners—the public toilets. This is where male prostitutes offer their services and where underage boys are quite often to be found.

The police section assigned to combating homosexuality knows all these places very well, and their secret agents monitor them continuously. However, arrests and subsequent trials are comparatively rare, for even in cases in which an agent is sure that two men who exchange a couple of words in a public toilet and then go off somewhere together really are homosexuals, and do indeed intend to engage in sexual relations, he will not arrest them. There would be no sense in doing so, since, if arrested, they would both naturally deny their intent, and the agent would have no evidence to use against them.

In recent years, however, the Moscow police have resorted to blatant entrapment methods. The *agent provocateur* pretending to be a homosexual (or sometimes a homosexual in fact) lures his partner into a trap where the police catch him unawares, and then acts as a witness for the prosecution.

One criminal case that was tried in the Moscow Municipal Court in the 1970s revealed that the police had organized some schoolboys into a special task force for combating homosexuals. The members of this group had to appear in public toilets and act as bait for homosexuals. In the end, however, the boys themselves wound up on trial, but not for entrapment. Having quickly realized the utter defenselessness of the homosexuals and their fear of seeking protection from the authorities, they began robbing them, and it is those robberies that they were charged with.

Even with the illegal entrapment methods that they use, the police are unable to halt the growth of male homosexual prostitution.

Since finding an apartment or a hotel room in which to carry on a regular business is a very complicated matter, large cities have seen the growing popularity of the prostitution taxi. Regular cooperation between taxi drivers and stable groups of prostitutes was noted as far as I know more than fifteen years ago by the Criminal Investigation departments of Moscow, Leningrad, and Kiev.

In Moscow the groups of prostitutes and the taxis with whose drivers they are in league are concentrated around the stations and a few restaurants traditionally considered to be centers of prostitution.

Both prostitutes and drivers cruise the stations around the clock. They congregate around the restaurants at closing time and solicit clients—mainly very drunken ones—at the exit. Some of the more elegant and good-looking prostitutes actually solicit clients inside the restaurants.

According to an unwritten rule, restaurant doormen do not allow unaccompanied women or pairs of women to enter restaurants in the evening. In actual fact, the doormen know all the prostitutes working in the vicinity by sight and readily let them inside for three rubles. Some of them even try to solicit clients from among the diners, and recommend prostitutes of their acquaintance to them. In such cases they are paid both by the clients and the girls.

Just as one of these restaurants is about to close, lines of vacant taxis form outside. But any attempt by an ordinary passenger to hire one would be in vain, for all the drivers are waiting for their own regular clients and are not interested in ordinary passengers.

Around the stations the prostitution taxi picture is not as obvious. In each station there is a special inspector on duty who makes sure that drivers of available taxis pick up passengers waiting on line immediately. This is why taxi drivers who are working with prostitutes hide with their cars in nearby lanes with their green lights off. A driver agrees with a prostitute on a place where his car will be parked, and once she has a customer she knows exactly where to find it.

The driver knows his business. Once the couple is seated, he drives them impassively and without turning around for thirty minutes or an hour through the dark deserted streets or else sits in the car, with his lights off, in some deserted courtyard or alley.

The way the taxi drivers and prostitutes settle accounts depends on who is playing the leading role. Sometimes the prostitute acts independently: she solicits a client, chooses the driver, and pays him out of the money she gets from her customer. In such a case the driver will get 10 to 15 rubles out of the 25 or 30 paid by the client.

In other cases the leading role belongs to the taxi driver. He is the one who receives an order for a woman from the client and gets in touch with the prostitute, who is either waiting in an appointed place nearby or is at home, expecting the driver's phone call. In such cases the driver is paid by the client and settles up with the prostitute, giving her 10 or 15 rubles and keeping between 15 and 20 for himself.

As such activities become ever more widespread among taxi drivers, the characteristics of organized pimpdom become increasingly obvious. Stable groups of prostitutes emerge who work with one or two drivers on a permanent basis. These groups usually divide up the territories among themselves, whether near the stations or at the restaurants. Sometimes these groups amalgamate to push out interlopers —drivers and prostitutes who have intruded into what they consider to be their zone. In the struggle for power, such methods are used as denouncing the competition to police officers, with whom good relations are enjoyed (relations based, naturally, on bribery). In addition, fights among wrench- and crowbar-wielding taxi drivers take place, and prostitutes beat up prostitutes belonging to a rival group. (According to eyewitnesses, fights among women are distinguished by their particular cruelty and a heavy dose of sadism.)

Misunderstandings also occur among taxi drivers belonging to the same group when, for example, one tries to lure over a woman working for another driver, which is considered inadmissible behavior. The methods by which these misunderstandings are settled include the same cruel, bloody fights and beatings and the same denunciations.

In the Soviet Union railway stations are always packed with weary passengers waiting to get onto a train. They can easily find themselves waiting a whole day, and will quite often have to spend the night at the station as well. These people are potential clients for a special category of prostitute: the station prostitute.

In the Moscow stations, the station prostitutes wander about in search of clients among the bored provincials who do not know how to kill the waiting time or how to partake of the delights and temptations of the capital. Anyone who has spent even a few hours in a large station in Moscow and is a good observer of life around him will have seen them, singly or in pairs, roaming around the halls, speaking to men. Often their solicitation meets with a negative gesture or rejoinder, but sometimes a man will pick up his suitcase and follow a woman somewhere. (Quite often two or three will go off with the same woman.)

There can be no doubt that these women are prostitutes; their behavior and their appearance make it glaringly clear. Usually they are no longer young women; they have let themselves go and are poorly and sloppily dressed, with crudely daubed faces, bloated from habitual drinking.

People who work in the Criminal Investigation Department told me that these are the lowest and cheapest category of prostitutes. They are at the rock bottom of the prostitution world—to which the dregs naturally sink. They usually find their clients among the provincials or the soldiers on their way home on leave, grown weary in their barracks from an absence of women. Not an affluent clientele, but not a fussy one either. Since these clients have luggage with them and are confined to the station, the prostitutes take them to the remote railway sidings where old and abandoned passenger cars are parked—a haven for beggars and tramps. Not a very comfortable spot, but on the other hand free.

In addition to this, there are always empty passenger cars in these sidings waiting to be attached to trains; their conductors will readily allow prostitutes and their clients to use them for a fee of one or two rubles.

The railway police know all the prostitutes very well, and arresting them would present no difficulties. But the bribes they receive from them are an ongoing source of income, apart from which they make great use of these prostitutes as secret informers. As they usually have connections with the station thieves, they can easily provide useful information about their criminal activities.

Although prostitutes are officially banned from hotels in the Soviet Union, hotel prostitutes nevertheless do exist as a separate category. Their entire business is founded on permanent, close contacts with hotel desk clerks and, especially, with the *dezhurnaya*. In the first place, the prostitutes need such contacts in order to be allowed into the hotels with their clients, but this is not the limit of their relationship. The Criminal Investigation Department has information from its agents to the effect that the *dezhurnaya* themselves solicit clients and then summon to the hotel the prostitutes with whom they maintain connections.

Even in cases in which a prostitute solicits her own clients from among hotel guests, she will usually do so with the help of the *dezhurnaya,* who will have given her information about a suitable prospect having checked into such and such a room.

I flew into Riga one evening, and my clients immediately drove me to the Hotel Riga, the best in town. We went up to my room and discussed our work plans for the following day, after which my clients left. I was just unpacking my suitcase when the telephone rang: "Ivan Nikolaevich?" asked a woman's voice.

"No, you've made some mistake; there's no one here by that name."

"Oh, he's already left, then! Well, it doesn't matter. Wouldn't you like some fun? I could drop by whenever it's convenient."

I declined her offer of "fun" politely but firmly, and there was no repetition of such phone calls. However, when I returned to the same hotel two weeks later and checked into a different room on another floor, I received a similar call.

What happened to me in Riga is part of everyday hotel life in any large town. Desk clerks not only give prostitutes the information they need but also solicit clients for them. It is quite common for a guest in a hotel in Moscow, Leningrad, Kiev, or one of many other cities to return to his hotel after a day of work and be asked sympathetically by the desk clerk whether he doesn't find it dull to while away the evening on his own and whether he would not like to know a "nice girl."

I know from court case material and from information given to me by people from the Moscow Criminal Investigation Department that hotel prostitution has become very widespread in Moscow. In virtually any large hotel a guest can have relations with a prostitute—unless he is a foreigner. Even if, for reasons of caution, the *dezhurnaya* does not offer to introduce the guest to a "nice girl," there will always be the telephone calls to the room with women's voices offering "fun" or "an evening together." If the guest is interested, a woman will appear in his room and remain there the whole night without encountering any difficulties from the *dezhurnaya,* who gets her 10 rubles from the 25 to 30 paid by the client.

The most expensive prostitutes in the Soviet Union are the foreign-currency prostitutes, the ones who meet mainly or exclusively with foreign clients and receive payment from them in convertible Western currencies.

As I have mentioned before, there is a chain of shops in the Soviet Union run by the *Beryozka* ("Birch") organization which accepts only Western currencies—not rubles. There one can buy top-quality imported merchandise and produce that cannot be purchased for rubles in the ordinary stores. This is why prostitutes who are available only for dollars, pounds, or marks are called *beryozki* in the Soviet Union.

They go about their soliciting mostly in places frequented by foreigners—at ballet performances in the Bolshoi Theater or in bars that accept only Western currencies. A beautiful, elegantly dressed woman with a smattering of some foreign language can easily meet and strike up an acquaintance with foreigners in the foyer of the Bolshoi Theater during the intermissions.

Soviet citizens, even if they do have some foreign currency, are allowed into foreign-currency bars only as guests of foreigners. An exception is made, however, for the foreign-currency prostitutes. They are not admitted free of charge, of course; the manager of the bar receives ten rubles from each of them as an admission charge.

These high overheads are quickly covered, however; the *beryozki* earn a great deal of money. Their clients pay them in hard currency or in vouchers that can be used in the Beryozka stores. (These vouchers are normally obtained at a special bank in exchange for foreign currency.)

Foreign currency and Beryozka vouchers are very highly rated on the black market. One can get 4 or 5 rubles for a dollar, which is worth 63 kopecks at the official rate, and 6 to 8 rubles for a voucher with a face value of one ruble. Hence a *beryozka* who is paid $25 or $30 in cash or 20 to 25 rubles in vouchers for a session with a client (this was the average rate in the late 1970s in Moscow and Leningrad) can earn 120 to 150 rubles in a few hours—the equivalent of a month's wages for an average manual or office worker.

In order to enter this elite class of Soviet prostitution a woman must possess not only physical charms but also the ability to behave in society, a minimum knowledge of foreign languages, and skill in dressing elegantly. (These qualifications do not apply to the foreign-currency prostitutes who work in port cities and who meet with foreign sailors. It is sufficient for them to have a few expressive gestures and to know a bit of sign language plus a couple of words familiar to people the world over—such as "dollar.")

This elite group of prostitutes has grown up in Moscow and Leningrad over the past ten or fifteen years. Its members naturally change, but they increasingly include young women with higher education (graduates of foreign-language institutes are particularly numerous). Here are two portraits:

Portrait 1. She graduated from one of Moscow's drama schools but did not succeed in making an artistic career and works as a model. The work is not regular and leaves her with a lot of free time. She speaks quite good English. She is bright and sufficiently well read to keep up a conversation about new trends in painting or about a ballet performance. She dresses with elegance. With her earnings from prostitution she has acquired a two-room cooperative apartment that allows her to receive her clients in comfort. She meets only with foreigners, and her regular clients include diplomats and permanent representatives of foreign firms trading with the Soviet Union. She gives information about her clients to a KGB official who is her regular contact, and so she can quietly carry on her trade without fear of arrest.

Portrait 2. She graduated from the Foreign Language Institute in Moscow and teaches French in a Moscow school. She started working as a prostitute while still a student at the institute, making extra money for clothes to supplement her state stipend and the allowance her parents sent her from home, which covered only food and very basic essentials. Before graduating from the institute she married a well-off, although by no means young, man so as to be able to settle down in Moscow and not have to return to the provinces. She was soon divorced, after which she retained the apartment that had belonged to her husband. As she is not interested in her regular salary, she works very little at the school and is involved mainly in her dates with foreigners. She has both regular and casual clients, all resulting from acquaintanceships struck up in hotel lobbies or foreign-currency bars. She is poorly educated and speaks bad French, but is always lively and cheerful. She is a pleasant partner for all kinds of entertainment and therefore has no shortage of clients.

There are no real brothels in the Soviet Union such as those that masquerade as massage parlors or clubs in the West. Nor could they possibly exist, since it is impossible to buy or rent a house in a large city. The very best a person can do —and then only if he belongs to the privileged circles—is to become the owner of four rooms in an apartment house, where there are many neighbors and an elevator operator who keeps a constant eye on all comings and goings and is always an informer for the local police.

Accordingly, any apartment that is regularly visited by a large number of people is bound to attract attention from neighbors and from the elevator operator—and, in turn, from the police. This is fraught with danger, since, while prostitution is not punishable by law in the Soviet Union, one can easily end up in the camps for five years for procuring or for running a brothel.

And yet brothels of a sort do exist in the Soviet Union. One can obtain a fairly comprehensive picture of how they operate, who runs them, what sort of clients they attract, and who services them from court case material and evidence collected by the Moscow Criminal Investigation Department from its agents.

The kind of people who run brothels are usually middle-aged single women. The center of operations of such an establishment is a three-room apartment. (Sometimes even two rooms will serve.) In such an apartment, which has been adapted as a brothel, only people who are personally known to the owner or who have been recommended are received, and then only by prior arrangement. The prostitutes called to meet the respective clients have to arrive one by one and do their best to make sure that the elevator operator does not guess which apartment they are going to. Then, one by one, the pairs disappear into the available rooms.

According to my informant from the Criminal Investigation Department, that is the procedure in a typical establishment whose clients are of the more down-to-earth variety and whose owners have not kept abreast of the achievements of the West in this area and have never seen pornographic films. (These, fortunately for the population, are never shown in the Soviet Union.) There are, however, deviations from the norm. On the basis of information received from Criminal Investigation Department employees and a few underground businessmen, it is possible to construct a picture of one of these "fantasy" brothels.

The owner of the three-room apartment is a nice-looking, middle-aged divorcée. She was never a professional prostitute, but since her divorce she has always had well-to-do patrons (sometimes several at the same time). She has many acquaintances among Moscow's doctors, lawyers, underground businessmen, and party and state officials in fairly lofty positions. They and their friends help to make up a more or less stable contingent of clients.

This brothel only rarely accepts individual clients; usually a party of men—no fewer than three or more than six— arrive together. Each guest hands over his payment to the lady of the house: twenty-five rubles, a bottle of vodka or brandy, and some sort of appetizer (a can of something or half a pound of sausage or ham).

The table is set in the largest room. Facing the table is a large ottoman. While the guests are drinking and nibbling, three naked girls are demonstrating lesbian sex techniques on this ottoman.

After dinner and the lesbian sex demonstration the girls go off into the bedroom and the guests visit them one by one in turn. Sometimes, for an additional payment, group sex games with financial stakes are held, the description of which would be appropriate in the scenario for a porno film.

Thanks to the owner's caution and her good relations with the local police officer—who received a sizable sum of money each month—and thanks also to those of her patrons and clients who occupied fairly powerful positions in the Moscow hierarchy, the brothel continued to function for many years, and as of 1977 I had heard no information about its having closed down.

The owner of the brothel I have described never ended up in court, and her clients escaped the unpleasant duty of having to appear as witnesses in a sensational court case. Nevertheless, while they are not frequent, such scandalous court cases do occur. A few years ago two of them received particularly wide publicity. I was able to gain access to the documents of both cases and was present during the court hearings.

The principal defendant in the first trial, which was held in the Moscow Municipal Court, was a woman of about fifty whom we will call Inna and whose nickname was "Inna First Aid," a name she had acquired before the Second World War, when she was a professional hotel prostitute. At that time she organized and headed a team of several prostitutes who regularly served the guests of the Moskva Hotel, where important officials from the provinces would stay when in Moscow on business. She was in regular contact with the *dezhurnya,* who would let her know when her "first aid" was called for. Then she would either dash over herself or send one of her team, in which case she would receive a cut from their earnings.

After the war Inna gave up prostitution herself but expanded her organizational activities substantially. She also expanded her circle of clients and of girls and women who were involved in professional prostitution. She no longer confined herself to serving visiting provincials, and sought clients from the privileged strata of Muscovite society, including important functionaries in the city's ruling apparat.

Clients would phone her, and she would send women to whatever address they indicated, but eventually her business expanded so much that she had to find a permanent base of her own. She was helped in this by her accomplice and co-

defendant E——, a small-time journalist with vast connections and a very wide circle of acquaintances. He found a
four-room apartment for five hundred rubles a month, and
they used this apartment as their base and set up a brothel
that became quite well known in certain circles. The service
became a big business. Over ten underage girls were used as
prostitutes in the brothel, and they were instructed in their
craft by Inna herself.

It was painful to hear the testimony of these fifteen-year-
olds as they gave an account of their training period to the
court. Their manner was completely unemotional, calm and
matter-of-fact, as they described the whole process in great
detail, using obscene words as they did so. They told of the
perversions that Inna taught them as she explained how to
serve masochists and sadists, and how she taught them to
perform oral sex, first on a model of a penis and then on a
real person.

As far as I know, not a single one of the guests at Inna's
salon was prosecuted for having had sexual relations with
minors. But many of them did not escape the public disgrace
of being questioned as witnesses in a courtroom packed with
members of the public. They looked pathetic and confused
behind the witness barrier. I remember two of them in particular.

A middle-aged homeopathist, well known throughout
Moscow, stood beside the witness barrier listening to the
testimony of one young girl who told the court and the public
how embarrassed she had felt when "that old man" had
gotten undressed, given her the belt of his trousers, and
ordered her to "whip him good and hard—to make it really
painful." So crushed was he by the public disgrace that he
was unable to give a coherent answer to the judge's question, "Has the witness testified correctly?"

A famous composer, the writer of many highly popular
songs of the 1920s and 1930s, adopted a self-confident, even
free and easy manner when the girls took the witness stand

during the cross-examination and told of the filthy, masochistic acts that he had forced them to perform. He categorically denied everything, but no one, including members of the court, was in any doubt about the truth of the girls' testimony.

Both of these men got off with public disgrace. The homeopathist was helped by patients who occupied sufficiently exalted posts to rescue him, and the composer was protected by his long-standing patron and admirer Marshal Klim Voroshilov, who was at the time a member of the Politburo and the Chairman of the Presidium of the Supreme Soviet of the USSR.

Both Inna and her accomplice E—— were sentenced to terms of imprisonment. I do not know what became of Inna afterward, but E—— resurfaced in Moscow after serving his sentence, and once again became the star of a similar trial.

CONCLUSION

THUS THE Soviet Union is infected from top to bottom with corruption—from the worker, who gives the foreman a bottle of vodka to get the best job, to Politburo candidate Mzhavanadze, who takes hundreds of thousands of rubles for protecting underground millionaires; from the street prostitute, who pays the policeman ten rubles so that he won't prevent her from soliciting clients, to the former member of the Politburo, Minister of Culture Ekaterina Furtseva, who built a luxurious suburban villa at the government's expense—each and every one is afflicted with corruption.

I was born in that country and lived there for almost sixty years. Year after year since childhood and throughout my whole conscious life I watched as corruption ate more deeply into society until it turned the Soviet regime in the sixties and seventies into a land of corrupt rulers, ruling over a corrupted people.

Corruption has become a national phenomenon in the Soviet Union. But this does not mean that the average Soviet

297

citizen is immoral and inclines toward deceit. I lived my life with this people and I can attest that this is not so. The Soviet people are no better and no worse than others. *Homo sovieticus* is not immoral, he simply has two separate systems of morality.

Entering into relations with representatives of the government, dealing with industry, commerce, and services, the Soviet citizen, readily and without thinking about it, uses corruption to get what is necessary for him—most often what is vitally necessary. In the same automatic way, the average Soviet citizen gives a ruble to a salesman in a store to get a piece of meat, 300 rubles to an official of the Ministry of Communications to have a telephone installed in his apartment, or 3000 rubles to an official of the District Executive Committee to get a government apartment. If he does not pay these bribes his family will not have meat; he will be forced to wait five or six years before a telephone is installed; he will remain for years with his large family in a single room in a communal apartment.

The Soviet citizen gives all these bribes without thinking about the moral aspect of his actions, without any burden on his conscience. Usually he understands perfectly well that he is breaking the law, but he does not consider his actions immoral.

Such are the Soviet citizen's relations with the government. But in private dealings this same citizen will conduct himself in accord with the precepts of common human morality. He will lie to a representative of the government administration but be truthful and honest in relations with friends and neighbors; he is happy to steal twenty packs of cigarettes from a tobacco factory where he works but will not steal a penny from another person.

This double standard results from the complete alienation of the Soviet individual from governmental power. The Soviet citizen rarely comprehends the totalitarian character of the Soviet regime, rarely recognizes his negative relationship to it. He instinctively responds to material deprivations, to lack of freedom, to the complete corruption of those who rule him, to the immorality of the regime by excluding everything connected with the state and the economics of the state from the sphere of moral values.

"They"—who rule over us—take bribes, "their trade," "their services" are corrupt through and through, so in dealing with "them" the norms of human morality do not apply. Thus I might formulate the creed of dual morality.

The virus of corruption, which infects the ruling apparatus of the Soviet Union from top to bottom, is inevitably, by a natural law, spreading to the whole society, to all spheres of its life. To cure the country of this virus appears to be impossible. The powers that be try to fight against the corruption of both the ruling apparatus and the people. However, they do not do this energetically or consistently enough, partly because those who possess ultimate power are themselves predisposed to this or that degree of corruption (in any event, to legalized corruption). But the main reason is that all the remaining links of the ruling apparatus are completely infected by corruption. And that is why it is possible to destroy corruption in the party-government apparatus only by destroying the apparatus itself, which of course is unrealistic. After all, the apparatus ruling over regions, districts, and republics is the body that supports the whole regime.

But even if the ruling elite undertook a decisive battle against corruption, such an attempt would be doomed to failure, since at the root of the general corruption of the Soviet Union lies the totalitarian rule of the Communist party, single-handedly ruling the country. This power is checked neither by law nor by a free press. And the nature of any unrestricted power is such that it inevitably corrupts those who wield it and constantly generates the phenomenon of corruption. So it is that corruption has become the organic and unchangeable essence of the Soviet regime and can be eliminated only by a root-and-branch change in the means of government.

More than four years have passed since I was forced to leave my country. It is unlikely that its rulers will ever give me a chance to see once again the places where I passed my life, where people dear to me live, where the grave of my mother is. But they cannot take away my love for my country and for my people.

This is a book in which I describe only the dark side of my country's life, only those people who found themselves drawn into corruption. I have not mentioned the many beautiful things about that country which the totalitarian regime could not destroy. I have not mentioned the many wonderful people with whom I lived in that country. I have written a book about corruption, not about the upright.

And now, finishing this book, I ask myself: What next? What is the future of the country?

And I answer my own question with bitterness: The Soviet government, Soviet society, cannot rid itself of corruption as long as it remains Soviet. It is as simple as that.

Index

Index

Silberg case investigated by,
150
in store corruption, 78–79
dezhurnaya, 278–79, 288, 289
dissidents, legal counsel for, 12
distribution of goods, 267–68
district executive committees, 25,
33
drivers' licenses, 183–84
drugs, illegal, 61
dvorniki, 279

economy:
bribery in ministries of, 136–37
centralization of, 133
information on, 128
official vs. unofficial systems
in, 134, 140
planning in, 133–34, 135
shabashnichestvo as factor in,
258–61
education, higher, 231–42
climate for corruption in, 235
"collective guarantee" system
in, 239–41
competitive examinations for,
231
corruption integral to, 235–36
entrance examination bribes in,
231–32, 235
fake middlemen in, 236–37
favoritism practiced in, 232–33
free, corruption in, 229–42
Jews discriminated against in,
232–35
medical school mafia in, 237–38
middlemen in, 236
trials for corruption in, 231–32
elite, ruling, 35–64
bugging of, 52–53
in Central Committee, 45–46
Central Committee in charge
of, 52
clothing for, 42–43
corruption ingrained in, 47, 51–
52

corruption tolerated among, 52,
53, 64
Council of Ministers in charge
of, 52
district corruption accepted by,
83
district elite and, 68
family ties in, 54, 55
food for, 35, 40–42
furnishings provided for, 36–37
government shelter for, 44–45
health services for, 43–44
hierarchy of privileges for, 45–
46
housing for, 36–37, 44, 46–47
impact of loss of position on,
50–51
impunity felt by, 52
inaccessibility of, 38, 50
isolation of, 36, 38, 50
KGB surveillance of, 52–53
Kremlyovka stores for, 40–42
as Politburo members, 46–47
psychology of, 47, 50
salaries for, 39
"second men" in, 48
secrecy surrounding, 50
servants of, 36, 37–38, 52
special services for, 39
elite, rural district, 65–76
acceptance of corruption
among, 72–73
attempt to expose corruption
in, 72
cars for, 73
composition of, 68
cooperative shop payments to,
71–72
gifts and services received by,
73–74
gift system structure in, 70–71
hierarchy in, 71, 75, 76
homes built for, 74
illegal payments to, 68
inspectors in, 76
lands designated for, 74